FUTURES TRADER PRO COMPREHENSIVE GUIDE TO S&P 500 E-MINI FUTURES

This is a work of nonfiction. While every effort has been made to ensure accuracy, the author and publisher assume no responsibility for errors or omissions, or for any outcomes related to the use of the information contained herein.

Published by: ALPHA BETA OMEGA ONE PUBLISHING COMPANY

ISBN:979-8-9994716-0-4
First Edition: July 13, 2025

Disclaimer: The information contained in this book is for educational and informational purposes only and should not be construed as financial or investment advice. Trading financial instruments, including but not limited to stocks, futures, options, and other derivatives, carries significant risk and may not be suitable for all investors. The strategies, examples, and opinions expressed in this book are based on personal experiences and research and are not guarantees of future performance.The author and publisher are not registered financial advisors, brokers, or investment professionals. Before making any financial decisions or implementing the strategies discussed in this book, readers are strongly advised to seek the advice of a qualified financial professional. Any reliance on the information provided in this book is solely at the reader's own risk. The performance of past trades or market examples provided in this book does not guarantee future results. Market conditions can change rapidly, and the risks associated with trading and investing may result in significant financial loss, including the loss of your entire investment. Readers should only trade with funds they can afford to lose. Neither the author nor the publisher shall be held responsible for any direct, indirect, consequential, or incidental losses or damages arising from the use of the information contained in this book. By reading this book, you acknowledge and agree to assume full responsibility for your trading and investment decisions. Trading involves complex financial instruments and strategies that require a thorough understanding of the markets.

CONTENTS

Dedication

To my beloved mother, who taught me the meaning of unconditional love and perseverance,

To my father, whose wisdom and strength have always been my guiding light,

You are my greatest inspiration and the foundation of all that I am.

With eternal gratitude and love.

Preface

Trading is more than just a profession—it's a blend of art, science, and psychology, deeply intertwined with human ambition and ingenuity. For years, I have been actively involved in trading across a variety of financial instruments, including stocks, ETFs, futures, and options. This book emerges from my journey, shaped by countless lessons learned, mistakes made, and successes celebrated. I'm writing it at a transformative time in the financial world—the rise of Artificial Intelligence. Algorithms, Quantum Computing, and machine learning are reshaping the trading landscape, introducing unprecedented speed and efficiency. Yet, amid these advances, the principles of trading rooted in human ingenuity and discipline remain as vital as ever.

This book is a guide to navigating the complexities of trading in an age where humans and machines coexist on the trading floor. I believe that while AI can augment our abilities, it cannot replace the depth of human thinking, intuition, and problem-solving. These uniquely human qualities, when refined and paired with structured strategies, can create formidable traders capable of competing in any market.

But let's face it—trading is not easy. It demands resilience, discipline, and a willingness to embrace failure as part of the learning process. Many claim it takes a decade or more to master this craft, and I agree. But I also believe that by adopting the right mindset, tools, and practices, you can accelerate your journey toward success. This book aims to equip you with the knowledge and framework to transform yourself from a reactive, emotionally driven trader into a methodical, rule-based professional.

Why We Trade and Why We Struggle

Trading is both deeply personal and universally human. At its core, trading taps into our innate desire to predict, control, and profit from the future. It's exhilarating to buy into a rising market and see your judgment vindicated as prices climb. But it's also humbling to watch a well-thought-out trade unravel due to unforeseen market conditions.

Why do we trade? Some seek financial independence, while others are drawn to the intellectual challenge of interpreting market movements. For many, it's the adrenaline rush—the thrill of risk and reward. But with these motivations come challenges. The human mind, while powerful, is also susceptible to vulnerability. We are creatures of emotion, and emotions—fear, greed, hope, and regret—are the greatest adversaries of successful trading.

Unlike computers, which execute trades based on predefined algorithms, we humans think, feel, and adapt. This ability to think deeply is our greatest strength, but it can also be our undoing. How often have you entered a trade out of fear of missing out, only to regret it moments later? Or sold too early, paralyzed by the fear of a potential loss? These emotional impulses can lead to costly mistakes.

Machines, on the other hand, lack emotion. They consistently and unemotionally follow rules, giving them a distinct edge in specific trading scenarios. However, this doesn't mean human traders are destined to lose. By understanding our emotional tendencies and implementing strategies to counteract them, we can level the playing field—and even outperform the machines in specific contexts.

The Journey to Becoming a Disciplined Trader

Success in trading requires a blend of technical skill, psychological resilience, and a methodical approach to decision-making. Here are some foundational principles that will guide you toward becoming a disciplined and effective trader:

Set Your Risk Parameters

Every trade begins with a plan. Define your risk tolerance and establish clear profit targets before you enter the market. A well-placed stop-loss order is your safety net, protecting you from significant losses when the market moves against your expectations. Likewise, setting a take-profit level ensures you lock in gains before emotions tempt you to hold out for more.

Trading without predefined risk parameters is like sailing without a compass—it's only a matter of time before you're lost. Make this non-negotiable in your trading practice.

Create and Refine Your Rules

Trading is not a game of chance; it's a structured process guided by rules. Develop a set of criteria for entering and exiting trades, and adhere to them with discipline. These rules should be based on sound analysis, whether technical, fundamental, or a combination of both. As you gain experience, refine your rules to reflect your evolving understanding of the markets.

Documenting your trading process is equally important. Keep a detailed journal of every trade you make, noting the reasoning behind it, the outcome, and the lessons learned. Over time, this journal will become an invaluable resource, revealing patterns in your trading behavior and helping you identify areas for improvement.

Embrace a Growth Mindset

Success in trading is not about avoiding failure—it's about learning from it. Many traders celebrate their victories but neglect to analyze their losses. This is a missed opportunity. Your mistakes, blunders, and failures are your most powerful teachers. Write them down, reflect on them, and commit to not repeating them. Similarly, document what works and strive to replicate those strategies consistently.

Surround yourself with a community of traders who share your passion for learning and growth. Engaging in discussions with peers can challenge your thinking, introduce you to new perspectives, and strengthen your understanding of the markets. Remember, you're not alone in this journey.

Trading as a Lifelong Journey

Whether you're an occasional trader or a full-time professional, trading is a journey that demands perseverance. There will be days when the markets test your resolve—days when losses feel insurmountable, and doubt creeps in. However, remember that every seasoned trader has faced these moments. What sets successful traders apart is their ability to rise after a fall.

Think back to when you learned to walk. You stumbled countless times before finding your footing. Trading is no different. Each setback is an opportunity to learn, adapt, and grow stronger. The key is to keep moving forward.

What you will learn from this book:

This book is not just a collection of strategies; it's a companion for your trading journey. I wrote it to help you navigate the market's challenges with confidence and clarity. My goal is to equip you with the tools, mindset, and discipline needed to become a risk-aware, logical, and ultimately successful trader.

As you embark on this journey, remember that trading is not about perfection. It's about progress, building on each experience, learning from each mistake, and constantly striving to improve. Whether you're just starting or have been trading for years, there is always room to grow.

So let's begin. Together, we'll tackle the complexities of trading, develop strategies to overcome its challenges, and work toward achieving consistent success. I wish you the best of luck, not just as a trader, but as a lifelong learner and explorer of the fascinating world of financial markets. Let's take the first step.

CHAPTER ONE

Introduction to S&P 500 Futures

Imagine having a tool that lets you harness the movements of the entire U.S. stock market, profiting whether it climbs or falls. That's precisely what S&P 500 futures offer—a dynamic gateway to trading the pulse of the financial markets. These futures contracts are agreements to buy or sell the value of the S&P 500 index, a benchmark that tracks 500 of America's leading companies. By speculating on the index's future value, traders can capitalize on market trends without ever owning a single stock.

Whether you're a speculator chasing profit or a hedger seeking to shield your portfolio from market volatility, S&P 500 futures hold immense potential. Their appeal lies in their versatility and focus, allowing traders to zero in on a single, robust instrument.

In the vast sea of financial opportunities, success often hinges on specialization. As a trader, honing your skills in one well-defined area is crucial for consistent profitability. Through years of experience, I've found that the S&P 500 Emini futures are one of the most rewarding instruments to master—a market rich with opportunities for those who are prepared. Let's dive into this fascinating world and uncover how you can turn knowledge into a trading edge.

Why do I recommend trading S&P futures over other options? The reasons are compelling and numerous, as outlined below:

- **Unmatched Leverage**: S&P 500 futures provide some of the best leverage available in the market, allowing traders to control a prominent position with a relatively small amount of capital.

- **Risk Management Tools**: Traders can effectively manage their risk by utilizing well-defined stop-loss orders and predetermined profit-taking levels.
- **High Liquidity**: These futures are among the most heavily traded instruments in the US markets, ensuring ample liquidity and smooth execution of trades.
- **No Time Decay**: Unlike options, S&P futures do not suffer from theta decay, meaning their value doesn't diminish over time.
- **Simplicity**: There is no need to worry about complex Greek calculations such as delta, gamma, or theta, making it easier for traders to focus on market trends.
- **Macro-Level Perspective**: Trading S&P futures allows traders to follow broader macroeconomic trends rather than being influenced by the specific conditions of individual stocks.

How Price Movements Determine Profit and Loss

E-mini contracts offer a compelling gateway to profit by mirroring the movements of the underlying index they represent. Take the E-mini S&P 500 (ES), for example: when the S&P 500 rises by 10 points, the ES follows suit, climbing the same 10 points. Here's where the opportunity shines—each point in the ES is worth $50. That means a simple 10-point move translates to a $500 swing in value per contract.

With the right strategy and timing, even small market movements can yield substantial gains, making E-mini contracts a powerful tool for traders looking to capitalize on market fluctuations. This level of leverage opens the door to potentially lucrative returns, turning market trends into actionable profit opportunities.

Calculating Profit and Loss (P&L)

The number of points determines the P&L in E-mini trading, or the number of ticks the price moves in your favor (or against you), and the number of contracts you are trading.

Per Tick Movement: Tick size for ES: 0.25 points.
Value per tick: $12.50.

Per Point Movement: 1 point = 4 ticks (0.25 x 4).
Value per point: $50.

Example: Profit Calculation

Suppose you buy 2 ES contracts at 4,000 and sell them at 4,010. The price has moved 10 points in your favor.

Profit Calculation: 10 x points × $50 x (value per point) × 2 contracts
= 10points×$ 50(value per point)×2contracts=+$1,000

Example: Loss Calculation

Suppose you buy 1 ES contract at 4,000 and the price falls to 3,990 before you exit.

The price has moved 10 points against you.

Loss Calculation: – 10 points × $50 (value per point) × 1 contract
= −10points×$ 50(value per point)×1contract=−$500

What You Need to Get Started

Before diving into S&P 500 futures trading, it is essential to ensure you have the proper tools and resources in place. Below is a checklist to guide you:

1. **Capital Requirements**: Before embarking on your journey into S&P 500 futures trading, it is crucial to ensure you have adequate capital to manage both your trading positions and potential market fluctuations. While the initial margin requirement to trade one E-mini S&P 500 futures contract typically ranges between $13,000 and $15,000, depending on the broker and prevailing market conditions, it is advisable to have additional funds to cushion against adverse price movements.
2. **Approved Trading Account**: Ensure your brokerage account is approved for futures trading and meets any regulatory requirements. There are few trading platforms that offer a competitive platform for trading futures contracts. Shop around and find one that suits your needs, comparing commissions and other features such as the availability of chart setups and indicators.
3. **Practice with Paper Trading**: Use paper trading features to simulate trades and build confidence without risking real money.

4. Charting Software: Invest in a reliable charting platform, such as TradingView, which includes a live data subscription, typically costing around $20 per month.
5. **Technical Analysis Skills**: Develop a solid understanding of supply and demand levels across multiple timeframes, such as 5-minute, 15-minute, 30-minute, and 1-hour charts.
6. **Risk-Reward Strategy**: Establish a clear risk vs. reward ratio to determine how much you are willing to risk for potential profit.
7. **Trading Rules**: Create a set of written trading rules tailored to your strategy and commit to following them under all circumstances.
8. **Time**: Dedicated trading time, you need to have several hours of undisturbed time for this adventure, the last thing you need is that you need to take a call from your boss or have some office meeting while you are in the trade that effects your decision making on the trade for profit taking!

Various Trading Platforms for S&P 500 Futures (E-mini)

Many platforms allow S&P 500 futures, each having its fee structure and advantages and disadvantages. Try a few and see what suits your specific needs and trading style. I intentionally refrain from recommending any particular trading platform in this book to maintain objectivity and independence. Choosing the right platform is a highly personal decision that depends on your unique trading style, preferences, and needs. I encourage you to research various platforms, contact their support teams, and ask relevant questions about features, fees, tools, and overall usability. Additionally, consider using their paper trading or demo account features to test the platform in a risk-free environment. This hands-on approach will help you determine which platform aligns best with your trading goals and provides the comfort and functionality you require.

Contract Specifications: S&P 500 futures are standardized contracts that track the value of the S&P 500 Index. These contracts are traded on the CME Group's Globex platform, offering electronic access to global participants.

Contract Size: Each Emini S&P 500 futures contract represents 50 times the value of the S&P 500 Index. For instance, if the index is trading at 4,000, the notional value of one contract is $200,000.

Tick Size: The minimum price movement is 0.25 points, equivalent to $12.50 per tick.

Trading Hours: S&P 500 futures trade nearly 23 hours a day, five days a week, allowing traders to react to global market events.

Margin Requirements: Brokers set initial and maintenance margin requirements, typically a fraction of the contract's notional value, to control risk.

Calendar of S&P 500 Futures:

The S&P 500 futures contracts are identified by the ticker symbol "ES", while the Micro S&P 500 futures, which are smaller-sized contracts, trade under the symbol "MES". The Micro S&P 500 futures are exactly one-tenth the size of the E-mini S&P 500 futures (ES), making them a more accessible option for traders with smaller accounts or those looking to manage risk more precisely.

Both types of contracts have specific expiration dates, which are listed in the table below. Traders must keep track of these dates and ensure they roll over their positions to the next contract before the last trading day of the current contract. This avoids being caught in an expiring contract and ensures continuity in trading:

Contract month	Ticker Code	Last day to trade
Mar 2026	ESH26	20 Mar 2026
June 2026	ESM26	18 Jun 2026
Sep 2026	ESU26	18 Sep 2026
Dec 2026	ESZ26	18 Dec 2026

Order Types

To execute trades effectively, understanding order types is essential:

- **Market Orders**: Execute immediately at the best available price.
- **Limit Orders**: Specify the maximum or minimum price at which you are willing to buy or sell.
- **Stop Orders**: Trigger a market order when a specified price is reached, often used for risk management.

- **Bracket Orders**: Combine stop-loss and profit-taking levels in a single order to automate trade management.

Settlement

S&P 500 futures are cash-settled, meaning no physical delivery of the underlying securities occurs. Instead, gains or losses are credited or debited to the trader's account daily based on the contract's closing price (a process known as mark-to-market).

Role of the CME Group

The CME Group plays a central role in facilitating S&P 500 futures trading by:

- **Providing a Reliable Marketplace**: Ensuring a secure and transparent trading environment.
- **Acting as a Clearinghouse**: Guaranteeing the financial integrity of trades.
- **Offering Risk Management Tools**, Such as daily price limits to prevent excessive volatility.

Practical Tips for Trading S&P 500 Futures

- **Start Small**: Begin with a single contract to minimize risk while gaining experience.
- **Focus on Liquidity**: Trade during peak market hours of 9.30 EST through 4 PM EST for tighter spreads and better execution. It is generally better not to trade outside peak trading hours unless absolutely necessary.
- Monitor Economic Indicators: Stay informed about key data releases and Federal Reserve announcements that can impact the broader market. Stay out of taking trades before and after such major announcements because that might adversely affect your trades.
- **Use Technical Analysis**: Employ tools like moving averages, trend lines, and support/resistance levels to identify trading opportunities.
- **Stay Disciplined**: Stick to your trading plan and avoid emotional decision-making.

By understanding and applying these mechanics, traders can approach S&P 500 futures with confidence and precision, setting the stage for long-term success.

Know your risk of trading S&P 500 Futures.

- **Leverage Risks**: While leverage can amplify profits, it also magnifies losses. Traders can lose more than their initial investment if the market moves against them.
- **Complexity**: Futures trading requires an understanding of margin requirements, daily settlement processes, and contract specifications, which can be intimidating for beginners.
- **High Volatility**: The S&P 500 futures market can experience significant price swings, requiring traders to have robust risk management strategies.
- **Margin Calls**: If a trader's account falls below the maintenance margin level, they may face a margin call, requiring additional funds to maintain their position.
- **Emotional Challenges**: The fast-paced nature of futures trading can lead to emotional decision-making, resulting in impulsive trades and potential losses.

Understand your risks when trading options on S&P Futures.

Trading options on S&P futures comes with significant challenges that can outweigh the benefits for many traders. The complexities of options pricing, influenced by factors such as implied volatility and time decay, make it challenging for traders to consistently generate profits. Time decay, in particular, can erode the value of options, leading to losses even if the market moves in the anticipated direction. The steep learning curve and the necessity of mastering advanced concepts, such as those used by the Greeks, further complicate options trading. These disadvantages highlight the inherent risks and challenges, making options on S&P futures unsuitable for most traders, especially those without extensive experience in trading options. I recommend traders stay away from trading options on S&P futures and use their energy on trading E-mini futures for better results.

CHAPTER TWO

Market Participants and Market Structure

Understanding the S&P 500 Futures Market

The S&P 500 futures market is one of the most liquid and widely traded financial instruments globally. Serving as a cornerstone for both institutional and retail traders, it offers opportunities for speculation, hedging, and portfolio diversification. Grasping the dynamics of its market participants and the unique structure of its trading hours is essential for anyone aiming to trade these futures successfully.

Key Participants in the S&P 500 Futures Market

1. Institutional Investors

Institutional investors dominate the S&P futures market due to its depth and their ability to manage large capital allocations efficiently. These entities include hedge funds, mutual funds, insurance companies, and proprietary trading desks. Their trades often represent significant volumes, influencing overall market behavior.

Roles and Impact:

Institutional investors utilize S&P futures to hedge against market downturns or manage their exposure to equity indices, eliminating the need to buy or sell individual stocks. Their large-scale trading activities significantly enhance market liquidity, ensuring smooth and efficient execution for all participants. Moreover, these institutions conduct extensive research and often take the lead in setting the tone for price movements during main trading hours, playing a pivotal role in the price discovery process. Through these functions, institutional investors not only protect their portfolios but also contribute to the overall stability and transparency of the S&P futures market.

Trading Strategies of Institutional Investors:

Institutional investors employ various trading strategies in the S&P futures market to optimize their positions and enhance returns. One such approach is directional trading, which involves speculating on market trends based on economic data, earnings reports, or announcements from the Federal Reserve. Additionally, these investors engage in arbitrage, exploiting price differences between the S&P futures and the underlying SPX index or ETFs like SPY to secure risk-free profits. Furthermore, they utilize algorithmic strategies, leveraging quantitative models to capitalize on minor price discrepancies that occur during periods of high liquidity. These diversified strategies enable institutional investors to effectively manage their portfolios, mitigate risks, and contribute to the overall efficiency and stability of the S&P futures market.

2. Retail Traders

Retail traders have become increasingly significant in the S&P futures market due to the accessibility of electronic platforms, low margin requirements, and round-the-clock trading capabilities. While individual traders trade smaller volumes, their collective activity can influence short-term market movements.

Roles and Impact:

Retail traders engage in short-term speculation by focusing on intraday movements and overnight volatility, taking advantage of the high leverage available in futures trading. Their activities often act as volatility amplifiers, particularly during periods of significant economic announcements or unexpected geopolitical events, where retail trading volumes can spike significantly. Additionally, retail traders have a more pronounced impact during the Globex session, a time when institutional activity is lower, allowing their trading decisions to more directly influence price movements. This heightened involvement during quieter trading hours underscores the critical role retail traders play in shaping the dynamics of the S&P futures market.

Challenges:

Retail traders often face significant challenges in the S&P futures market, including an increased susceptibility to emotional decision-making, especially during low-volume Globex hours when market conditions can become more volatile and stressful. This emotional vulnerability can lead to impulsive trades and poor risk management. Additionally, retail traders often face challenges in competing with institutional-grade algorithms during periods of high liquidity. These sophisticated algorithms can execute trades with remarkable speed and precision, frequently outpacing the capabilities of individual traders. As a result, retail traders may find it challenging to achieve consistent profitability and maintain an edge in such a highly competitive environment.

3. Market Makers and Specialists

Market makers are essential participants in the S&P futures market, ensuring continuous liquidity by providing bid-ask quotes across trading sessions. Although the market does not rely on traditional floor-based specialists, certain trading firms and proprietary desks perform similar roles to maintain order flow.

Operations:

Market makers operate by maintaining a bid-ask spread, which allows them to earn profits through the difference between their buy and sell quotes. They engage in inventory management by holding and adjusting their positions to meet market demand, particularly during periods of high activity in the main trading hours. During Globex hours, market makers continue to operate but reduce their activities in response to lower trading volumes, ensuring that they remain responsive to the market's needs without overextending in quieter periods.

The presence of market makers has a significant impact on the S&P futures market, enhancing liquidity and ensuring price continuity. By providing ample liquidity, especially during the main trading session when trade sizes are larger, market makers facilitate smoother and more efficient transactions for all participants. Additionally, their continuous activity helps minimize price gaps, even during times of market stress, thereby maintaining stability and reducing volatility. This ensures that the market remains orderly and that price movements reflect a balanced interplay of supply and demand.

Trading Hours in the S&P 500 Futures Market

Understanding the distinct trading hours is crucial for developing effective trading strategies. The S&P futures market operates primarily during two periods:

Main Trading Hours: 9:30 AM - 4:00 PM ET

Globex Hours: 6:00 PM - 9:30 AM ET

Main Trading Hours (9:30 AM - 4:00 PM ET)

The main trading session aligns with the operating hours of the U.S. stock market, resulting in peak liquidity for the S&P 500 futures. During this period, the market experiences high volume and volatility, as the large number of buyers and sellers ensures narrow bid-ask spreads and efficient execution of trades. Additionally, futures prices exhibit strong correlation with the S&P 500 cash index and its underlying stocks, reflecting synchronized price movements. Institutional investors play a dominant role in this session, accounting for a significant portion of the trading volume. Their activity is often driven by economic releases, earnings reports, and other market-moving events, further contributing to the dynamic and active nature of the main trading hours.

Strategic Considerations:

Traders seeking high liquidity and smoother execution should focus their activities during these hours. Aligning strategies with institutional trading patterns can enhance performance and effectively manage risk.

Globex Hours (6:00 PM - 9:30 AM ET)

Globex, the electronic trading platform for CME Group, facilitates the trading of S&P futures for 23 hours each day, with a one-hour downtime from 5:00 PM to 6:00 PM ET. The overnight session on Globex exhibits unique dynamics that differentiate it from the main trading hours. During this period, trading activity significantly decreases, especially after 8:00 PM ET, which results in wider bid-ask spreads and less liquidity. Additionally, price movements are often influenced by events in Asian and European markets, introducing an international dimension to the trading environment. The reduced number of participants during Globex hours can lead to more erratic and volatile price fluctuations, making it challenging to execute large trades without impacting market prices. These factors collectively create a trading landscape that requires careful consideration and strategic planning for those participating in the overnight sessions.

Strategic Considerations:

While Globex hours offer opportunities to react to international news and overnight trends, retail traders are generally advised to concentrate their trading efforts during the main session. The increased risks of slippage and unexpected volatility make Globex hours more suitable for experienced traders who can navigate these challenges.

For our discussion, we will categorize the trading hours as follows:

Time in Eastern time	Trade Volume and Volatility	Authors Comments
9.30 AM - 11.00 AM	High volume and high volatility	Suitable for experienced traders, if you trade this hour, take profit quickly with proper stop loss protection
11.00 AM - 1.00 PM	Moderate volume	Ideal for beginners and swing trading
1.00 PM - 3.50 PM	Moderate volume	Unexpected moves are suitable for experienced traders
3.50 PM - 4.00 PM	High volume and high volatility	Do not trade if you are a beginner trader.
4.00 PM - 5.00 PM & 6.00 PM - 9.30 AM	Globex hours, low volume	Do not trade unless necessary to close existing open trades.

9.30 AM - 11.00 AM: Opening Session

The first 90 minutes of the trading day are often the most dynamic and volatile period, during which the market typically establishes the day's high and low points. This early activity allows traders to discern the directional trend, providing valuable insights into the market's momentum for the rest of the day. Although this session experiences significant volatility initially, the intensity generally subsides by the end of the first 90 minutes, creating a more precise and more stable environment for trading activities later in the day. Consequently, beginner traders should observe and familiarize themselves with the market movements during this period rather than entering trades prematurely. By patiently watching the initial fluctuations, novice traders can gain a better understanding of market behavior and avoid the risks associated with high volatility without sufficient experience.

11:00 AM - 1:00 PM: The Midday Session

During the midday session, which coincides with the lunch break for many traders, market activity tends to decrease significantly. On trending days, if a clear trend is established in the morning, it may continue but at a slower pace, allowing the momentum to persist without the intense volatility seen earlier. Additionally, this quieter period can present reversal opportunities, where the market may change direction from the trends set during the opening session, offering potential chances for traders to capitalize on trend continuation or reversal patterns. This reduced volatility and steadier market movement make the midday session particularly suitable for beginner traders, who can look for potential trading opportunities with lower risk and greater manageability. By taking advantage of the calmer conditions, novice traders can develop their strategies and gain confidence without being overwhelmed by the rapid fluctuations typical of more active trading periods.

1:00 PM - 3:50 PM: The Afternoon Session

The afternoon session alternates between periods of idleness and sudden bursts of activity. During the Low Activity Zone, which occupies the middle portion of this period, the market often experiences minimal movement as price action fluctuates within a narrow range, reflecting a period of consolidation and equilibrium. However, this relative calm is typically disrupted during the Power Hour Momentum phase, the final hour before the market closes. In this time frame, renewed momentum emerges as traders position themselves for the end of the trading day, leading to significant price movements and increased volatility. This surge in activity requires traders to remain disciplined and avoid impulsive decisions that could undermine earlier gains. Consequently, the afternoon session is particularly suitable for experienced traders who possess the expertise to navigate sudden market movements and capitalize on the opportunities that arise during these dynamic shifts.

3:50 PM - 4:00 PM: The Closing 10 Minutes

The final 10 minutes of the trading day are among the most unpredictable periods, characterized by high volatility and significant price swings. Institutional orders executed during this period can cause sharp price movements, making the market highly volatile and difficult to predict. Due to the unpredictable nature of these price fluctuations, traders should avoid entering new positions during this window to minimize potential risks. Instead, this period is best utilized for reflection and record-keeping. Traders should use the last few minutes of the day to review their trading activities, documenting both profits and losses, as well as key takeaways. This reflective practice helps in refining future strategies, enhancing overall trading performance, and ensuring that lessons learned from the day's activities contribute to more informed and disciplined trading decisions in subsequent sessions.

Challenges in the Modern Era:

Algorithmic Dominance: High-frequency trading (HFT) firms significantly influence short-term price action during the main trading hours, thereby increasing market complexity.

Overnight Volatility: In the absence of institutional activity, retail traders and global news often dictate Globex prices, leading to heightened volatility.

Conclusion

The S&P 500 futures market is a vibrant and dynamic environment shaped by its diverse participants and distinct trading structure. Institutional investors provide depth and stability during main trading hours, while retail traders inject energy and exploit opportunities during low-volume Globex sessions. Market makers and specialists ensure liquidity and price continuity, and electronic platforms have revolutionized trading accessibility and efficiency. By understanding the roles of these participants and the unique characteristics of trading hours, traders can navigate the complexities of the S&P futures market more effectively.

CHAPTER THREE

Candlestick Patterns

The history of candlestick patterns dates back to the 18th century in Japan, where a legendary rice trader named Munehisa Homma revolutionized market analysis. In the bustling Dojima Rice Exchange of Osaka, Homma observed that price movements were driven not only by supply and demand but also by the emotions of traders. He developed the first candlestick charts to visually capture these market dynamics. Each candlestick told a story of optimism, fear, greed, and hesitation—emotions that still govern markets today. This method became so effective that Homma reportedly amassed immense wealth, earning him a place in trading folklore. Over centuries, candlestick analysis spread to Western markets, evolving into a universal tool for traders across stocks, commodities, and futures. Its rich blend of art and science, rooted in human psychology, makes it as relevant and intriguing today as it was in Homma's era.

In this chapter, we delve into the foundational candlestick patterns essential for developing a strong trading strategy. While a single candlestick might not tell the whole story, the patterns formed by subsequent price movements provide critical insights into market behavior. These patterns serve as a visual language of price action, helping traders interpret the ongoing battle between buyers and sellers and anticipate what may lie ahead. By mastering these patterns, you'll gain a valuable toolset for predicting trends, identifying reversals, and navigating the complexities of the financial markets with confidence.

1. Doji

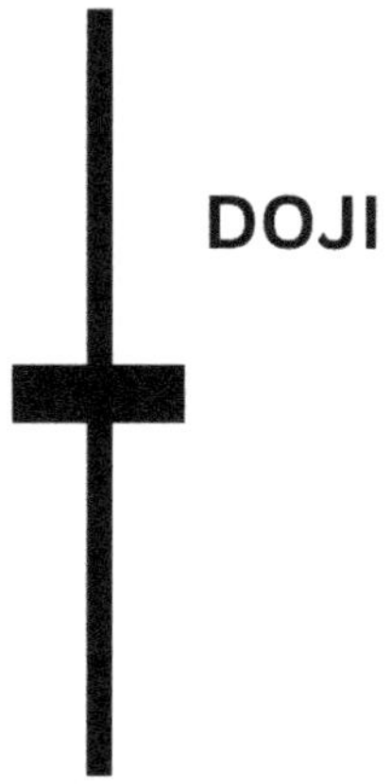

A Doji forms when the open and close prices are nearly identical, reflecting market indecision. It signals potential reversals or continuation, depending on the surrounding candles, and requires confirmation for clarity.

A Doji is a candlestick pattern that represents indecision in the market, forming when the opening and closing prices are nearly identical. It visually appears as a cross or plus sign, reflecting a balance between buying and selling pressures. This pattern indicates a tug-of-war between buyers and sellers, with neither side gaining a decisive advantage. Its significance lies in its ability to signal a potential reversal or continuation of the current trend, depending on the context provided by the surrounding candles. Traders often regard a Doji as a moment of hesitation in the market, where momentum may shift.

The context of a Doji is crucial for accurately interpreting its meaning. For example, when a Doji appears after a prolonged uptrend, it may suggest exhaustion among buyers and signal a potential reversal to the downside. Conversely, in a downtrend, it might hint at waning selling pressure and a possible shift upward. However, a Doji's signal is not standalone and requires confirmation from subsequent price action, such as a breakout or a follow-through candle in the direction of the trend. By understanding the nuances of a Doji within broader market conditions, traders can make more informed decisions about their entries and exits.

2. Dragonfly Doji

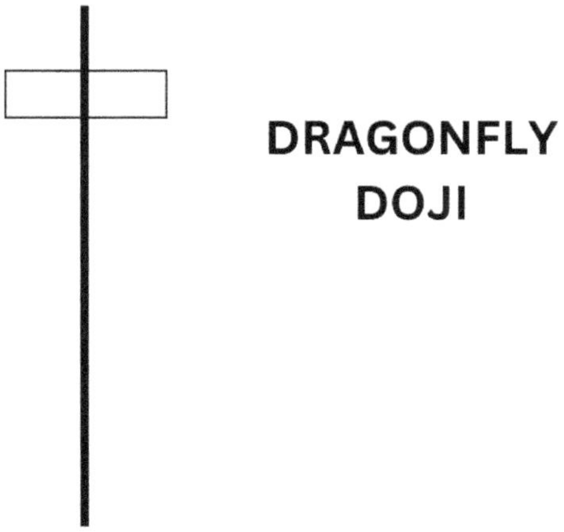

This pattern features a long lower wick, with the open, high, and close all occurring near the high. It suggests strong buying pressure after an initial period of selling dominance, often signaling a bullish reversal when confirmed.

The Dragonfly Doji is a unique candlestick pattern that forms when the opening, high, and closing prices are nearly identical, creating a small or nonexistent real body, accompanied by a long lower wick. This pattern emerges when sellers initially dominate the session, driving prices significantly lower. However, intense buying pressure later steps in, recovering the losses and pushing the closing price back near the opening level. The result is a candlestick that resembles a "T" shape, symbolizing a shift in market sentiment.

The Dragonfly Doji is often seen as a potential reversal signal, particularly when it appears after a sustained downtrend. Its long lower wick reflects robust buying interest at lower price levels, suggesting that the market may be nearing a turning point. While this pattern indicates that buyers regained control after a sell-off, it does not guarantee a reversal. Traders should view it as an early warning of a possible shift rather than a definitive signal.

The importance of the Dragonfly Doji in price action analysis lies in its ability to highlight areas where buyers are stepping in aggressively. For the pattern to hold greater significance, it is often accompanied by key support levels or high trading volumes, which can reinforce its reliability. However, traders are advised to wait for a bullish confirmation candle, such as a strong upward close that breaks above the Doji's high, before committing to long trades. Pairing this pattern with other technical tools, such as trendlines, moving averages, or oscillators like RSI, can further enhance its effectiveness in identifying high-probability entry points for a potential upward reversal.

3. Gravestone Doji

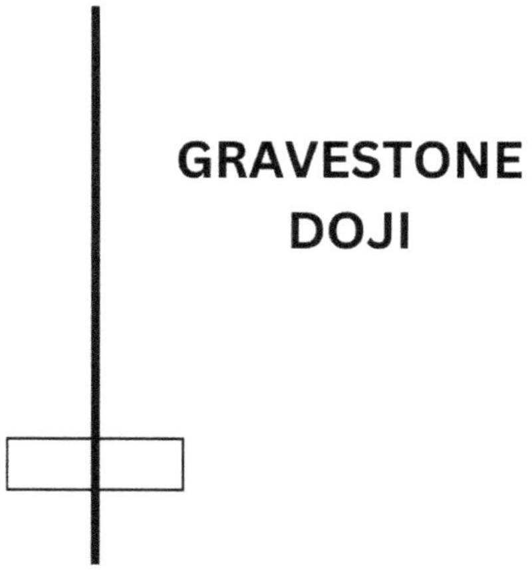

Characterized by a long upper wick with the open, low, and close near the session low, it signals buyer exhaustion and potential bearish reversals, especially near resistance levels.

The Gravestone Doji is a candlestick pattern that serves as the opposite of the Dragonfly Doji, characterized by a long upper wick and a small or nonexistent real body, with the opening and closing prices near the low of the session. This formation occurs when buyers initially attempt to push prices higher during the trading period, creating the long upper wick. However, their efforts are ultimately overcome by sellers, who drive prices back down to close near the opening level. The pattern visually resembles a gravestone, symbolizing a potential end to upward momentum.

The Gravestone Doji is often considered a warning sign of a bearish reversal, particularly when it appears at or near the top of an uptrend. It signals that buyers may be losing control and that selling pressure is beginning to dominate the market. This makes it a crucial pattern for traders looking to identify potential market tops or areas of resistance where the uptrend might stall or reverse.

The importance of the Gravestone Doji in price action analysis lies in its ability to highlight areas of strong selling interest. However, like most candlestick patterns, it is not a standalone signal and should be confirmed by additional factors. A bearish confirmation candle, such as a strong red candlestick closing below the low of the Doji, significantly strengthens the signal, providing traders with more confidence to enter short positions.

4. Hammer

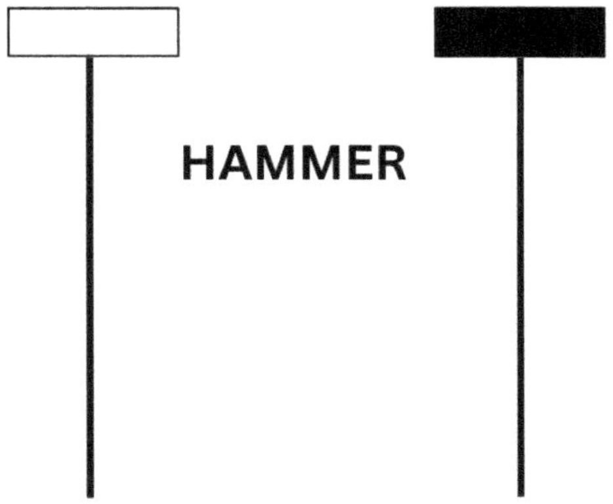

A small body near the top of the range and a long lower wick define the Hammer. Found in downtrends, it signals potential bottoming and reversal, confirmed by a bullish follow-up candle.

The Hammer is a candlestick pattern that typically forms at the bottom of a downtrend, signaling a potential reversal in market sentiment. It is characterized by a small real body near the top of the candle's range and a long lower wick, which is at least twice the length of the body. This structure reflects the market dynamics during the session: sellers dominated initially, driving prices significantly lower, but strong buying interest emerged, pushing the price back up toward the opening level by the close. The result is a hammer-shaped candlestick, symbolizing that the market may be "hammering out" a bottom.

The significance of the Hammer lies in its ability to mark a potential trend reversal and signal that buyers are stepping in aggressively at lower levels. This suggests that the bearish momentum is waning, and bulls are beginning to regain control, creating the potential for an upward price movement. The pattern is particularly impactful when it appears at key support levels or after a prolonged downtrend, where traders are looking for signs of a reversal.

However, the Hammer alone does not confirm a trend change; it serves as a warning of a possible shift in sentiment. Traders must wait for a bullish confirmation candle, such as a strong green candle closing above the Hammer's high, to validate the reversal and provide a safer entry point for a long position. This confirmation reduces the risk of false signals and increases the probability of a successful trade.

5. Hanging Man

Similar to the Hammer but forming in an uptrend, the Hanging Man suggests building selling pressure and a potential bearish reversal when confirmed by subsequent price action.

The Hanging Man is a candlestick pattern that forms at the top of an uptrend and is visually similar to the Hammer, but its implications are distinctly bearish. It features a small real body near the top of the price range and a long lower wick, typically at least twice the length of the body. This pattern emerges when sellers manage to push prices significantly lower during the session, but buyers step in to regain some control, driving the price back up near the opening level by the close. Despite the higher close, the long lower wick suggests that selling pressure is beginning to build, potentially signaling the exhaustion of the uptrend.

The significance of the Hanging Man lies in its ability to serve as a warning of a potential bearish reversal. It highlights a moment of vulnerability in the uptrend, where buyers may be losing momentum, and sellers are starting to assert themselves. This pattern often appears near resistance levels or after an extended upward move, where traders are on the lookout for signs of a reversal.

However, the Hanging Man is not a definitive signal on its own and requires confirmation before taking action. Traders should wait for the next candle to provide a clear bearish signal, such as a strong red candle closing below the Hanging Man's low. This confirmation indicates that selling pressure has intensified, increasing the likelihood of a reversal and making it a safer entry point for short positions.

6. Inverted Hammer

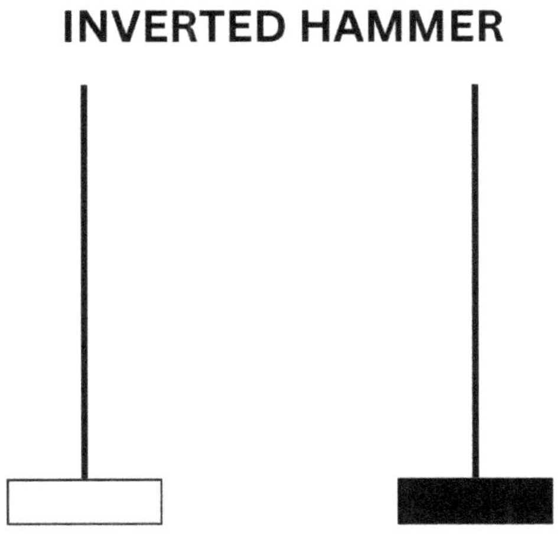

The Inverted Hammer is a candlestick pattern that typically forms at the end of a downtrend, signaling a potential reversal in market sentiment.

It is characterized by a small real body near the lower end of the candle's range and a long upper wick, which is at least twice the length of the body. This structure reflects the market dynamics during the session: buyers made an attempt to push prices significantly higher, as evidenced by the long upper wick, but sellers regained control and pushed the price back down near the opening level by the close. Despite the close near the session low, the pattern suggests that selling momentum may be waning and that buyers are starting to test the waters.

The significance of the Inverted Hammer lies in its ability to hint at a potential reversal in a bearish trend. While the pattern does not guarantee a shift in direction, it serves as an early indication that the downtrend may be losing steam. This is particularly meaningful when the Inverted Hammer appears near a key support level or after a prolonged decline, where traders are actively seeking signs of a potential bottom.

However, the Inverted Hammer is not a definitive reversal signal on its own and should always be accompanied by confirmation. Traders are advised to wait for a bullish confirmation candle, such as a strong green candlestick closing above the high of the Inverted Hammer, before entering an extended position. This confirmation provides greater confidence that the buying pressure seen during the formation of the pattern is likely to continue, reducing the risk of false signals.

7. Shooting Star

The Shooting Star is a bearish candlestick pattern that typically forms at the top of an uptrend, serving as a potential warning of a reversal in market sentiment. It is characterized by a small real body near the lower end of the candle's range and a long upper wick, which is at least twice the length of the body. This pattern forms when buyers initially dominate the session, driving prices significantly higher. Still, sellers gain control later in the period, pushing the price back down near the opening level by the close. The resulting candle visually resembles a shooting star, symbolizing a fading upward momentum.

The Shooting Star's significance lies in its ability to signal a potential exhaustion of the uptrend. The long upper wick reflects an unsuccessful attempt by buyers to maintain higher price levels, indicating growing selling pressure and a possible shift in control from bulls to bears. This pattern is significant when it occurs near resistance levels, following an extended upward move, or in overbought market conditions where traders are expecting a pullback.

However, the Shooting Star is not a guaranteed reversal signal on its own. Traders should wait for confirmation before taking action. A bearish confirmation candle, such as a strong red candlestick closing below the low of the Shooting Star, is crucial to validate the pattern and indicate that selling pressure is likely to persist. This confirmation provides traders with a higher-probability signal to enter short positions, reducing the risk of false signals.

8. Bullish Engulfing

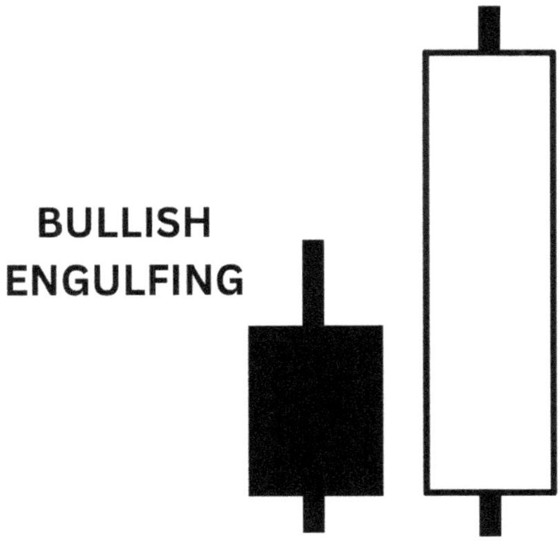

The Bullish Engulfing pattern is a powerful candlestick formation that occurs during a downtrend and signals a potential reversal in market sentiment. It consists of two candles: a smaller bearish candle followed by a larger bullish candle. The body of the bullish candle completely engulfs the body of the preceding bearish candle, demonstrating a dramatic shift in momentum. This pattern indicates that buyers have stepped in forcefully, overpowering sellers and potentially marking the beginning of an upward trend.

The significance of the Bullish Engulfing pattern lies in its ability to highlight intense buying pressure at lower levels. It suggests that bearish sentiment is weakening, and bulls are regaining control, signaling a critical reversal. This pattern is particularly impactful when it appears near key support levels, after a prolonged decline, or in oversold conditions, as these contexts add weight to the potential for a reversal.

For traders, the Bullish Engulfing pattern serves as a clear visual signal of a shift in market dynamics. However, as with any reversal pattern, confirmation is crucial. Traders often wait for the engulfing candle to close and, in some cases, for additional confirmation such as a higher high on the next candle or increased volume accompanying the pattern. These elements help to validate the reversal and reduce the risk of false signals.

9. Bearish Engulfing

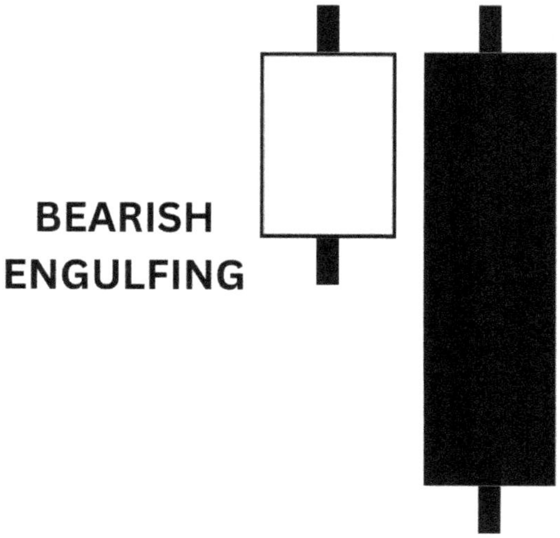

The Bearish Engulfing pattern is a significant candlestick formation that serves as the opposite of the Bullish Engulfing pattern. It occurs when a larger bearish candle completely engulfs the body of the preceding bullish candle, signaling a decisive shift in momentum from buying to selling pressure. This pattern reflects a decisive rejection of higher prices, as sellers overpower buyers and drive prices lower. It is significant when it forms at the end of an uptrend, as it often signals a potential bearish reversal and the exhaustion of upward momentum.

The Bearish Engulfing pattern's significance lies in its ability to highlight a key turning point in market sentiment. It indicates that sellers are gaining control after a period of bullish dominance, making it an essential pattern for traders looking to identify potential market tops or areas of resistance. This pattern is especially impactful when it appears near key resistance levels, after an extended rally, or in overbought market conditions, where a reversal is more likely.

While the Bearish Engulfing pattern is a strong visual indicator of a potential trend reversal, traders should wait for confirmation before taking action. A bearish confirmation candle, such as another red candle closing below the low of the engulfing candle, adds confidence to the signal and reduces the likelihood of a false reversal. This confirmation provides a safer entry point for short trades and helps traders manage risk effectively.

10. Morning Star

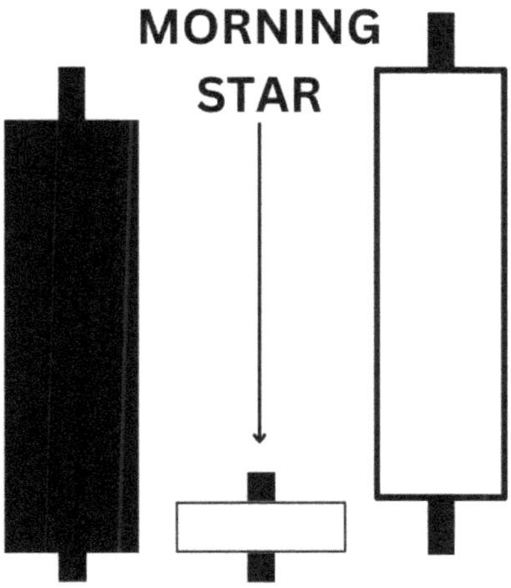

A three-candle bullish reversal pattern with a large bearish candle, a smaller indecision candle, and a strong bullish candle

that closes above the first candle's midpoint. It marks the transition from bearish to bullish sentiment.

It typically forms at the bottom of a downtrend and consists of three distinct candles:

a. **The first candle** is a large bearish candle that reflects intense selling pressure, continuing the prevailing downtrend.
b. **The second candle** is smaller, often a Doji or a small-bodied candlestick, which indicates indecision or a pause in the market. This candle represents a balance between buyers and sellers as the downward momentum starts to weaken.
c. **The third candle** is a strong bullish candle that closes well into the body of the first bearish candle, signaling that buyers have regained control and a potential trend reversal is underway.

The Morning Star pattern holds significant importance in technical analysis because it marks a potential bottom in the market, often appearing at key support levels or after a prolonged decline. It reflects a transition in sentiment: sellers lose momentum, and buyers step in with enough strength to push prices higher, potentially initiating a new uptrend.

For traders, the confirmation of the Morning Star is essential before entering long positions. This confirmation comes when the third bullish candle closes above the midpoint of the first bearish candle, reinforcing the validity of the reversal signal. A close above this level suggests that the buying pressure is strong enough to overpower the previous selling momentum, offering a higher-probability setup for long trades.

11. Evening Star

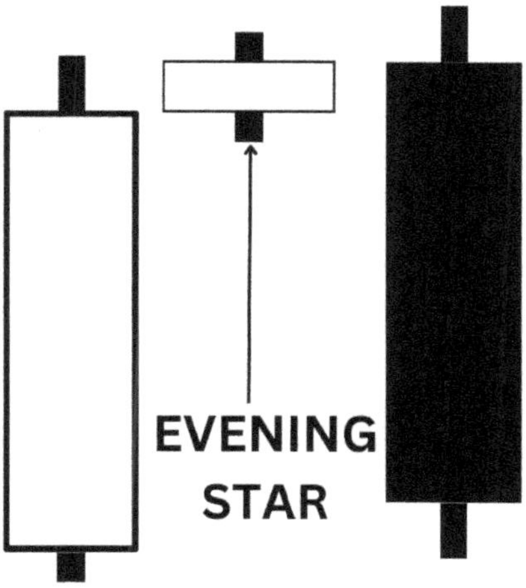

The bearish counterpart to the Morning Star, this three-candle pattern consists of a large bullish candle, an indecision candle, and a strong bearish candle, signaling a potential reversal at market tops.

The Evening Star is a well-known three-candlestick bearish reversal pattern that typically forms at the top of an uptrend, signaling a potential shift in market sentiment from bullish to bearish.

a. **The first candle** is a large bullish candle that reflects intense buying pressure, continuing the prevailing uptrend.
b. **The second candle** is smaller, often a Doji or a small-bodied candlestick, which indicates indecision in the market. This candle suggests that the upward momentum is beginning to wane as buyers and sellers reach a temporary balance.
c. **The third candle** is a strong bearish candle that closes well into the body of the first bullish candle, confirming that sellers have taken control and signaling a potential reversal.

The Evening Star pattern is significant because it marks a potential top in the market, often appearing near resistance levels or after an extended upward move. It demonstrates a transition in sentiment: buyers lose momentum, and sellers step in with enough force to push prices lower, suggesting the beginning of a downtrend. This pattern is particularly impactful when it appears in overbought conditions or alongside bearish divergence in technical indicators.

Traders should exercise caution and seek confirmation before acting on the Evening Star pattern. The bearish reversal is confirmed when the third candle closes below the midpoint of the first bullish candle. This confirmation provides a more reliable signal that the uptrend is losing steam and that a downtrend may be forming. Without this confirmation, the pattern could result in a false signal.

12. Piercing Line

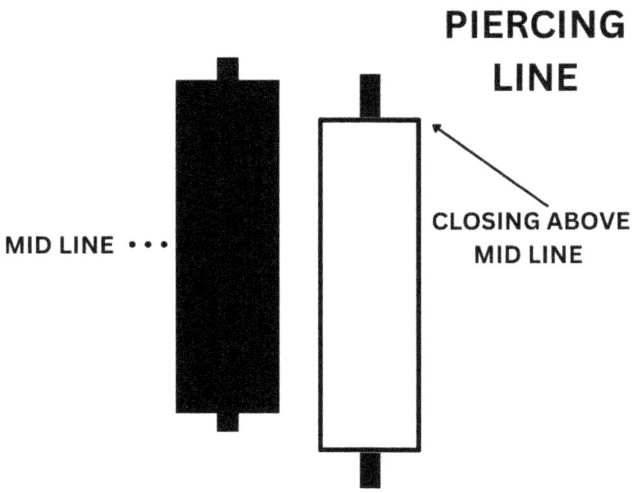

The **Piercing Line** candlestick pattern is a two-candle bullish reversal pattern that signals a potential shift in market sentiment from bearish to bullish. It typically forms after a downtrend and highlights the emergence of intense buying pressure. The pattern consists of two distinct candles:

a. **The first candle** is a large bearish candle, reflecting sustained selling pressure and the continuation of the existing downtrend.
b. **The second candle** opens below the low of the first candle, signaling an initial bearish extension. However, buyers step in aggressively, pushing the price higher, and the candle closes above the midpoint of the first bearish candle. This close demonstrates a significant recovery and a potential reversal in market sentiment.

The Piercing Line pattern is significant because it indicates that buyers are regaining control after a sell-off. The intense buying pressure evidenced by the second candle's close above the midpoint of the first candle signals a potential bottom and the possibility of an upward reversal. This pattern often appears near key support levels or in oversold conditions, where buyers are expected to step in and counteract selling momentum.

For traders, the confirmation of the Piercing Line pattern is essential before taking action. Confirmation is provided by the second candle's close above the midpoint of the first candle, which suggests that the bullish momentum is strong enough to counteract the prior bearish pressure. Many traders use this confirmation as a signal to enter long positions, targeting subsequent resistance levels or the beginning of a new uptrend.

13. Dark Cloud Cover

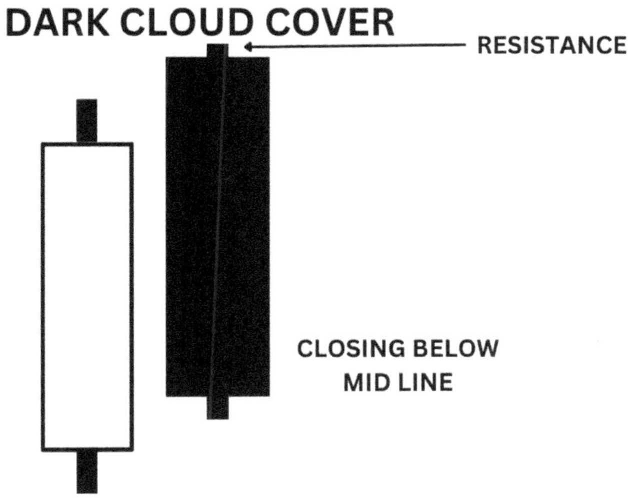

The Dark Cloud Cover is a two-candle bearish reversal pattern and the counterpart of the Piercing Line pattern. It typically forms at the top of an uptrend or near a resistance level, signaling a potential shift in market sentiment from bullish to bearish. This pattern consists of two distinct candles:

a. **The first candle** is a large bullish candle that reflects intense buying pressure, continuing the prevailing uptrend.
b. **The second candle** opens above the high of the first bullish candle, creating a gap up, but sellers take control during the session, driving the price down. The second candle closes below the midpoint of the first bullish candle, signaling a significant shift in momentum.

The Dark Cloud Cover pattern is significant because it highlights a bearish reversal and suggests that the uptrend may be losing steam. The gap up at the beginning of the second candle initially gives the impression of continued bullish strength. However, the subsequent bearish move and the close below the midpoint of the first candle indicate that sellers have regained control and are likely to push prices lower. This pattern is particularly significant when it forms near resistance levels, as it increases the likelihood of a reversal.

For traders, confirmation of the Dark Cloud Cover pattern is essential before taking action. The bearish reversal is validated when the second candle closes below the midpoint of the first candle. This confirmation provides a more reliable signal to enter short positions, as it reflects a decisive shift in market sentiment. Many traders place stop-loss orders above the high of the second candle to manage risk effectively.

14. Three White Soldiers

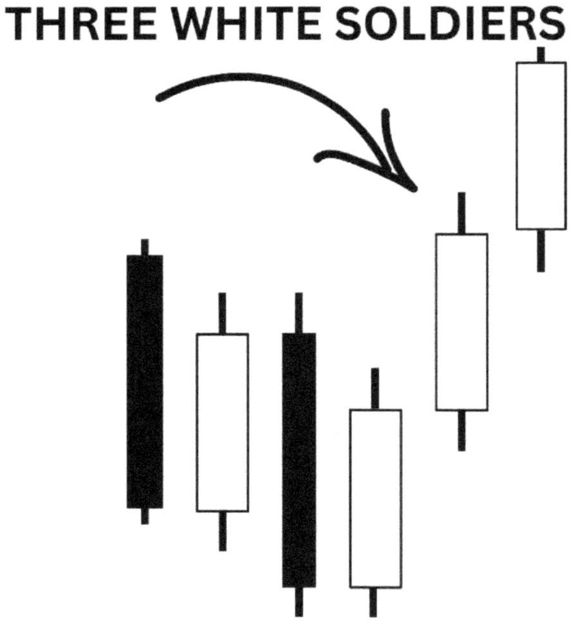

This pattern features three consecutive long bullish candles with higher closes, showcasing strong buyer momentum and trend continuation or reversal after a downtrend.

The Three White Soldiers candlestick pattern is a bullish formation that consists of three consecutive long bullish candles, each closing higher than the previous one. This pattern reflects strong upward momentum and is considered a reliable signal of trend continuation or a reversal from a prior downtrend. The consistently higher closes and long bodies of the candles indicate persistent buying pressure, with bulls firmly in control of the market.

Each candle in the Three White Soldiers pattern provides critical insights into market sentiment:

a. **The first candle** signifies the initial push by buyers, reversing bearish momentum or strengthening an existing uptrend.
b. **The second candle** builds on the first, opening near or slightly below the previous close and closing higher, reinforcing the dominance of buyers.
c. **The third candle** confirms the strength of the upward move, closing even higher and signaling that the bullish trend is well-established.

The significance of the Three White Soldiers pattern lies in its ability to showcase persistent and increasing buying pressure over multiple sessions. This pattern is significant when it appears after a downtrend, as it indicates a reversal and the start of a potential uptrend. It can also occur during an uptrend, acting as a continuation signal that suggests further bullish momentum.

For traders, the Three White Soldiers pattern offers a clear entry point for long positions. Many traders choose to enter after the close of the third bullish candle, as it confirms the pattern's strength. To manage risk effectively, stop-loss orders are often placed below the low of the first candle in the pattern, protecting against unexpected market reversals.

15. Three Black Crows

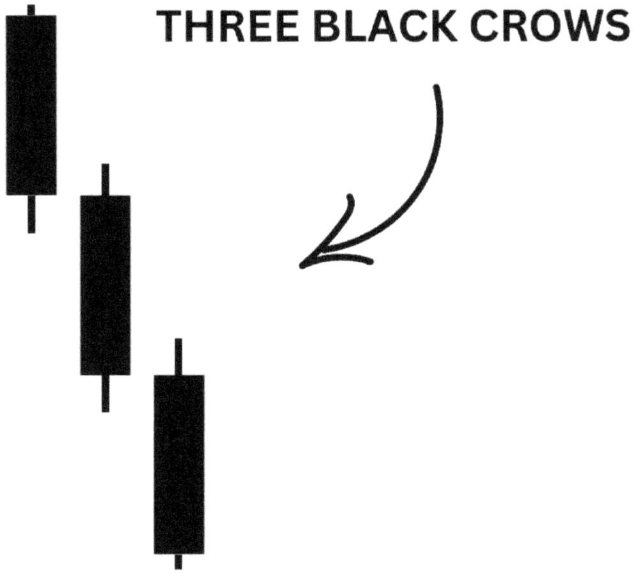

The Three Black Crows pattern has three long bearish candles with lower closes, signaling sustained selling pressure and potential trend reversal.

This pattern typically forms at the top of an uptrend or after a period of consolidation, signaling a substantial shift in market sentiment from bullish to bearish. The consistently lower closes and long bodies of the candles reflect sustained selling pressure, with bears taking control of the market.

Each candle in the Three Black Crows pattern provides essential insights into the transition of market momentum:

a. **The first candle** initiates the reversal, signaling that sellers have begun to overpower buyers after a period of bullish or neutral sentiment.
b. **The second candle** confirms the bearish momentum, opening near or slightly above the previous close and closing even lower. This reinforces the strength of the downward move.
c. **The third candle** solidifies the pattern, closing significantly lower and leaving little doubt that the bears are now firmly in control.

The significance of the Three Black Crows pattern lies in its ability to identify sustained bearish momentum and signal a potential trend reversal. When it appears near key resistance levels, overbought conditions, or after an extended uptrend, it often marks the beginning of a downtrend. The pattern is helpful for traders seeking to anticipate bearish reversals and capitalize on shifts in market sentiment.

For traders, the confirmation of the Three Black Crows pattern comes after the third candle closes, which provides a clear signal to enter short positions. Stop-loss orders are typically placed above the high of the first candle to manage risk effectively. This placement ensures protection against unexpected price rebounds while maintaining a favorable risk-reward ratio.

16. Tweezer Tops

Two candles with nearly identical highs signal resistance and potential bearish reversals. Confirmation from a bearish follow-up candle strengthens the signal.

The Tweezer Tops candlestick pattern is a bearish reversal formation that consists of two candles with nearly identical highs, typically appearing at the top of an uptrend. This pattern signals strong resistance and the potential for a reversal in market direction. The equal highs on the two candles reflect a rejection of higher prices, indicating that buyers are struggling to push the price further upward while sellers are starting to assert control.

The structure of the Tweezer Tops pattern provides essential insights into market sentiment:

a. **The first candle** is often bullish, reflecting the continuation of the uptrend as buyers push prices higher.
b. **The second candle** may open near the previous close but fails to break above the high of the first candle, forming a near-equal high. This candle can be bearish, reflecting an inability to sustain higher prices as selling pressure increases.

The Tweezer Tops pattern's significance lies in its ability to highlight key resistance levels and a potential shift in momentum. It shows that buyers are losing strength and that sellers are stepping in to defend the resistance zone. This pattern is significant when it appears near psychological price levels, historical resistance, or in overbought market conditions, where reversals are more likely.

For traders, confirmation of the Tweezer Tops pattern is essential before taking action. A bearish confirmation candle following the Tweezer Tops, such as a strong red candle closing below the low of the pattern, is a critical signal to validate the reversal. This confirmation provides a safer entry point for short positions, reducing the risk of false signals.

17. Tweezer Bottoms

Two candles with nearly identical lows highlight support and potential bullish reversals. A bullish confirmation candle enhances reliability.

The Tweezer Bottoms candlestick pattern is a bullish reversal formation that serves as the counterpart to the Tweezer Tops. It consists of two candles with nearly identical lows, typically appearing at the bottom of a downtrend. This pattern signals strong support and the potential for a shift in market sentiment from bearish to bullish. The equal lows on the two candles indicate that sellers are struggling to push prices lower, while buyers are stepping in to defend the support zone, potentially marking the beginning of an upward reversal.

The structure of the Tweezer Bottoms pattern provides valuable insights into market dynamics:

a. **The first candle** is usually bearish, continuing the prevailing downtrend as sellers dominate the session and push prices lower.
b. **The second candle** often opens near the previous close but finds strong buying interest at the same low as the first candle. This results in a near-equal low, signaling that sellers are losing momentum while buyers gain strength. The second candle is typically bullish, underscoring the transition in control.

The significance of the Tweezer Bottoms pattern lies in its ability to highlight key support levels and suggest a potential reversal. It reflects a strong defense by buyers at lower price levels, where selling pressure diminishes and bullish momentum begins to build. This pattern is particularly impactful when it forms near historical support levels, psychological price zones, or in oversold conditions, where reversals are more likely.

For traders, confirmation of the Tweezer Bottoms pattern is crucial before entering long positions. A bullish confirmation candle following the Tweezer Bottoms, such as a strong green candle closing above the high of the pattern, provides the necessary validation that buying pressure is likely to continue. This confirmation reduces the risk of false signals and offers a safer entry point.

18. Harami (Bullish and Bearish)

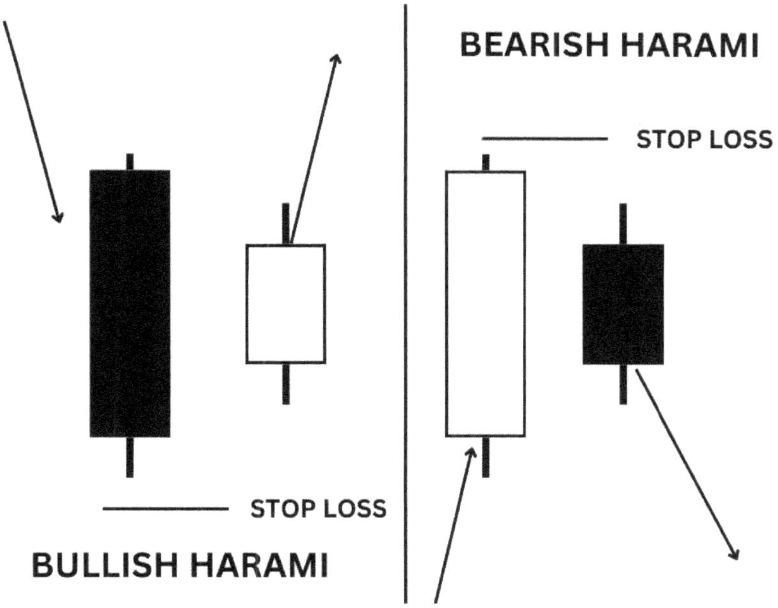

A Harami is a candlestick pattern that signals a potential shift in market momentum, often indicating a reversal or a period of consolidation. The term "Harami" is derived from the Japanese word for "pregnant," reflecting the visual appearance of the pattern, where a smaller candle is entirely contained within the body of the preceding larger candle. This two-candle formation can occur in both bullish and bearish contexts, depending on the direction of the prior trend.

Structure of a Harami Pattern:

a. The first candle is a large candle that reflects the prevailing market trend. In an uptrend, it will be a bullish candle, and in a downtrend, it will be bearish.
b. The second candle is smaller, often with a contrasting body color, and forms entirely within the range of the first candle's body. This smaller candle indicates a pause in the dominant momentum, with neither buyers nor sellers asserting precise control.

Interpretation and Significance:

The Harami pattern is significant because it highlights a shift in momentum, suggesting that the dominant trend may be weakening. In a downtrend, a Bullish Harami indicates that selling pressure is diminishing, and buyers may be stepping in, potentially signaling an upward reversal. Conversely, in an uptrend, a Bearish Harami suggests that buying momentum is fading, and sellers are gaining strength, potentially leading to a downward reversal.

This pattern can also indicate consolidation, where the market takes a breather before resuming its previous trend. The context in which the Harami forms—such as near key support or resistance levels or alongside overbought or oversold conditions—can help determine whether it signals a reversal or continuation.

Trading the Harami Pattern:

For traders, confirmation is essential before acting on a Harami pattern. This often involves waiting for a breakout from the range of the Harami's two candles. In a Bullish Harami, a breakout above the high of the larger candle confirms a potential upward move, signaling a buying opportunity. In a Bearish Harami, a breakout below the low of the larger candle confirms bearish momentum, signaling a shorting opportunity.

19. Kicker Pattern (Bullish and Bearish)

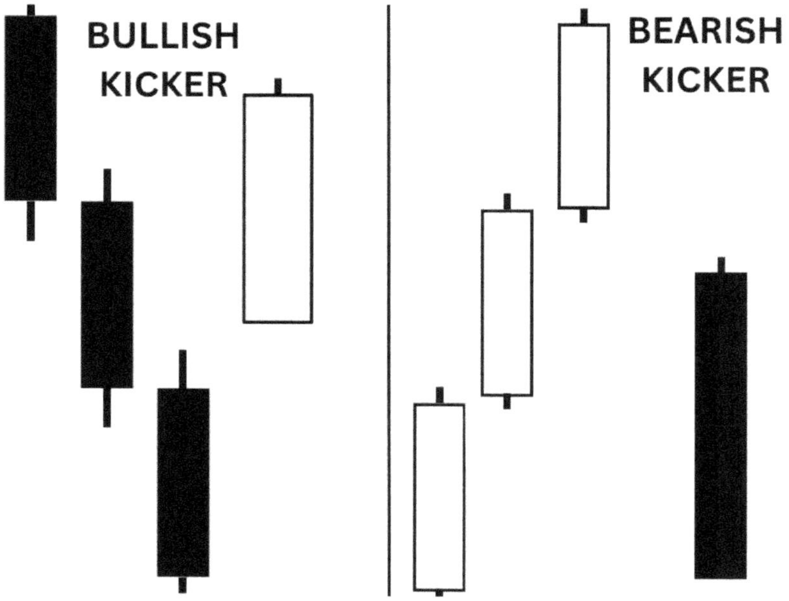

The Kicker Pattern is a powerful candlestick formation that signals an abrupt and decisive reversal in market sentiment. This pattern is characterized by a sharp change in direction, typically marked by a gap and no overlap between the two candles involved. The Kicker is considered one of the most reliable and impactful reversal patterns, often leading to substantial and sustained price movements in the direction of the second candle.

Structure of the Kicker Pattern:

a. The first candle reflects the current market trend and sentiment. In a bearish kicker, the first candle is bearish, continuing a downtrend. In a bullish kicker, the first candle is bullish, extending an uptrend.
b. The second candle opens with a gap in the opposite direction of the first candle and moves powerfully in that direction throughout the session. There is no overlap between the body of the first candle and the second candle, creating a visual gap that underscores the dramatic shift in sentiment.

Interpretation and Significance:

The Kicker Pattern signifies a sudden and forceful reversal in market dynamics, often triggered by unexpected news, economic data, or a shift in market sentiment. Its significance lies in its ability to signal strong and reliable trend reversals, as the sharp gap and the decisive movement of the second candle reflect overwhelming dominance by either buyers or sellers.

In a Bullish Kicker, the market abruptly shifts from bearish to bullish sentiment, with the second candle gapping up and closing strongly higher. This pattern often marks the beginning of a robust upward trend. Conversely, in a Bearish Kicker, the market transitions from bullish to bearish sentiment, with the second candle gapping down and closing significantly lower, signaling the onset of a strong downward trend.

Trading the Kicker Pattern:

Traders typically enter positions in the direction of the Kicker candle, as it confirms the momentum of the reversal. In a bullish kicker, traders look to buy, while in a bearish kicker, traders look to short. The lack of overlap between the candles and the decisive movement of the second candle provides a clear signal of the new trend.

20. Spinning Top

A Spinning Top is a candlestick pattern characterized by a small real body positioned near the middle of the candle's range, accompanied by long upper and lower wicks. This formation reflects market indecision, where neither buyers nor sellers can gain precise control during the session. The small body represents a minimal difference between the opening and closing prices. At the same time, the long shadows indicate significant price movement in both directions before the market settled near its open.

Interpretation and Significance:

The Spinning Top is an essential signal in technical analysis as it often warns of a potential pause or reversal in the current trend. When it appears during an uptrend, it suggests that bullish momentum is weakening, and a reversal or consolidation may be imminent. Conversely, in a downtrend, it indicates that selling pressure is diminishing and that a reversal to the upside or a period of sideways movement may follow.

The Spinning Top does not provide a definitive direction for future price movement but instead highlights market indecision. Its significance is heightened when it occurs near key support or resistance levels, where market participants are likely to reevaluate the trend. The small body of the Spinning Top is the key feature, signaling that the balance between buyers and sellers is shifting, even if the outcome remains unclear at that point.

Confirmation and Context:

While the Spinning Top suggests a potential change in the market, it requires confirmation from the following candle to determine the likely direction. If the next candle is bullish and closes above the high of the Spinning Top, it may confirm a continuation or reversal to the upside. Conversely, if the next candle is bearish and closes below the low of the Spinning Top, it may confirm a continuation or reversal to the downside.

The size of the wicks on either side of the Spinning Top is less important than the small body itself, which emphasizes the lack of decisive movement during the session. The long shadows illustrate attempts by both buyers and sellers to push the price in their favor, but the small body underscores that neither side succeeded in asserting dominance.

Application in Technical Analysis:

The Spinning Top is often used in conjunction with other technical tools and indicators to enhance its predictive power. For example:

a. If it forms near a support level in a downtrend, it may suggest that the trend is losing strength, and a reversal could be on the horizon.
b. If it forms near a resistance level in an uptrend, it may signal that the bullish move is stalling.

In summary, the Spinning Top is a versatile and valuable candlestick pattern that highlights a market's hesitation and alerts traders to the possibility of a change in trend. By waiting for confirmation from the next candle and analyzing the broader market context, traders can use this pattern to anticipate potential pauses, reversals, or shifts in momentum with greater accuracy.

21. Long-Legged Doji

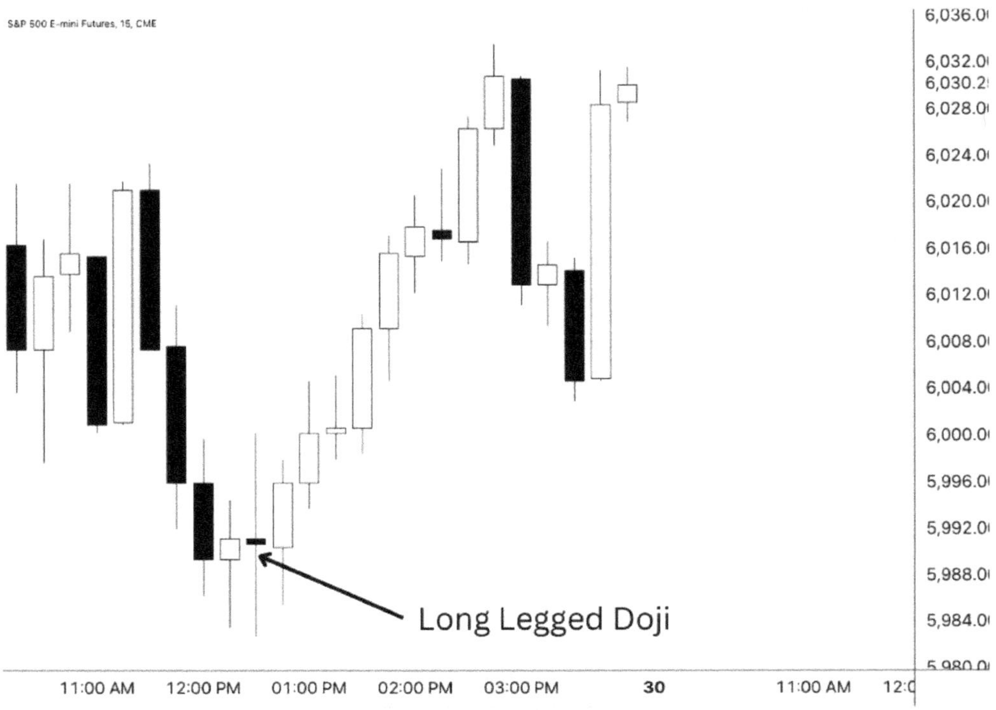

The Long-Legged Doji is a distinctive candlestick pattern characterized by its exceptionally long upper and lower wicks and a small or nonexistent real body. This formation reflects significant indecision in the market, as both buyers and sellers actively push prices far from the opening level during the session, only for the cost to return close to its opening by the close. The result is a Doji with long shadows extending in both directions, signaling a balance of power between bulls and bears.

Interpretation and Significance:

The Long-Legged Doji serves as a clear indication of market indecision, where neither buyers nor sellers have managed to gain the upper hand. Its formation suggests that both sides attempted to assert dominance, driving the price significantly higher and lower during the session, but ultimately failed to maintain control. This pattern is particularly noteworthy when it appears after a strong trend, as it can signal potential trend exhaustion or a pause in momentum.

In an uptrend, the Long-Legged Doji may indicate that buying momentum is weakening and that a reversal or consolidation could follow. Conversely, in a downtrend, it suggests that selling pressure is subsiding, raising the possibility of a bullish reversal or sideways movement. Its presence at key support or resistance levels can amplify its importance, as these are areas where market indecision often leads to significant price shifts.

Confirmation and Context:

While the Long-Legged Doji is a strong warning of potential trend exhaustion, it does not provide a clear indication of future direction on its own. Traders should wait for confirmation from the next candle before taking action. If the next candle closes above the high of the Long-Legged Doji, it may confirm a bullish reversal or continuation of an uptrend. Conversely, if the next candle closes below the low of the Long-Legged Doji, it may confirm a bearish reversal or continuation of a downtrend.

The pattern's significance is heightened when it forms in specific contexts:

a. Near a support level in a downtrend, it could signal that sellers are losing strength and buyers may begin to take control.
b. Near a resistance level in an uptrend, it suggests that buyers are struggling to maintain momentum, opening the door for a potential reversal.

Application in Technical Analysis:

To enhance the reliability of the Long-Legged Doji, traders often combine it with other technical tools and indicators. For instance:

a. High trading volume during the formation of the Long-Legged Doji indicates intense activity and adds weight to its significance as a potential turning point.
b. Support and resistance levels provide additional context, as the pattern often forms near these critical zones where market indecision is most pronounced.

By itself, the Long-Legged Doji is a valuable signal of uncertainty and potential trend exhaustion. However, traders should use it in conjunction with confirmation from subsequent price action and other technical analysis tools to determine the likely direction of the next move. When interpreted correctly, the Long-Legged Doji can serve as a critical early warning of a change in market dynamics, offering traders a valuable edge in anticipating reversals or pauses in the trend.

22. Inside Bar

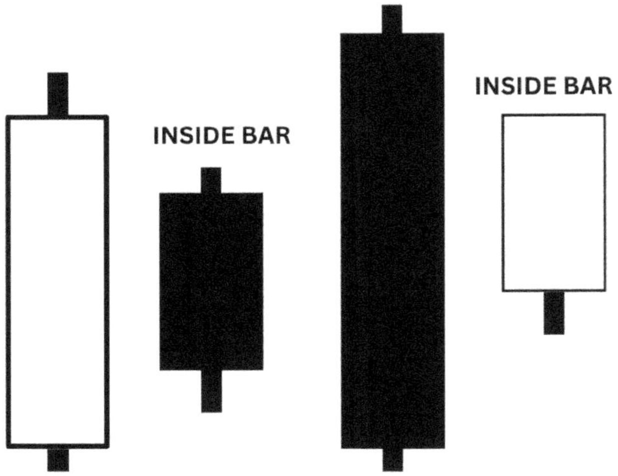

An Inside Bar is a two-candle pattern where the second candle forms entirely within the range of the first candle, including its high and low. The smaller second candle reflects a period of market consolidation, indecision, or reduced volatility following a larger movement. This pattern often serves as a precursor to a breakout, as it represents a pause in the prevailing trend before the market decides on its next direction.

Structure of the Inside Bar:

a. The first candle, often referred to as the "mother bar," is larger and reflects the dominant trend or market sentiment.

b. The second candle, called the "inside bar," has a smaller range, with its high being lower than the mother bar's high and its low being higher than the mother bar's low. This smaller range shows that the market is temporarily contracting, with neither buyers nor sellers asserting dominance.

Interpretation and Significance:

The Inside Bar is significant because it highlights a pause in market activity that often precedes a breakout. This period of consolidation reflects a temporary balance between buyers and sellers, with reduced price volatility. Traders interpret this pattern as a build-up of potential energy, which is typically released in the form of a strong price move when the market breaks out of the inside bar's range.

In an uptrend, an Inside Bar indicates that the market is taking a breather before potentially resuming its upward trend. In a downtrend, it means a potential pause in bearish momentum before resuming its decline. When an Inside Bar appears at key support or resistance levels, it may signal an impending reversal rather than continuation.

Trading the Inside Bar:

The Inside Bar is a versatile pattern, but its actual value lies in its ability to predict breakouts. Traders often wait for the price to break above or below the inside bar's range before entering a trade in the direction of the breakout.

For example:

a. A breakout above the high of the inside bar signals bullish momentum, providing an entry point for long positions.
b. A breakout below the low of the inside bar signals bearish momentum, providing an entry point for short positions.

The strength of the breakout and the direction of the trend often determine the significance of the move. Inside Bars that form in the direction of the prevailing trend are more likely to result in continuation. In contrast, those forming at key reversal points, such as resistance or support levels, may indicate a trend change.

23. Outside Bar

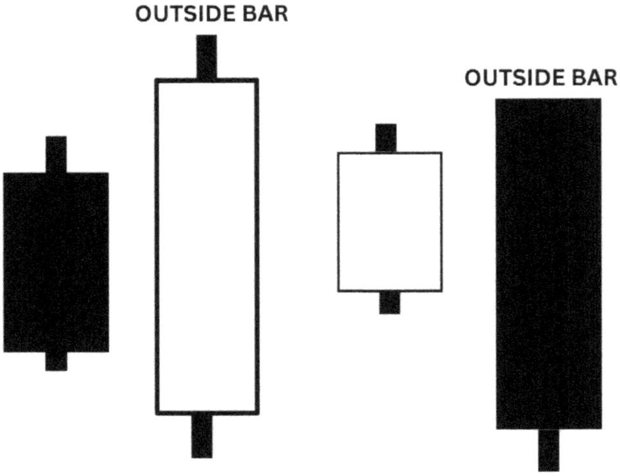

The Outside Bar, also known as an Engulfing Bar, is a powerful candlestick pattern that occurs when a candle's range completely engulfs the range of the previous candle. This means the Outside Bar's high is higher than the previous candle's high, and its low is lower than the previous candle's low. This pattern can signal either a sharp reversal or continuation of the current trend, depending on the context in which it forms. The extensive range of the Outside Bar reflects heightened market activity and strong momentum, making it a key signal for traders.

Structure of the Outside Bar:

a. **The first candle** reflects the existing market sentiment or trend. It is smaller in range compared to the second candle.
b. **The second candle**, the Outside Bar, completely engulfs the high and low of the first candle, indicating a significant shift in market dynamics. This candle may close in either direction, depending on whether it signals a reversal or continuation.

Interpretation and Significance:

The Outside Bar is significant because it highlights a surge in market momentum, as reflected in the larger range of the second candle. This surge often follows periods of lower volatility or consolidation, marking a decisive move by either buyers or sellers.

a. In a bullish context, the Outside Bar may signal that buyers have taken control, especially if it closes near its high. This scenario often indicates a continuation of the trend or a reversal from a prior downtrend.

b. In a bearish context, the Outside Bar suggests that sellers have overpowered buyers, especially if it closes near its low, indicating potential trend continuation to the downside or a reversal from an uptrend.

The pattern's relevance is heightened when it occurs at key support or resistance levels or after a prolonged trend, as it often marks the beginning of a strong price move in the breakout direction.

Trading the Outside Bar:

Traders use the Outside Bar as a reliable signal to enter positions in the direction of the breakout. Key entry strategies include:

a. Bullish breakout: Enter long positions when the price breaks above the high of the Outside Bar, confirming upward momentum.
b. Bearish breakout: Enter short positions when the price breaks below the low of the Outside Bar, confirming downward momentum.

The size of the Outside Bar relative to the surrounding candles provides additional clues about the strength of the breakout. A significantly larger Outside Bar indicates firm conviction and a higher likelihood of a sustained move in the breakout direction.

Contextual Importance:

The location of the Outside Bar within the broader market structure is critical to its interpretation. For example:

a. If an Outside Bar forms near a support level in a downtrend, it may indicate a bullish reversal.
b. If it forms near a resistance level in an uptrend, it may suggest a bearish reversal.
c. Within a strong trend, an Outside Bar often acts as a continuation signal, reinforcing the dominant momentum.

24. Abandoned baby

The Abandoned Baby candlestick pattern is a rare and highly reliable three-candle reversal formation that signals a significant shift in market sentiment.

This pattern is characterized by a gap between the first and third candles, with a Doji or small-bodied candle isolated in the middle. The Doji remains entirely separated from the first and third candles by gaps on both sides, emphasizing its distinct nature. This pattern represents a firm rejection of prior price levels and often precedes a sharp reversal in the prevailing trend.

Structure of the Abandoned Baby Pattern:

a. **The first candle** is a large, directional candle that reflects the dominant trend. In a bullish reversal (Abandoned Baby Bottom), the first candle is a strong bearish candle. In a bearish reversal (Abandoned Baby Top), the first candle is a strong bullish candle.

b. **The second candle** is a Doji or small-bodied candle that forms with a gap, completely isolated from the first and third candles. This Doji indicates market indecision or equilibrium between buyers and sellers. Its isolation highlights a moment of hesitation or uncertainty, as neither side asserts control.

c. **The third candle** moves decisively in the opposite direction of the first candle, confirming the reversal. In a bullish reversal, this is a strong bullish candle that gaps above the Doji and closes well into the body of the first bearish candle. In a bearish reversal, this is a strong bearish candle that gaps below the Doji and closes well into the body of the first bullish candle.

Interpretation and Significance:

The Abandoned Baby pattern is significant because it combines several elements of market psychology into a clear and visually striking formation. The gaps before and after the Doji symbolize a dramatic rejection of prior price levels, indicating that the prevailing trend has lost momentum. The isolated Doji reflects a state of indecision or balance between buyers and sellers, while the third candle decisively resolves this uncertainty in the direction of the reversal.

In an Abandoned Baby Bottom, the pattern signals that selling pressure has exhausted, and buyers are stepping in forcefully, marking a potential shift to an uptrend. In an Abandoned Baby Top, the pattern indicates that buying momentum has faded, and sellers are now taking control, suggesting the start of a downtrend.

Trading the Abandoned Baby Pattern:

Traders typically wait for confirmation before entering positions based on the Abandoned Baby pattern. The confirmation comes in the form of the third candle, which closes firmly in the direction of the reversal. Entry strategies include:

a. For bullish reversals (Abandoned Baby Bottom): Traders enter long positions when the confirmation candle closes above the high of the Doji or the gap area.
b. For bearish reversals (Abandoned Baby Top): Traders enter short positions when the confirmation candle closes below the low of the Doji or the gap area.

The distinct gaps on either side of the Doji provide clear levels for setting stop-loss orders, often just below the gap in bullish setups or above the gap in bearish setups.

Contextual Importance:

The gaps on either side of the Doji are critical to the uniqueness and reliability of the Abandoned Baby pattern. These gaps visually highlight the rejection of previous price levels and the market's abrupt shift in sentiment. The isolation of the Doji is a hallmark of the pattern, symbolizing a distinct pause or hesitation before a decisive move.

Summary:

The Abandoned Baby is a rare and powerful three-candle reversal pattern that provides traders with a clear and reliable signal of a significant trend change. Its combination of gaps, an isolated Doji, and a strong confirmation candle makes it one of the most distinctive reversal patterns in technical analysis. By waiting for confirmation and integrating additional tools such as volume analysis and momentum indicators, traders can effectively capitalize on the sharp price movements that often follow this pattern.

CHAPTER FOUR

Ichimoku Cloud

Mastering the Ichimoku Cloud for S&P Futures Trading

In the vast universe of technical analysis, where lines, dots, and squiggles often compete for your attention, the "Ichimoku Kinko Hyo" stands out like a wise old sensei at a karate tournament. Usually called the "Ichimoku Cloud," this indicator is less a tool and more a philosophy—a complete system for analyzing price action, elegantly wrapped in a visual masterpiece that looks like someone decided to draw a weather forecast on your trading chart. Created by the visionary Japanese journalist Goichi Hosoda in the mid-20th century, it was initially used for Japanese equities. But much like sushi and anime, it has transcended borders to become a global favorite, particularly for traders in the high-stakes S&P 500 futures market.

So, what exactly is this colorful web of lines and shaded areas? Think of the Ichimoku Cloud as the Swiss Army knife of indicators—it's got everything you need: momentum, trend direction, support, resistance, and even a sneak peek into future price action.

Refer to the chart on the following page. This black and white visual masterpiece adeptly captures an upward-trending market within a 5-minute candlestick framework. The Ichimoku Cloud distinctly outlines a bullish pattern, providing robust support along its lower boundary. As the trading session progresses, the bullish momentum begins to wane, culminating in the price action falling towards the cloud support and testing the cloud. This decisive breach effectively signals the end of the bullish phase that sustained the market from 9 AM to 2 PM, illustrating how the Ichimoku Cloud serves as both a guide and a sentinel in discerning trend reversals.

This chapter will demystify the Ichimoku Cloud by breaking it down into its core components: the Tenkan-sen (Conversion Line), Kijun-sen (Base Line), Senkou Span A and B (the Cloud), and the mysterious yet oddly reliable Chikou Span (Lagging Line). Together, they form a system so comprehensive it's like having a weather report, GPS, and fortune teller all on your chart. Trust me, by the end, you'll know when it's sunny skies or storm clouds ahead in your trading world.

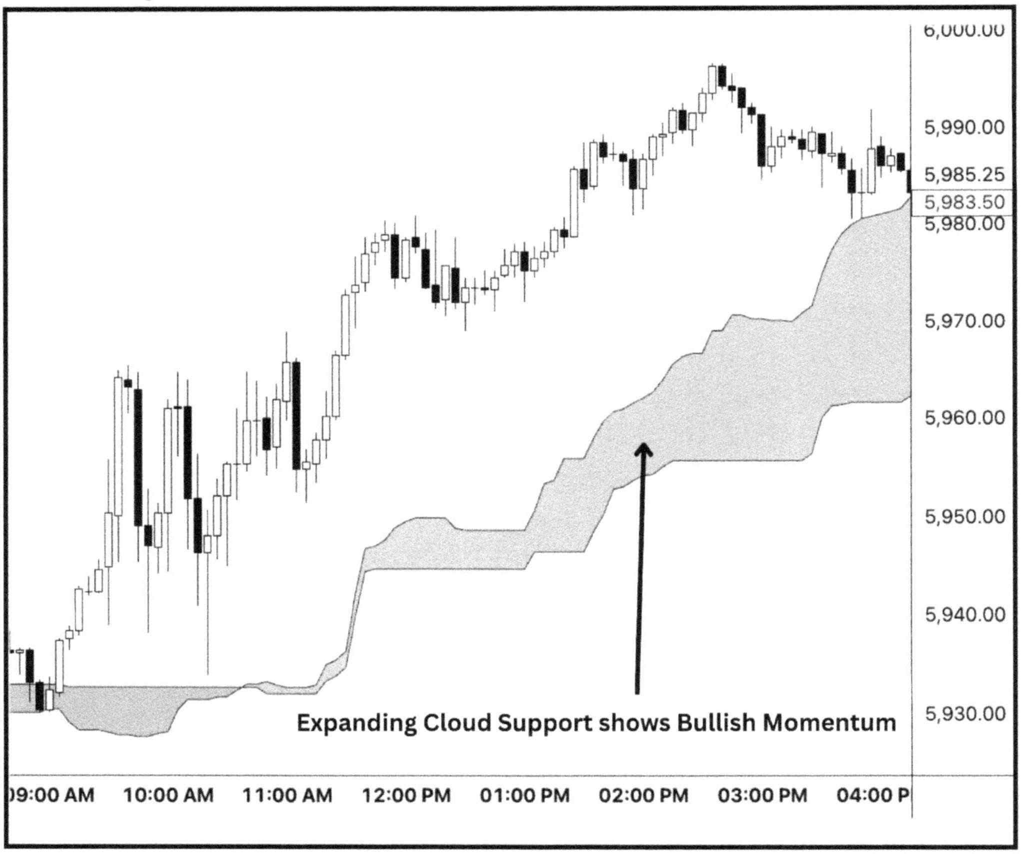

What makes the Ichimoku Cloud particularly special for S&P futures is its adaptability. Whether you're trading during the early morning volatility of U.S. market hours or navigating the more subdued overnight sessions, the Cloud offers signals that are as reliable as your morning coffee, assuming your coffee doesn't spill on your keyboard when the market suddenly drops. It's perfect for intraday scalping, swing trading, or simply confirming longer-term trends. Just remember: the Cloud doesn't eliminate the need for a solid trading plan—it's an assistant, not a genie.

Understanding the Ichimoku Cloud Components: The Ichimoku Cloud is composed of five distinct lines, each calculated from averaging price data over specific periods. When plotted together, these lines form a "cloud" on the price chart, combined with leading and lagging spans that paint a complete picture of current and future potential support, resistance, and trend bias. The five key components are:

Tenkan-sen (Conversion Line): Calculated as the midpoint of the highest high and lowest low over the last 9 periods, the Tenkan-sen functions like a short-term moving average. It provides a quick gauge of momentum. On an S&P futures chart, if prices trade consistently above the Tenkan-sen, it indicates a relatively strong short-term trend.

Kijun-sen (Base Line): Similar to the Tenkan-sen, but calculated over the last 26 periods, the Kijun-sen provides a more medium-term reference point. Its slower calculation makes it a steadier benchmark of the underlying trend. Traders often consider the Kijun-sen as a pivot point: when the price is above it, the medium-term bias is bullish; when below, it's bearish.

Senkou Span A (Leading Span A): This line is calculated by averaging the Tenkan-sen and Kijun-sen and then plotting the result 26 periods ahead. This forward-shifted line forms the first boundary of the Ichimoku "cloud," offering a glimpse into potential future support/resistance levels. If the S&P futures price is above Senkou Span A, it suggests underlying strength.

Senkou Span B (Leading Span B): Senkou Span B represents the midpoint of the highest high and lowest low over the past 52 periods, projected 26 periods into the future. Being based on a longer timeframe, it tends to move more slowly. When combined with Senkou Span A, it completes the cloud. Thin clouds reflect lower volatility and less "depth" in support/resistance, while thick clouds suggest more substantial barriers.

Chikou Span (Lagging Span): The Chikou Span plots today's closing price 26 periods behind, serving as a measure of momentum and trend confirmation.

If the Chikou Span is above the price from 26 periods ago, it often confirms a bullish environment; if below, it may confirm a bearish environment.

Interpreting the Cloud: Trend, Bias, and Momentum: One of the most compelling aspects of the Ichimoku Cloud is how it reveals trend direction and potential future support/resistance at a single glance. Consider these guidelines:

Price Relative to the Cloud: Above the Cloud: The market is generally considered bullish. For S&P futures, this might mean the index is broadly supported by positive sentiment or favorable macro conditions.

Below the Cloud: The environment is considered bearish. Persistent trading below the cloud suggests market participants view valuations as too high or expect further downside.

Inside the Cloud: The market is in a state of equilibrium or transition. It's often best to wait for a clear break above or below the cloud before making significant trading decisions.

Color and Thickness of the Cloud: When Senkou Span A is above Senkou Span B, the cloud is typically shaded green (in many charting packages), denoting a bullish-forward bias. When Senkou Span B is on top, the cloud is shaded red, signaling a more bearish undertone. Thick clouds generally provide more substantial support or resistance—if S&P futures are attempting to break through a dense cloud from below, it may require significant buying momentum to succeed.

Crosses of Tenkan-sen and Kijun-sen: The Tenkan-Kijun cross can offer early indications of trend changes. A bullish cross occurs when the Tenkan-sen moves above the Kijun-sen, while a bearish cross occurs when the Tenkan-sen drops below the Kijun-sen. While these signals alone don't guarantee success, they can be potent when combined with price relative to the cloud. For instance, a bullish cross above the cloud is considered a strong bullish signal, whereas a bullish cross below the cloud is less reliable.

Chikou Span Confirmation: The Chikou Span acts as a final filter. If you're uncertain about the validity of a breakout or a trend change, check where the

Chikou Span is in relation to historical prices. If it confirms the direction (for example, Chikou Span above past prices in a breakout scenario), you can have greater confidence in the signal.

Applying Ichimoku to S&P Futures Day Trading: While the Ichimoku Cloud was initially developed for longer-term timeframes, day traders have adapted it to intraday charts, such as 5-, 15-, or 30-minute charts, to gain a structural understanding of market conditions. The principles remain the same, though some adjustments and interpretations may be necessary to deal with increased noise.

1. **Identifying the Dominant Intraday Trend**: On a 15-minute chart of S&P futures, you might begin your day by examining where the price is relative to the cloud. If at the start of the U.S. session (around 9:30 AM EST), the futures are comfortably above a green-colored cloud and the Tenkan-sen is above the Kijun-sen, you have a bullish baseline scenario. This suggests looking for long trades on pullbacks rather than trying to fade the uptrend.
2. **Trading Pullbacks to the Kijun-sen or Cloud Support**: If the S&P futures are trending higher above the cloud, a common strategy is to wait for the price to pull back toward the Kijun-sen or the upper edge of the cloud. These areas often serve as dynamic support. If price stabilizes there and the Chikou Span remains comfortably above historical prices, consider going long, anticipating a continuation of the bullish trend.
3. **Exploiting Cloud Breakouts**: When S&P futures have been trapped inside the cloud for several hours, perhaps leading up to a major economic report, traders know that this indicates indecision. A definitive break above or below the cloud after the news can signal the start of a trend. If price breaks above the cloud and the Tenkan-sen crosses above the Kijun-sen simultaneously, it can provide a clear bullish entry signal.
4. **Monitoring Market Transitions**: Day traders frequently encounter rapid shifts in market sentiment. If a bullish market quickly turns south due to unexpected headlines, watch how the Ichimoku lines react. A sudden drop below the cloud, with the Tenkan-sen crossing below the Kijun-sen and the Chikou Span dipping under historical prices, confirms the shift to a bearish environment. This allows you to adapt your strategy and start looking for shorting opportunities on rallies into cloud resistance.

Combining Ichimoku with Other Indicators and Tools: While the Ichimoku system is designed as a stand-alone method of analysis, many traders find value in confirming Ichimoku signals with other tools. Since S&P futures are influenced by macroeconomic events, index fundamentals, and shifts in broader market sentiment, the additional confirmation can help reduce false signals.

Volume and Market Internals: Although Ichimoku excels in trend identification, it doesn't inherently incorporate volume data. Checking trading volume or market internals, such as the NYSE Advance/Decline lines, can help confirm the strength of an Ichimoku breakout. For example, if price breaks above the cloud on the S&P futures at the same time volume spikes and market internals improve, the bullish signal has more weight.

Key Support/Resistance Zones and Fibonacci Levels: The Ichimoku Cloud outlines dynamic support/resistance, but it can be beneficial to check static levels as well. If the top of the cloud aligns with a significant price level (e.g., a previous day's high or a Fibonacci retracement), that confluence suggests a more substantial barrier. A rejection at this level aligns well with Ichimoku's signals, increasing the probability of a successful trade.

Risk Management and Trade Execution with Ichimoku: Even the best signals fail at times, so prudent risk management is critical. The Ichimoku system, with its clear visual boundaries, lends itself naturally to effective stop placement and position sizing.

Using the Cloud as a Stop-Loss Level: When entering a long trade on a bullish Ichimoku signal, you could place a stop loss just below the cloud or the Kijun-sen line. The logic is that if price breaks back below these key levels, the bullish scenario you entered no longer holds. Similarly, for short trades initiated below the cloud, a stop above the cloud boundary can protect your position from a bullish reversal.

Adjusting Position Size Based on Cloud Thickness: If the cloud is thick, it may represent a substantial support/resistance zone, potentially allowing you to risk fewer points. Conversely, thin clouds signal weaker levels, and you should trade smaller position sizes or use tighter stops in those scenarios.

Partial Profit-Taking on Key Signals: If the S & P futures rally strongly above the cloud and you are in a profitable long position, you might consider taking partial profits if price stalls at a significant resistance level or if the Tenkan-sen and Kijun-sen start to Ichimoku lines flattening can hint at waning momentum, prompting cautious profit-taking.

Common Pitfalls and How to Avoid Them

Relying on Ichimoku Alone Without Context: While Ichimoku is comprehensive, no single indicator should be used in isolation. Understanding the broader context, such as upcoming Federal Reserve announcements, major economic data releases, or overnight news, ensures you're not caught off guard by sudden volatility shifts.

Ignoring Timeframes and Market Sessions: Market conditions can vary dramatically between different sessions. S&P futures trade nearly 24/5, but the most volume and volatility occur during U.S. market hours. Ichimoku signals on a low-volume overnight session might be less reliable. Consider time-of-day factors and, if necessary, switch between multiple timeframes to confirm your analysis.

Forcing Trades When Signals Are Weak: The cloud and lines can sometimes create ambiguous signals. If price is inside the cloud and the Tenkan-sen and Kijun-sen are flat, the market lacks a clear trend. Forcing trades in such conditions often leads to losses. Patience and the discipline to wait for clear signals are essential.

Real-World Example: Ichimoku Applied Intraday

Take a look at this daily timeframe chart, where each candle represents one day of price action. A robust and growing bullish cloud provides firm support, with prices testing the cloud during the final weeks of December 2024 and rebounding from this support on January 3, 2025. Traders can utilize this higher timeframe to identify the cloud support level and then zoom into lower timeframes to make informed swing trade decisions

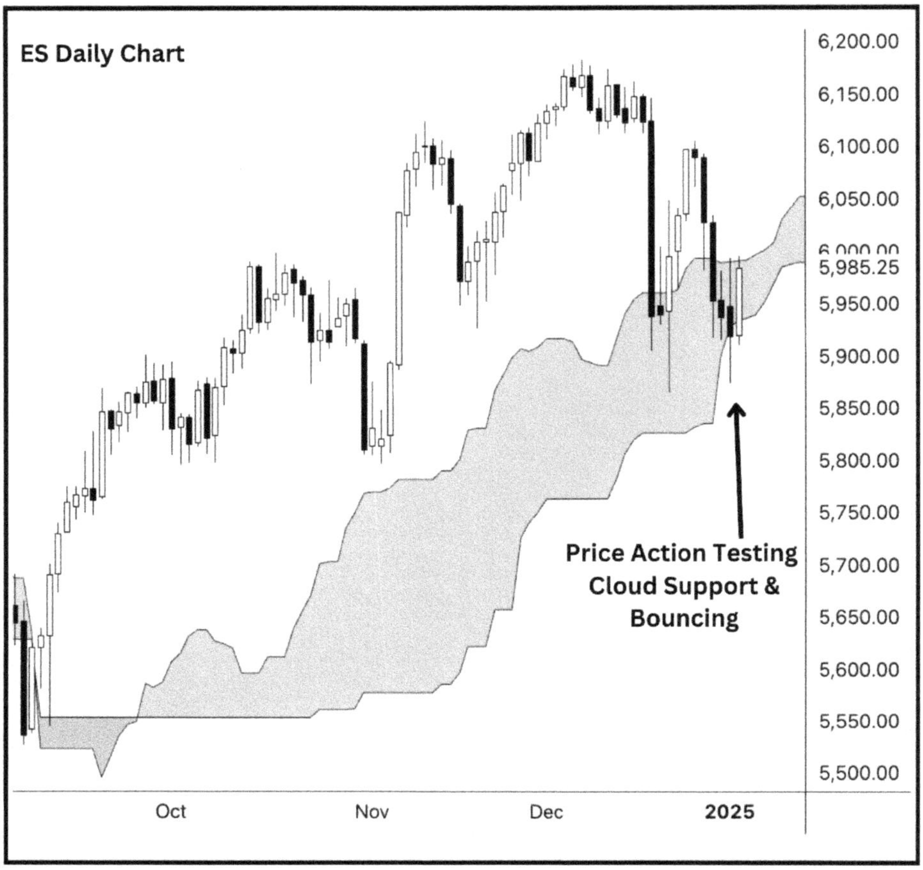

The following are the settings that I recommend for the Indicator setup:

- Search for the Indicator "Ichimoku" on your trading or charting platform that you use
- Input Conversion line length 9
- Input baseline length 26
- Input Leading span B length 52
- Input Lagging Span 26
- Select your Indicator "Style" tab and check Leading Span A, Leading Span B, and use the desired colors
- **Plot Backgrounds at desired colors,** preferably green and red variations to indicate bullish and bearish trends.

Conclusion: The Ichimoku Cloud is more than just another technical indicator; it's a comprehensive system designed to give traders a multifaceted view of the market. When applied to S&P futures trading, it offers insight into trend direction, potential support and resistance, and momentum, all at a single glance. Coupled with proper risk management and confirmation from other tools, the Ichimoku Cloud can become a powerful ally, guiding traders through the complexities of day-to-day price action in one of the world's most closely watched markets. Mastering the Ichimoku system takes practice and patience, as well as the ability to distinguish strong signals from weak ones. Over time, as you gain experience using Ichimoku on S&P futures charts, you'll learn to trust its signals, adapt to changing market conditions, and execute trades with greater confidence and precision. In essence, the Ichimoku Cloud can offer the clarity and perspective you need to navigate the ever-shifting seas of short-term futures trading successfully.

CHAPTER FIVE

Supply and Demand

The principle of supply and demand forms the cornerstone of financial markets, and S&P futures are no exception. Picture demand zones as **eager shoppers on Black Friday**, ready to snatch up bargains, and supply zones are like sellers lining up with a tidal wave of **sell orders**, prepared to **flood the market** as soon as price action reaches higher prices. Understanding these zones can feel like having a treasure map, only with fewer pirates and more profit potential. The concept of supply and demand zones not only highlights key reversal points but also provides traders with a framework for making well-timed entries and exits. By identifying these zones, traders can align their strategies with institutional activity, increasing the odds of success. Mastering these zones can transform your trading by uncovering high-probability opportunities that are often hidden in plain sight.

Refer to the 30-minute chart on the next page, prices reached the supply zone near 6175, reversing sharply downward as sellers overwhelmed buyers, confirming the presence of supply. Similarly, the prior day's low around 6115 acted as a demand zone, with prices finding support and reversing upward due to strong buying interest. These zones, formed by institutional orders, are key areas where future price reversals are likely, offering valuable insights for traders.

Identifying Demand Zones:

Look for sharp price movements originating from a base. These zones often signify areas where institutional investors have placed large buy orders. This is a price area where buying pressure exceeds selling, pushing the price higher. It's commonly located near support levels. Demand zones often align with psychological levels or areas of major news releases. For example, a demand zone might emerge around a Federal Reserve interest rate decision, where institutional buying propels the price upwards.

Spotting Supply Zones:

Supply zones are characterized by rapid price declines. This is a price area where selling pressure overwhelms buying, causing the price to fall. It's often found near resistance levels. Historical price action, combined with resistance levels, can serve as reliable markers. Supply zones frequently coincide with exhaustion of bullish momentum. Traders should be cautious when prices approach these zones, as reversals are common.

Identifying Supply and Demand Zones

Three key attributes characterize supply and demand zones:

Sharp Price Movement: Look for areas on the chart where the price made a decisive move away from a level, indicating a significant imbalance.

Base Formation: Before the sharp movement, the price often consolidates, forming a base. This base is the origin of the zone.

Unfilled Orders: These zones often have pending orders from institutional players, resulting in repeated reactions when revisited.

Mastering Supply and Demand Zones with a Multi-Timeframe Approach

A multi-timeframe approach is a powerful technique that enhances a trader's ability to identify supply and demand zones with greater accuracy. By analyzing charts across different timeframes, this method provides a comprehensive view of market dynamics, helping traders make more informed decisions.

In practice, this strategy involves examining multiple timeframes simultaneously to uncover key levels and trends that may not be immediately apparent on a single chart. For instance, during my regular trading sessions, I rely on a carefully structured chart layout. On the left, I monitor the 5-minute chart, which provides detailed insights into short-term price movements and entry points. On the right, I split the space into two halves, dedicating one to the 15-minute chart and the other to the 1-hour chart. This configuration allows me to maintain a broader perspective on the market's intermediate and longer-term trends while still focusing on granular intraday activity.

By synthesizing information from these timeframes, I can accurately identify zones of supply and demand, detect trend shifts, and align my trades with the prevailing market conditions. This multi-timeframe approach is a cornerstone of my trading strategy, ensuring that each decision is grounded in a thorough and holistic understanding of the market's behavior. Now let's discuss the process of identifying supply and demand zones.

Higher Timeframe (Macro View)

Start with a higher timeframe (e.g., daily or weekly charts) and it provides the "big picture," allowing you to identify central supply and demand zones where significant institutional activity has occurred. These zones act as strong support and resistance levels.

Steps:

a. Identify primary price levels where large candles or gaps occurred.
b. Mark these zones with horizontal rectangles, extending them into the future.

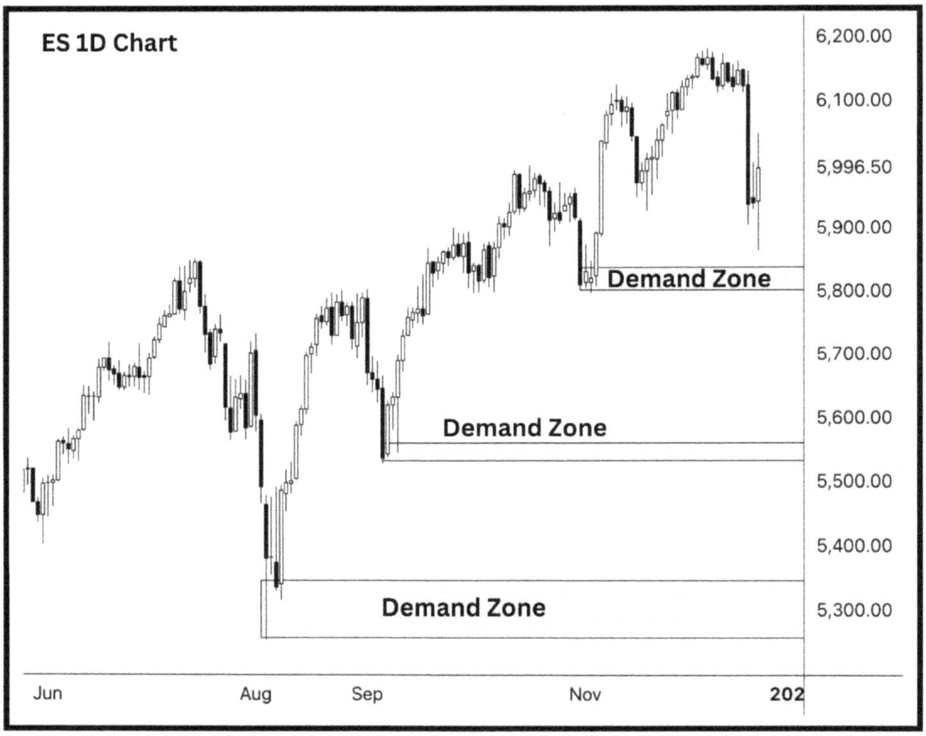

Take a look at the daily chart above. Each candlestick represents a single day of market activity, capturing the open, high, low, and close for that day. Notice the clearly defined demand and supply zones marked on the chart. These zones are critical for understanding the broader market context, as they highlight areas where the market has previously reversed or where trends have strengthened.

On this higher timeframe, we can identify significant demand zones around the 5300, 5550, and 5800 levels. These levels provide a roadmap for potential major reversals or trend continuations, offering traders valuable insights into where buyers or sellers are likely to step in and shift the market's direction.

Intermediate Timeframe (Trend Confirmation)

The intermediate timeframe (e.g., 1-hour or 4-hour charts) narrows the focus to trends within the higher timeframe zones. Here, you can validate whether the price is respecting the primary supply or demand levels identified earlier. This timeframe refines your zones and confirms whether they remain valid for current market conditions.

Steps:

a. Observe how the price reacts when it enters the higher timeframe zones.

b. Identify smaller bases or consolidation areas within the higher timeframe zones.

c. Look for confirmation signals such as candlestick patterns (e.g., pin bars, engulfing candles).

Observe the chart on the next page. This is a 4-hour chart, where each candlestick represents an hour of market activity. Here, we can see how patterns begin to take shape within this intermediate timeframe. Notice the clear supply zone around the 6165 level, where selling pressure has emerged, and the demand zone near the 5960 level and 5800 levels, where buyers have consistently stepped in. These zones provide valuable insight into how the market is balancing between buyers and sellers in the short term.

Lower Timeframe (Entry Timing)

The purpose of the lower timeframe, for instance, the 5-minute or 15-minute chart, is fine-tuning entries and trade management. You are searching for particular setups that will enable you to enter trades with minimum risk. This timeframe provides the precision needed to set tight stop-losses and optimal entry points. This layered approach allows us to understand how the broader market context relates to short-term movements, providing a clearer view of potential trading opportunities.

Steps:

a. Wait for the price to reach the supply or demand zones as identified by higher timeframes.
b. Look for either reversal patterns or breakout structure within these zones.
c. Use confirmation tools, such as trendlines, Fibonacci retracements, or moving averages, to confirm the entry.

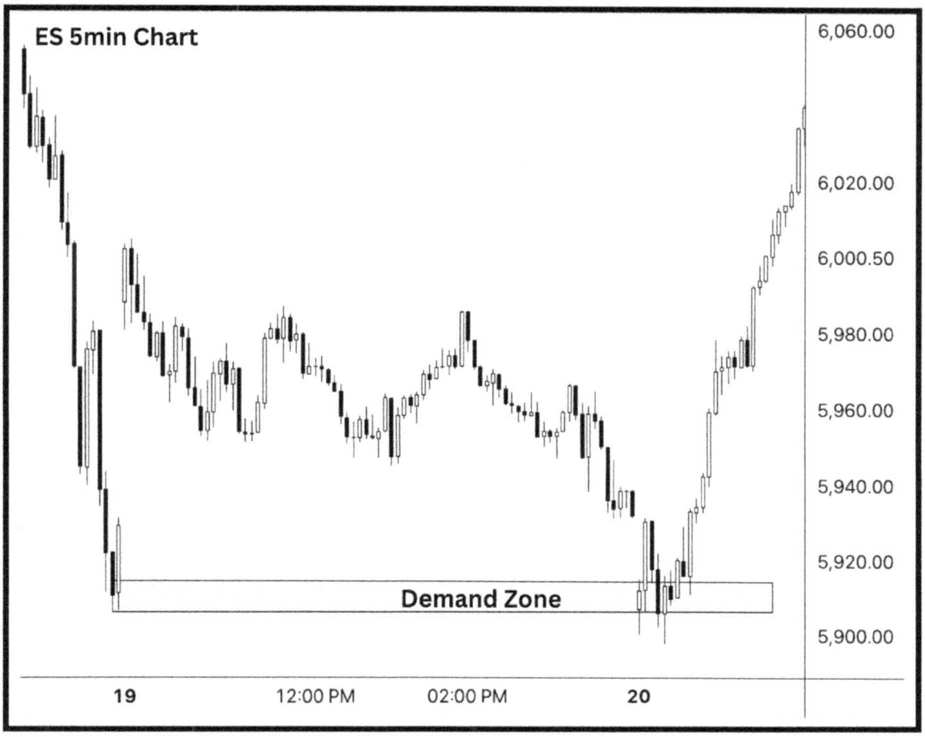

Practical Application: Combining Timeframes

Mastering supply and demand zones through a multi-timeframe analysis is a game-changer for understanding the financial markets. By combining higher timeframe zones to establish the broader context with lower timeframe zones for precise entry and exit points, traders gain both clarity and accuracy in identifying high-probability trading opportunities. This approach offers a comprehensive view of market dynamics, allowing you to align your trades with the dominant trends while capitalizing on short-term movements. With practice, patience, and disciplined execution, this powerful technique can become an indispensable tool in your trading arsenal.

How to use the supply and demand analysis conclusion for trading purposes:

a. A higher timeframe demand zone suggests looking for buy setups on lower timeframes.

b. A higher timeframe supply zone suggests looking for sell setups on lower timeframes.

This alignment increases the probability of success by ensuring your trades are supported by the broader market context.

Practice Patience and Discipline

Using multiple timeframes requires patience. Wait for price action on the lower timeframe to confirm your thesis from the higher timeframe. Avoid impulsive trades, and let the market come to you. Combining these timeframes not only improves accuracy but also minimizes risk. By incorporating multiple time frame supply and demand analysis into your trading, you create a structured, strategic approach that captures the big picture while allowing for precise, tactical execution. This method bridges the gap between long-term trends and short-term opportunities, giving you a more straightforward path to consistent trading success.

CHAPTER SIX

Chart Setup

For simplicity and faster execution, I suggest a minimalist approach of having a straightforward chart setup. Many beginner traders seek miracle indicators and experiment with everything out there in the charting world. I mean the following setup for S&P futures traders.

Chart 1 Setup:

a. 5 min Candlestick charts with plain background, white or black, depending upon color preference, suitable for your eyes
b. 20 bar Exponential moving average (EMA) line.
c. Pay for the required fee associated with live chart data on CME and get current live price details on ES S&P futures without any time delay
d. Split the screen into three segments, one segment on the left side for 5 5-minute chart, and the other two segments on the right side, split equally into top and bottom, for 1 1-hour and 15-minute chart types on the Emini futures ticker symbol.

The 1-hour chart offers a macro perspective for trend analysis, the 15-minute chart refines entries, and the 5-minute chart focuses on precise execution.

Chart 2 Setup

1. Another chart with ticker SPY at 5 5-minute time frame
2. VWAP (Volume Weighted Average Price)
3. POC (Point of Control).

Why do we use Chart 2 with SPY?

SPY, being an ETF, has higher trading volume and liquidity, which results in smoother and more accurate VWAP and POC calculations compared to ES futures

VWAP (Volume Weighted Average Price

The Volume Weighted Average Price (VWAP) is a trading indicator that provides the average price of a security, weighted by its trading volume, over a specific period. It represents the price at which the majority of trading occurred, combining both price and volume into a single value. VWAP helps identify whether the price is above or below the average price paid by traders:

Above VWAP: Bullish sentiment; buyers are willing to pay a premium.

Below VWAP: Bearish sentiment; sellers dominate.

Support and Resistance: Acts as a dynamic support or resistance level.

Institutional Use: Institutions often utilize VWAP to assess trade execution efficiency, aiming to buy below or sell above VWAP to minimize negative market impact.

Uses of VWAP in Trading

Intraday Benchmark: Commonly used in intraday trading to gauge fair value.

Entry and Exit Signals: Traders look for pullbacks to VWAP for entry or breaks below/above VWAP for exits.

Mean Reversion: Prices frequently gravitate toward the VWAP during sideways markets, offering reversion opportunities.

POC (Point of Control)

The Point of Control (POC) is a concept from Market Profile or Volume Profile analysis. It represents the price level at which the highest trading volume occurred during a specific period. POC highlights where the most trading activity took place, indicating a price level of significant interest to market participants.

High Volume Node: POC is part of the volume profile and typically aligns with a high volume node, an area where price consolidates due to balanced supply and demand.

Market Consensus: Reflects a consensus among buyers and sellers about the fair value of the security.

Dynamic Nature: POC shifts over time as new data emerges, reflecting changes in market sentiment.

Uses of POC in Trading

Support and Resistance: POC can act as a key support or resistance level since it indicates where the market feels "comfortable" trading.

Reversal Zones: Price often reacts strongly around the POC, either bouncing off or consolidating at this level.

Trend Continuation or Rejection: Breaks above or below the Point of Control (POC) suggest shifts in market sentiment, providing directional cues.

Streamlined Chart Setups for Faster Trade Execution:

A minimalist chart setup is recommended for simplicity and faster execution, avoiding the common mistake of overloading charts with indicators. For S&P 500 futures (ES), a 5-minute candlestick chart with a 20-bar exponential moving average (EMA) is paired with live CME data for accurate pricing. The screen is split into three segments: 5-minute, 15-minute, and 1-hour charts, allowing for a balance between macro and micro perspectives. A secondary setup utilizes the SPY ETF on a 5-minute timeframe, incorporating VWAP and POC indicators, which leverage SPY's higher liquidity for more accurate calculations. VWAP acts as a dynamic support and resistance level, signaling bullish or bearish sentiment. At the same time, POC identifies key price levels with the highest trading volume, serving as strong support or resistance. Together, these setups provide a clear and efficient framework for decision-making, with advanced indicators such as MACD and RSI, which will be covered in subsequent chapters.

CHAPTER SEVEN

Charting Tips

Charting Tip #1: Use Gann Lines in your weekend analysis for identifying potential swing trade research

Gann Lines are a set of technical analysis tools developed by the legendary trader W.D. Gann, who used them to predict future price movements in financial markets, including futures trading. Gann believed that markets follow specific patterns that can be mathematically calculated and predicted using angles and geometric concepts.

<u>Traders use the Gann Fan to:</u>

- Identify potential support and resistance levels.
- Spot trend reversals when the price interacts with one of the fan lines.
- Predict future price movements by observing how the market respects or breaks through the Gann Fan lines.

Key Points to Remember about Gann Lines:

Geometrical Nature: Gann lines are based on the idea that market movements are geometric, and price and time move in specific, predictable patterns.

Angles: The most commonly used angles are the 1x1, 2x1, and 3x1 lines, representing different rates of price movement.

Support and Resistance: Gann lines help traders identify potential support, resistance, and turning points by looking at where the price interacts with the angles or fan lines.

Market Timing: Gann lines are also used to time entries and exits, using price and time cycles.

Complexity: Gann's methods can be complex and require experience to interpret correctly. They are often used by advanced traders who are comfortable with more intricate chart analysis.

How to Use Gann Lines in Futures Trading:

1. Identify a Key Price Point: Start by identifying a significant high or low price point (e.g., the start of a trend or a major reversal point).
2. Draw Gann Angles: Use a charting tool to draw Gann angles from this key price point. The most essential angle is the 1x1 angle (45 degrees), which represents an equal relationship between price and time.

3. Observe Price Action: Watch how the price interacts with the Gann lines. A bounce off a line could indicate support, while breaking through a line could signal a breakout or trend continuation.
4. Combine with Other Tools: Gann lines are typically used alongside other technical analysis tools, such as trendlines, moving averages, and oscillators, to confirm trading signals and increase accuracy.
5. Time Cycles: Utilize the Square of Nine or other Gann tools to analyze the timing of market events, facilitating the prediction of when significant price movements are likely to occur.

Charting Tip #2: Using the Fibonacci tool in the charting

Fibonacci retracements are used to identify potential support and resistance levels during a pullback, with the most commonly applied levels being 23.6%, 38.2%, 50%, and 61.8%. Additionally, in bearish conditions, the Fibonacci tool can be used on a 5-minute chart to analyze recent highs and lows, such as 6050.75 and 6031.50. By extending these levels to -1, -2, and -3, the tool projects additional targets at 100%, 200%, and 300% of the distance between the high and low. This helps identify potential targets in a downtrend based on the same magnitude of the initial price move. You can also reverse the process in the bullish reversals to identify potential targets for taking profits.

Chart Tip 3: Measured moves

The concept of measured moves in S&P futures trading refers to a method used by traders to project potential price targets based on prior price movements. It relies on identifying a pattern where a price move in one direction (leg) is expected to be replicated or proportionally extended in a subsequent move. This concept is rooted in the idea that markets often move in symmetrical patterns due to psychological and technical factors.

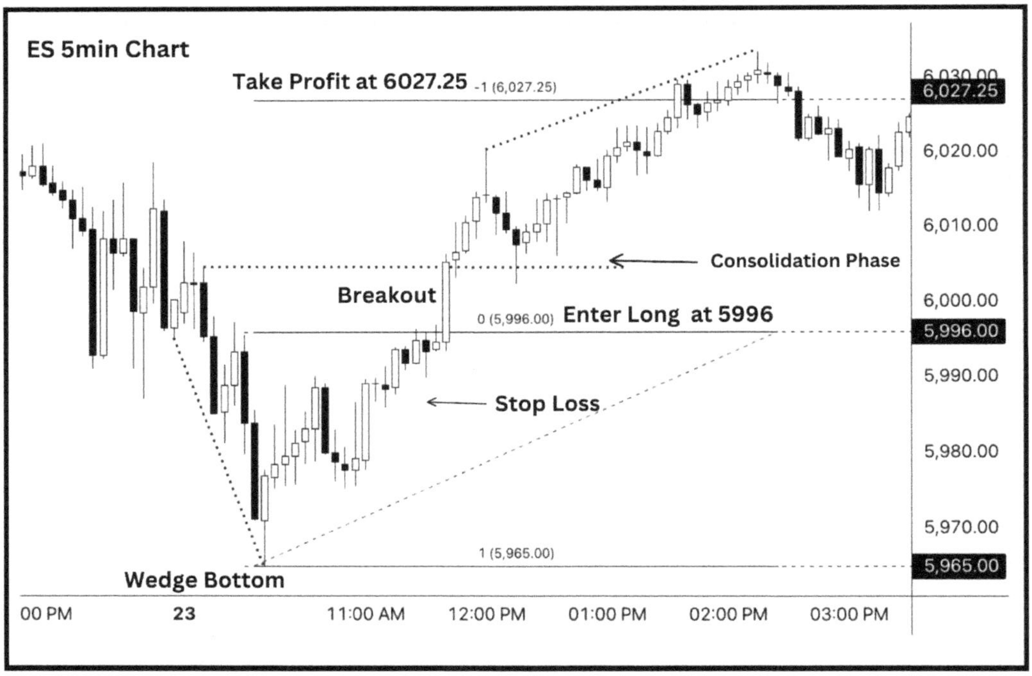

Measured moves start with an impulse move—the first leg—defined by strong momentum in a particular direction. In our example, the market rallies from 5965 to 5996, creating a 31-point surge. This initial climb establishes a blueprint for where prices might head next.

Following this first push, the market typically takes a breather in the form of a retracement. During this pullback or consolidation, prices often respect critical technical levels, such as a 50% Fibonacci retracement. Once the pullback finds support and shows signs of reversing back in the original trend direction, traders anticipate a second upswing.

That continuation move—the second leg—often mirrors the length of the initial leg. In this example, once prices break higher from the retracement, the market climbs another 31 points, extending from 5996 to 6027. The symmetrical nature of these two legs adds confidence to the idea that the market may be completing a measured move.

Charting Tip #4: Triangles and how to spot one

When drawing trend lines for triangles, start by identifying at least two or three clear pivot points that define each edge of the pattern. For an ascending triangle, draw a horizontal line across the swing highs that align roughly at the same price level, and then connect the successive higher lows with a rising diagonal line. Conversely, for a descending triangle, draw a horizontal line across the swing lows at a similar price level, and connect the successive lower highs with a descending diagonal line. Adjust and refine these lines as new price data comes in, ensuring they capture the most recent, significant pivot points without forced fits or unnecessary clutter.

Ascending Triangle:

An ascending triangle is a bullish continuation pattern characterized by a rising trendline connecting higher lows, combined with a horizontal resistance line at the top of the formation. For S&P futures traders, the typical strategy involves waiting for a breakout above that horizontal resistance, often confirmed by increased trading volume, before entering a long position. A stop-loss is usually placed just below the rising trendline or recent swing low, providing a defined risk level in case the breakout fails. Traders aim to capture a "measured move" by estimating the vertical distance from the triangle's base and projecting that same distance above the breakout point as a potential profit target.

Descending Triangle:

A descending triangle is a bearish continuation pattern formed by a descending trendline connecting lower highs and a horizontal support line at the bottom of the formation. For S&P futures traders, a common approach is to wait for a clean break below that support, ideally supported by a spike in trading volume, before entering a short position. To manage risk, traders often place a stop-loss just above the descending trendline or the most recent swing high. Similar to other technical patterns, a measured move can be used to project potential profit: measure the height of the triangle from the highest point to the support line, then subtract that distance from the breakout level to estimate the downside target.

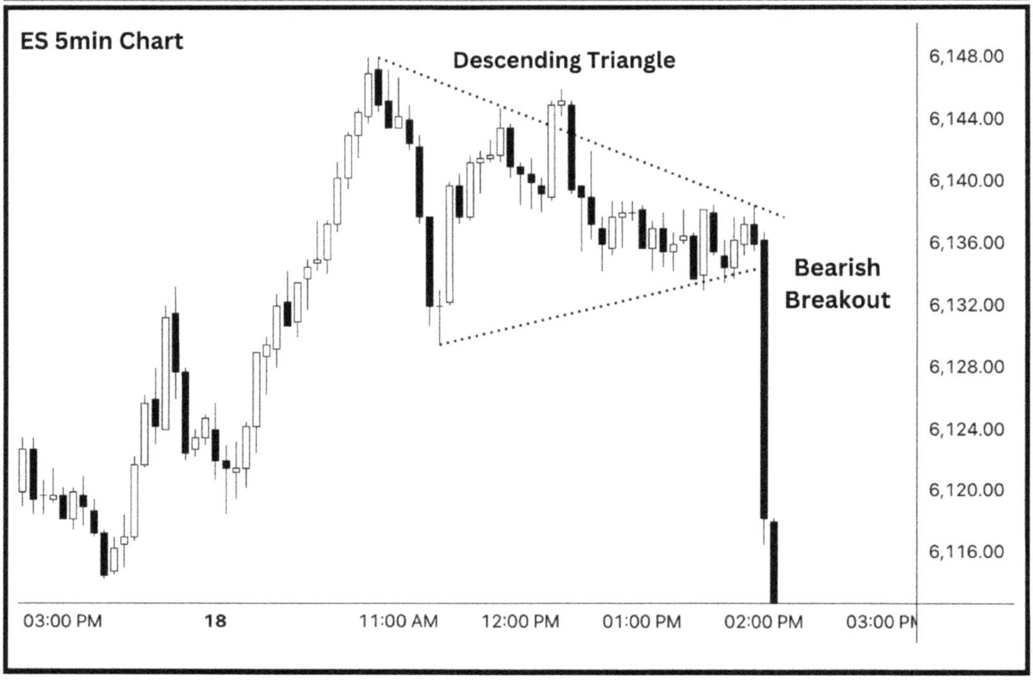

Refer to the chart image above; the price action spent approximately 3 hours within this descending triangle pattern before breaking downwards. In this type of descending price action, traders can enter a trade upon confirmation of a breakout right below the line of the bottom of the triangle at 6130, with a proper stop a few points above the top line of the triangle at 6140. Traders should enter short positions with a stop entry order method.

Charting Tip #5: Double Top and Double Bottom

The **Double Top** and **Double Bottom** are classic reversal chart patterns used by traders in S&P futures trading to identify potential trend reversals. These patterns reflect significant shifts in market sentiment, signaling the end of a prevailing trend and the beginning of a new one.

The **Double Top** pattern is a bearish reversal formation that appears after an uptrend has developed. It is characterized by two consecutive peaks at approximately the same price level, separated by a moderate decline, known as the trough. The first peak indicates resistance, where buying pressure starts to weaken. After a pullback, the price attempts to break the resistance again but fails, forming a second peak. The confirmation of the pattern occurs when the price breaks below the support level created by the trough between the two peaks. This breakout signals the start of a downtrend.

The **Double Bottom** pattern is the bullish counterpart, indicating a reversal from a downtrend. It consists of two consecutive lows at approximately the same price level, separated by a moderate recovery (the peak). The first low reflects intense selling pressure, but the price rebounds, suggesting potential support. After another dip to test the support level, the price rallies again, forming the second low. The pattern is confirmed when the price breaks above the resistance level created by the peak between the two lows, signaling the start of an uptrend.

To trade a **Double Top**, traders typically wait for the price to break below the support level. The entry point is often just below the breakout level, and the price target is calculated by measuring the height of the pattern (distance between the peaks and the trough) and subtracting it from the breakout point. For a Double Bottom, traders enter when the price breaks above the resistance level, with the price target calculated by adding the height of the pattern to the breakout point.

Both patterns are strengthened by volume analysis. In a **Double Top**, volume typically decreases as the second peak forms, and a surge in volume accompanies the breakdown below support. In a **Double Bottom**, volume often increases during the rally from the second low and surges during the breakout above resistance. This volume behavior confirms the validity of the breakout.

While these patterns are reliable indicators, they are not foolproof. False breakouts can occur, particularly in volatile markets such as S&P futures. Traders should confirm the patterns using additional tools such as trendlines, moving averages, or momentum indicators. Furthermore, the broader market context, including macroeconomic factors and news, should always be considered when trading these patterns.

By understanding and applying the Double Top and Double Bottom patterns effectively, traders can identify key reversal points in S&P futures and position themselves for significant price movements in the direction of the new trend.

Charting Tip # 6: Triple Top and Triple Bottom

The **Triple Top** is a bearish reversal pattern that forms after an uptrend has established itself. It is characterized by three peaks at approximately the same price level, separated by two troughs. Each peak represents a failed attempt by buyers to push the price higher, indicating weakening bullish momentum.

The key confirmation of the **Triple Top** occurs when the price breaks below the support level created by the troughs between the peaks. This breakout suggests that sellers have gained control, signaling the beginning of a downtrend.

Key Features of a Triple Top:

a. **Three Peaks:** The three highs occur near the same price level, showing strong resistance.
b. **Declining Momentum:** Each subsequent peak may have lower volume, reflecting diminishing buying interest.
c. **Breakout:** The pattern is confirmed when the price breaks below the support level, usually accompanied by a surge in volume.

Trading the Triple Top:

a. **Entry Point:** Enter a short trade when the price breaks below the support level at 6020.

b. Price Target: The target for this setup is typically located at the support level of 5998.

c. **Stop-Loss Placement:** Place a stop-loss slightly above the third peak to limit risk at 6027.50.

Triple Bottom

The **Triple Bottom** is the bullish counterpart of the Triple Top and forms after a downtrend. It consists of three lows at approximately the same price level, separated by two peaks. Each low represents a failed attempt by sellers to push the price lower, indicating weakening bearish momentum.

The pattern is confirmed when the price breaks above the resistance level created by the peaks between the lows. This breakout signals that buyers have regained control, and a new uptrend is likely to begin.

Key Features of a Triple Bottom Line:

a. Three Lows: The three lows occur at approximately the same price level, indicating strong support.

b. **Increasing Momentum:** Volume may increase during the rallies off each low, indicating growing buying interest.

c. Breakout: The pattern is confirmed when the price breaks above the resistance level, typically accompanied by a surge in volume.

Trading the Triple Bottom:

a. **Entry Point:** Enter a long trade when the price breaks above the resistance level.

b. **Price Target:** The target is calculated by measuring the height of the pattern (distance between the lows and the resistance level) and adding it to the breakout point.

c. **Stop-Loss Placement:** Place a stop-loss slightly below the third low to limit risk.

Another variation: Three push down

A three push down pattern, sometimes seen as a variation of the "three drives" or "triple thrust" pattern, occurs when price makes three consecutive lows, each typically accompanied by slowing momentum. Traders watch for each low to form near or slightly below the previous one, suggesting that selling pressure is losing steam even as the price continues to dip.

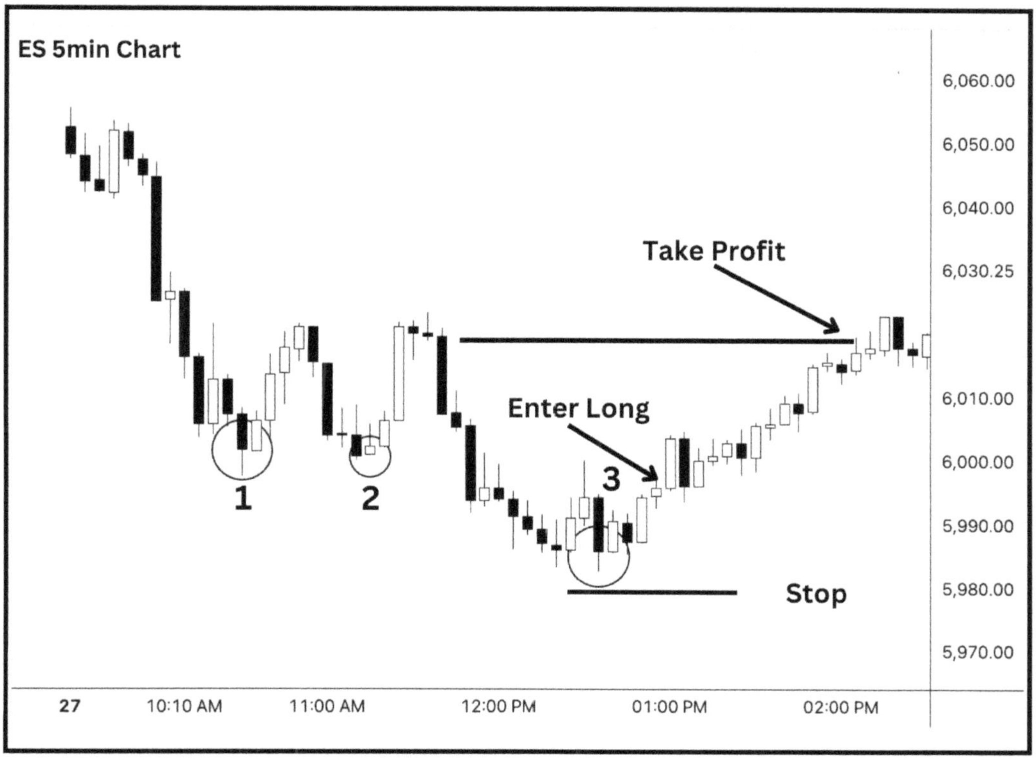

To trade this setup, a trader should look for confirmation of a reversal on the third push, such as a bullish candlestick pattern or an uptick in volume. An entry is often placed once price action closes above the short-term resistance formed near the second or third low. A stop-loss is typically set just below the final push to protect against a false breakout, and a profit target can be determined by identifying a key resistance level or a measured move based on the distance from the deepest low to the breakout area.

Charting Tip #7 Cup and Handle

The Cup and Handle is a bullish continuation chart pattern often used by traders in S&P futures trading to identify potential breakout opportunities. It resembles the shape of a teacup, where the "cup" is a rounded bottom and the "handle" is a consolidation phase that follows before a potential breakout.

The pattern begins with the cup, which represents a rounded bottom signifying a gradual change in market sentiment from bearish to bullish. The left side of the cup shows the decline, while the right side indicates the recovery back to previous highs. A smooth, rounded shape typically shows a strong foundation for future growth.

Following the cup is the handle, a consolidation or slight pullback phase. The handle usually forms as a small descending channel or sideways range. This reflects a temporary pause as traders digest gains before the breakout. The breakout occurs when the price breaks above the resistance level defined by the rim of the cup (the previous high before the decline). This breakout is typically accompanied by increased volume, signaling strong bullish momentum.

To trade the Cup and Handle pattern in S&P futures, traders first identify the pattern on the charts. The entry point is at the breakout above the resistance at the rim of the cup. For confirmation, traders often wait for a close above the resistance level or a volume spike. The price target is calculated by measuring the depth of the cup (distance between the rim and the lowest point of the cup) and adding it to the breakout point. For instance, if the cup's depth is 50 points and the breakout occurs at 4,500, the price target would be 4,550. Stop-loss orders are typically placed slightly below the handle's low or the midpoint of the cup, depending on risk tolerance.

The duration of the cup can vary, taking weeks to months in higher timeframes but forming more quickly on intraday charts. The handle usually lasts a few days to weeks on daily charts. Spotting such a cup and handle followed by a bullish breakout is a rare event in the intraday time frame, such as 5 5-minute chart. Volume patterns are crucial: during the cup formation, volume tends to decrease as the price declines and gradually increases during the recovery. The handle forms on low volume, while the breakout should occur on higher volume for confirmation.

While the Cup and Handle is a reliable pattern, it's essential to recognize its limitations. False breakouts can occur if the breakout isn't supported by volume or broader market sentiment.

Charting Tip # 8 Wedges (Rising and Falling)

In technical analysis, a wedge is a chart pattern formed by converging trendlines that often signals a period of price consolidation or indecision. There are two types of wedges: the rising wedge and the falling wedge. A rising wedge forms when both the support and resistance lines slope upwards, creating higher highs and higher lows, but the rate of ascent slows as the price narrows. This pattern is typically considered a bearish reversal signal, especially when it appears after an uptrend. A breakout below the lower trendline suggests the price may reverse downward, signaling a potential short (sell) position. (See the chart image below.)

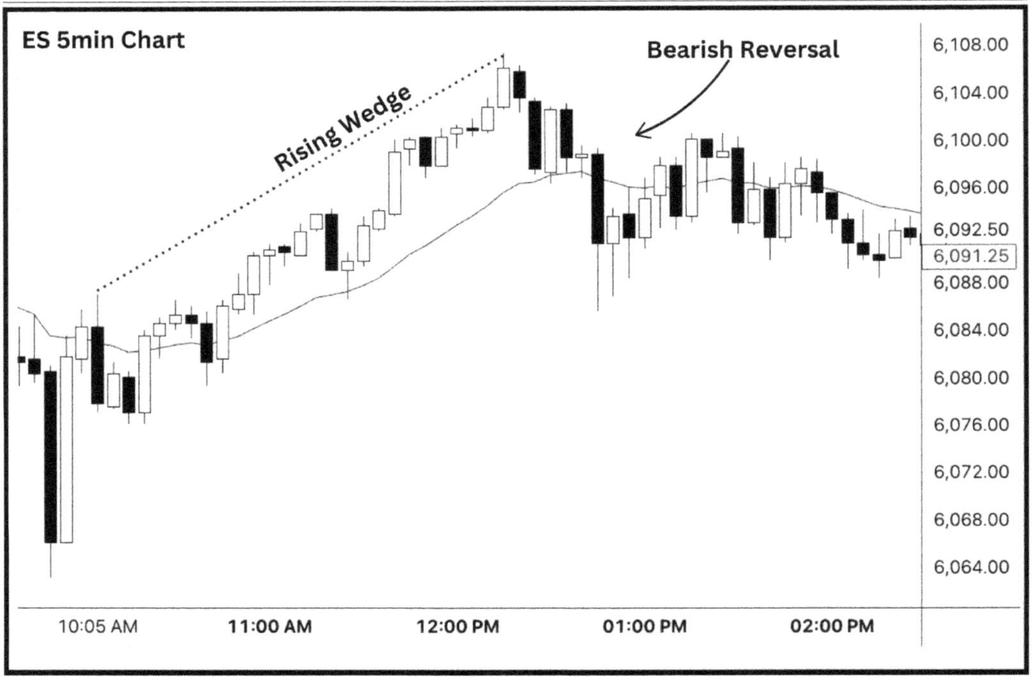

Conversely, a falling wedge forms when both the support and resistance lines slope downward, with lower highs and lower lows. It is generally seen as a bullish reversal pattern, especially after a downtrend, indicating a loss of bearish momentum. A breakout above the upper trendline suggests a potential upward move, signaling a long (buy) position. In both cases, volume typically decreases during the formation of the wedge and should increase when the price breaks out, confirming the breakout. Traders use these patterns to identify potential trend reversals, with the width of the wedge providing an estimate of the breakout's magnitude. It's crucial to combine wedge patterns with other technical indicators to confirm signals and manage risk.

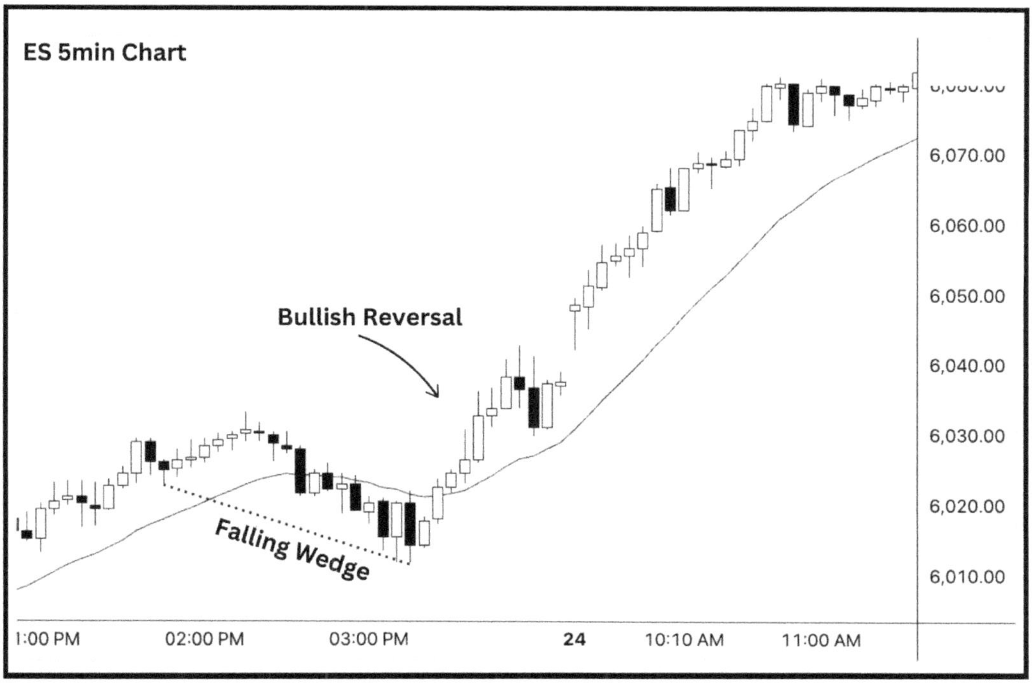

Charting Tip #9 Rectangles (Consolidation before breakout)

A **rectangle-shaped consolidation** is a chart pattern that forms when the price moves within horizontal support and resistance levels, creating a rectangular shape. This pattern is also known as a range-bound or box pattern. During this consolidation phase, the price oscillates between the established support (bottom) and resistance (top) levels, indicating indecision in the market as buyers and sellers are in equilibrium. The price doesn't make a clear upward or downward move. Instead, it "bounces" between these two horizontal boundaries. This consolidation typically occurs after a strong trend, and it often represents a period of indecision or pause before the market chooses its next direction. When the price eventually breaks out of the range, either above the resistance level or below the support level, it signals a potential continuation or reversal of the prior trend.

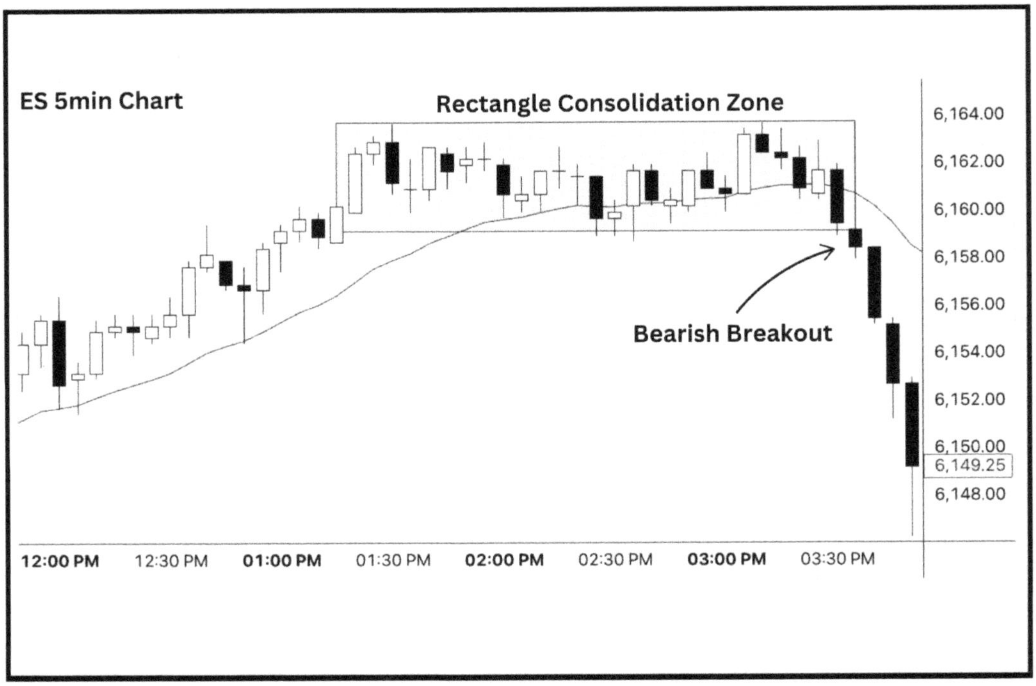

How to Trade Rectangle Consolidation:

Breakout Strategy: A breakout occurs when the price moves above the resistance level (for an upward move) or below the support level (for a downward move). Traders watch for a strong price movement and volume expansion after the breakout to confirm the new trend.

Entry: For a breakout above resistance, enter a long (buy) position, and for a breakout below support, enter a short (sell) position.

Stop-Loss: A stop-loss order is placed just outside the opposite side of the breakout point (e.g., below the breakout level for a long position).

Target: The target can be set by measuring the height of the rectangle (the distance between the support and resistance levels) and projecting it in the direction of the breakout from the breakout point. This gives an estimate of the potential price move after the breakout.

In general, a rectangle pattern indicates a period of accumulation or distribution, and a breakout from this consolidation phase is often followed by a strong price movement. However, it's essential to confirm the breakout with increased volume to reduce the risk of false breakouts.

Charting Tip #10 Pennants

Pennants are part of a continuation pattern. This pattern is marked by a sharp price movement, known as the flagpole, followed by a consolidation period where price action forms a small symmetrical triangle. The pennant resolves with a breakout in the direction of the preceding trend, often accompanied by high trading volume.

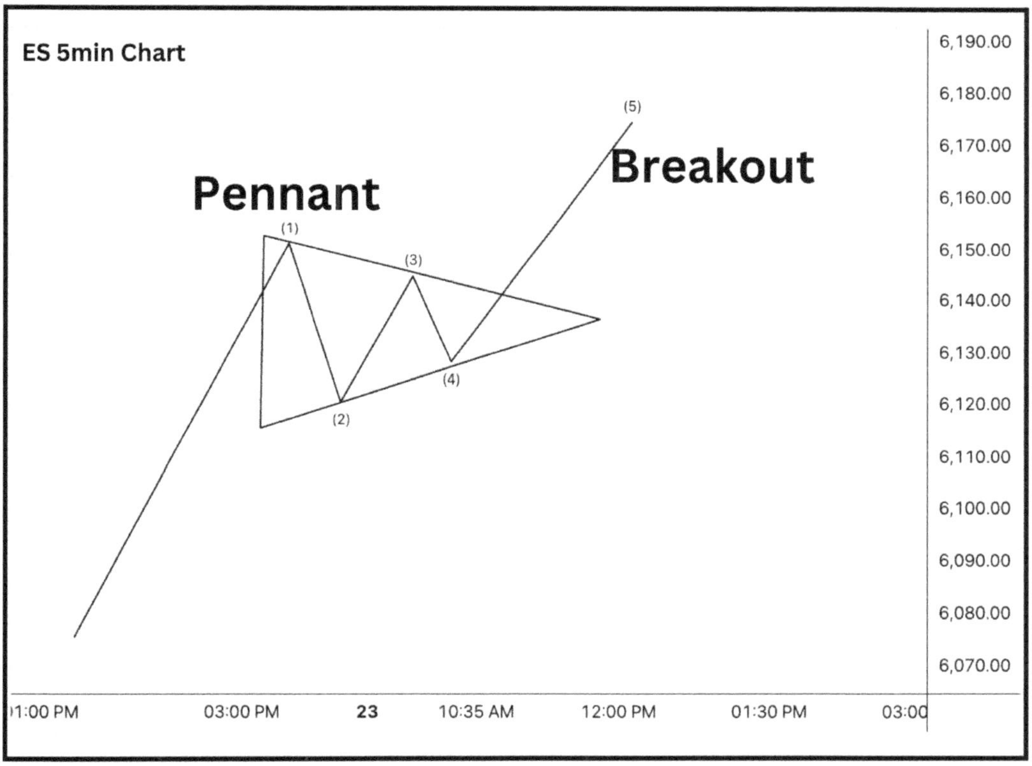

To identify a pennant, look for a strong price movement leading into a consolidation phase with converging trendlines. Volume typically decreases during this phase and spikes during the breakout. The breakout usually happens around two-thirds of the way through the pattern and continues in the direction of the original trend. Pennants are most effective on intraday charts, such as the 5-minute or hourly timeframe, but can also appear on daily charts.

The classic breakout strategy involves entering a trade when the price breaks out of the pennant in the direction of the trend. Use the length of the flagpole to estimate the price target and set a stop-loss just outside the opposite trendline. For those seeking a more aggressive approach, anticipatory entries can be made within the pennant, but this requires tighter stop-loss management due to the higher risk of false breakouts. Alternatively, traders can wait for a post-breakout retracement to enter, which offers added confirmation by testing the breakout level as support or resistance.

For example, in a bullish scenario, if the S&P futures price rises from 6120 to 6140 and consolidates between 6130 and 6140, a breakout above 6140 could target 6160, mirroring the flagpole's length. Conversely, in a bearish scenario, a drop from 6000 to 5980 followed by consolidation may lead to a breakout below 5980, targeting 5960.

Charting Tip #11 Bull Flags

The bull flag pattern is a continuation chart pattern that signals a potential upward price movement after a brief consolidation. It typically follows a strong upward price movement, known as the flagpole, which is followed by a period of consolidation or slight pullback, forming the flag. This pattern generally indicates that the prior uptrend is likely to resume once the consolidation phase is complete. The flag often takes the shape of a rectangular or downward-sloping channel, and when the price breaks out from this consolidation phase, it suggests that the upward trend is set to continue.

How to Spot a Bull Flag Pattern

To identify a bull flag pattern, look for a strong uptrend or a sharp price rise, which forms the flagpole. After this initial rally, the price typically enters a consolidation phase or a mild pullback, which forms the flag. This flag phase can either slope downward or move sideways, and it is generally contained within parallel support and resistance lines. As the flag forms, volume typically decreases, indicating that the buying momentum has paused but has not completely faded. The pattern is confirmed when the price breaks above the resistance level of the flag, signaling that the uptrend is likely to resume.

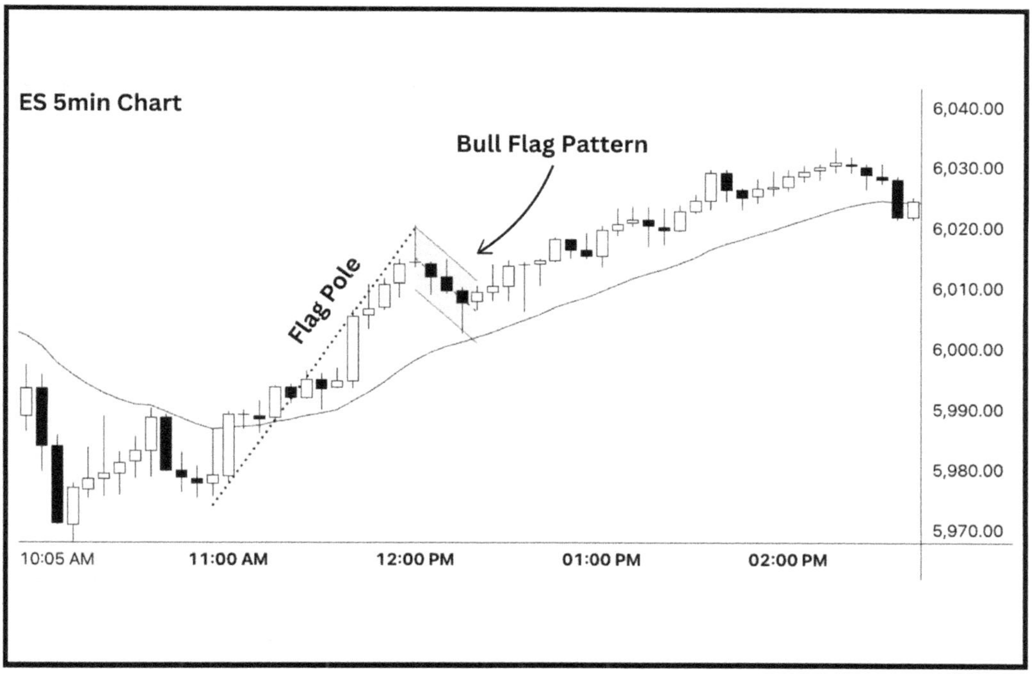

How to Trade the Bull Flag Pattern

When trading the bull flag pattern, the key action is to enter a long position once the price breaks above the upper boundary of the flag (the resistance line). This breakout is generally confirmed by an increase in volume, indicating a surge in buying interest. To protect your position, place a stop-loss just below the lower boundary of the flag or beneath the lowest point of the flag (the support level). This ensures that you limit potential losses in case the breakout fails. As for setting a target, measure the length of the flagpole (the initial sharp upward movement) and project that same distance upward from the breakout point to estimate the potential price move.

Key Characteristics of the Bull Flag Pattern

The bull flag pattern typically appears after a strong bullish trend, marking a temporary pause or consolidation before the trend continues. The flag part of the pattern usually slopes downward, signifying a mild pullback or consolidation. The duration of the consolidation phase can vary but is generally short to medium-term, with longer consolidations suggesting a stronger breakout. During the flag formation, volume should decrease, but a volume increase during the breakout confirms the strength of the continuation move. As with any chart pattern, using additional technical indicators (like RSI,

MACD, or moving averages) can help confirm the breakout and reduce the risk of false signals.

The bull flag is a powerful pattern that shows the market is gathering strength after a pullback, poised to continue its upward trajectory. With careful attention to volume and price action, this pattern can provide profitable opportunities for traders looking to ride the next wave of the trend.

Charting Tip #12 Bear Flags

A bear flag pattern is a bearish continuation chart pattern that occurs after a strong downward price movement, known as the flagpole, followed by a brief consolidation or upward pullback that forms the flag. This pattern typically signals that the prevailing downtrend is likely to continue once the consolidation phase concludes. To spot a bear flag, look for a sharp price decline, followed by a period where the price begins to move sideways or slightly upward, forming parallel support and resistance lines. The flag part of the pattern usually slopes upward or moves horizontally, indicating a pause in selling pressure. The pattern is confirmed when the price breaks below the lower boundary of the flag, signaling a continuation of the downward trend.

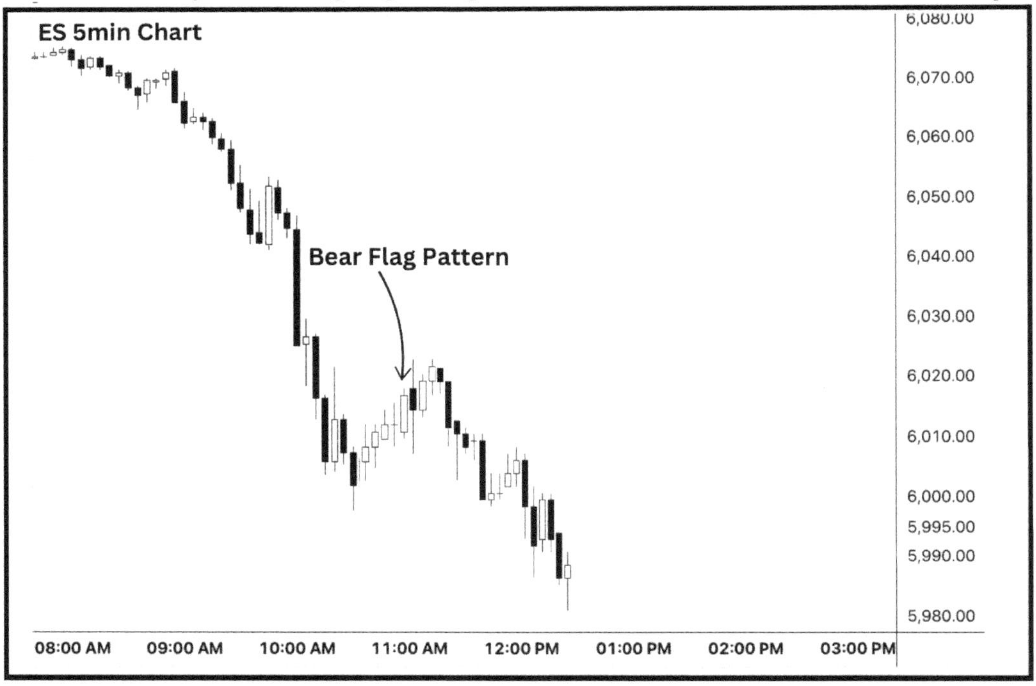

To trade a bear flag pattern, the best entry point is when the price breaks below the lower trendline of the flag, which indicates the resumption of the downtrend. This breakout is often accompanied by an increase in volume, confirming the strength of the downward movement. A short (sell) position is typically taken at this point. Traders place a stop-loss order just above the upper trendline or the highest point within the flag to protect against potential false breakouts. For setting a target, measure the length of the flagpole (the initial sharp price decline) and project that distance downward from the breakout point. This gives an estimate of the potential price move after the breakout. As with all chart patterns, it's crucial to confirm the bear flag signal with other technical indicators, such as volume and momentum indicators, to ensure the trade's validity and reduce the risk of false signals.

Charting Tip #13: Head and Shoulders

The Head and Shoulders pattern is one of the most well-known and reliable chart formations used by technical analysts to identify potential trend reversals. It typically appears at market tops (bearish head and shoulders) or bottoms (bullish inverse head and shoulders) and serves as a warning sign that the current trend may soon change direction.

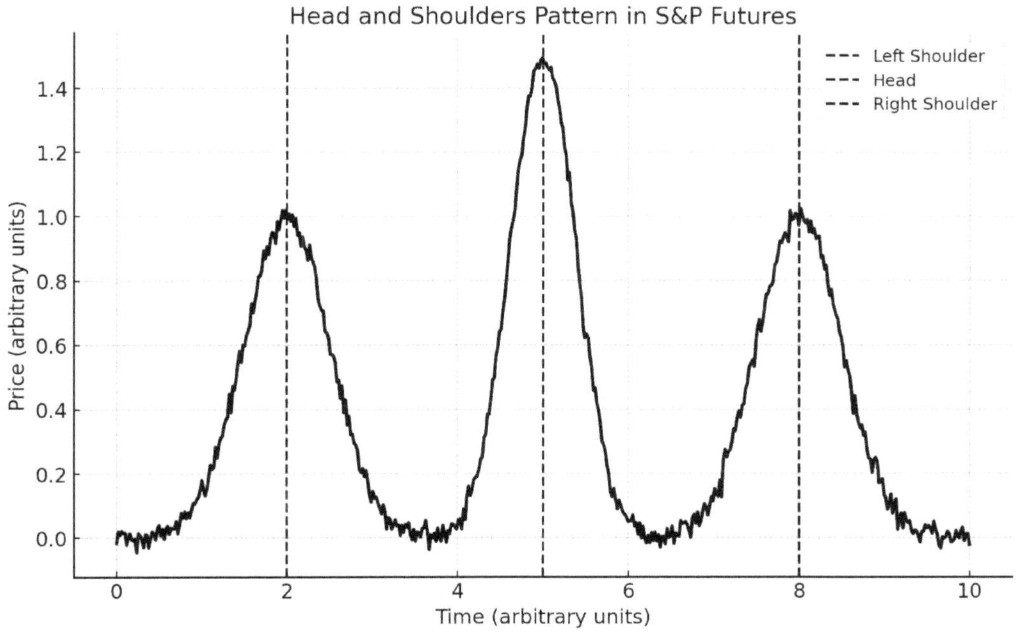

Key Features of the Pattern

The Head: The highest (or lowest in the case of an inverse pattern) peak in the formation. It stands out between the two smaller peaks or troughs (the shoulders).

The Shoulders: Two smaller peaks (or troughs) on either side of the head, roughly equal in size and height. Logically, the two shoulders are the supply zones.

The Neckline: A trendline connecting the lows (or highs in the inverse pattern) of the two shoulders. This is the key level that confirms the reversal once broken.

Trading the Head and Shoulders Pattern

Signal Confirmation: A break below the neckline (for bearish head and shoulders) or above the neckline (for bullish inverse) confirms the trend reversal.

Volume Dynamics: The break should ideally be accompanied by a noticeable increase in trading volume, reinforcing the strength of the reversal.

Price Target: Measure the distance from the head to the neckline and project it downward (or upward for inverse) to estimate the potential price target.

In the real world, the shoulders and head may not always align perfectly with a textbook setup. Instead, they often appear more irregular and resemble the chart shown below:

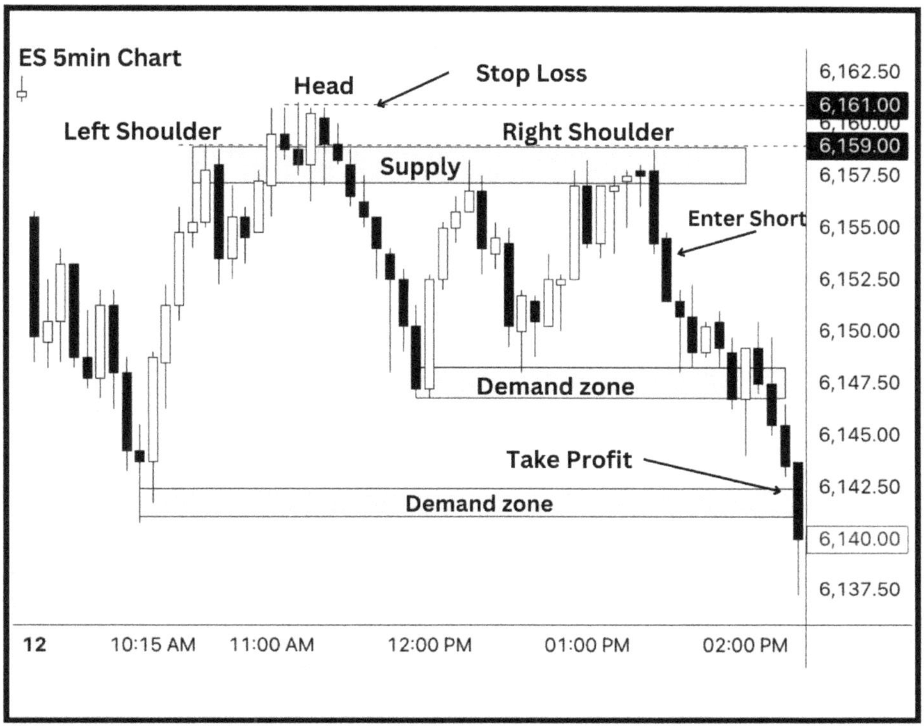

Charting Tip #14 Rounding Bottom

A rounding pattern, often referred to as a "saucer bottom," is a long-term chart formation indicating a gradual shift from bearish to bullish market sentiment. On a price chart, it appears as a wide, curved "U," reflecting a slow decline in selling pressure followed by a steady increase in buying interest. This pattern can span weeks or months, making patience a crucial skill for traders seeking to capitalize on the eventual reversal.

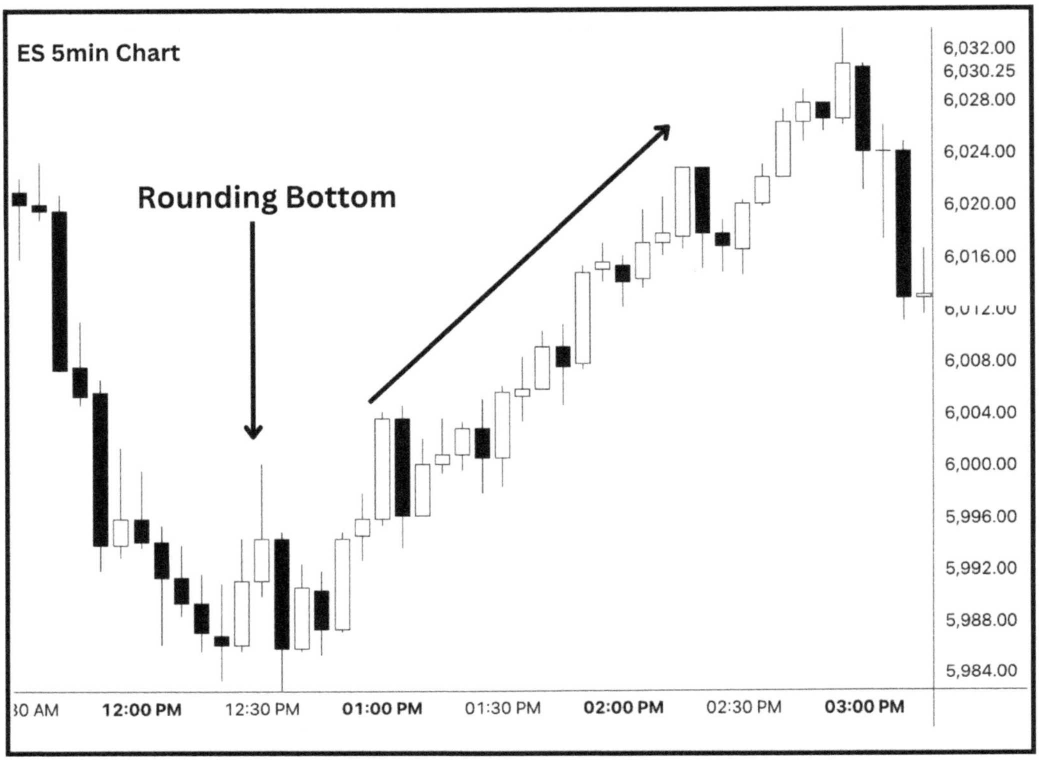

Key Features of the Pattern

A rounding bottom is characterized by a gradual decrease in price that levels off at a trough, then rises gently toward resistance. Volume behavior typically supports this formation, as it tends to be lower at the trough and increases as the price begins to climb. Additionally, the change in sentiment is rarely abrupt; instead, the market transitions slowly, allowing traders time to confirm the pattern before committing to a position.

Trading the Rounding Bottom Chart Pattern

When trading a rounding bottom in S&P 500 E-mini futures (ES), start by identifying a distinct curvature in the price action on daily or weekly charts. Draw a horizontal line at the resistance level, marking where the price last stalled before its decline. As the market arcs upward, watch for signals of strengthening momentum, such as increased volume or bullish indicator crosses (e.g., MACD or RSI).

Upon a strong close above the resistance, an aggressive trader might enter immediately, while a more conservative approach would be to wait for a successful retest of that level as support. Placing a stop-loss below the breakout zone helps safeguard against a failed move. A common profit target technique involves measuring the distance from the trough to the resistance line and projecting that magnitude above the breakout level. Throughout the trade, monitor price action closely and adjust stops to protect gains if the market continues to rally.

Conclusion

A rounding bottom offers a reliable signal of a potential long-term trend reversal, particularly in markets like the S&P 500 E-mini futures. Its formation indicates a gradual waning of bearish momentum and rising bullish interest, making it attractive for swing and position traders. By combining this pattern with disciplined risk management—through the use of stop-loss orders, volume analysis, and trade planning—traders can capitalize on a possible major shift in market sentiment and aim for substantial gains.

CHAPTER EIGHT

Mastering Trends

Trading S&P futures revolves around the ability to understand and capitalize on market trends. Trends serve as a foundational framework, guiding traders in making informed decisions about when to buy, sell, or hold positions. By aligning trades with the market's momentum, traders can enhance their chances of success while minimizing the risks of trading against the prevailing direction. This chapter explores the core principles of trend analysis, including techniques for identifying trends, drawing trend lines and channels, leveraging moving averages, recognizing trend reversals, and effectively navigating trading ranges.

Identifying Trends

A trend reflects the general direction in which the market is moving over time. Spotting trends early can make the difference between a profitable trade and a missed opportunity.

Three Types of Trends.

Uptrend: A sequence of higher highs and higher lows. For example, in an uptrend, the S&P 500 futures might move from 4200 to 4300, pull back to 4250, and then push higher to 4350. This pattern shows that buyers are in control, with each pullback being an opportunity to enter the trend.

Downtrend: A series of lower highs and lower lows. For instance, the S&P 500 futures might fall from 4300 to 4200, bounce to 4250, and then decline further to 4150, indicating seller dominance.

Sideways Trend: When prices oscillate within a defined range, failing to make significant higher highs or lower lows. For example, if the S&P 500 futures trade between 4300 and 4400 for weeks, this represents a consolidation phase.

Practical Example: Spotting a Trend

On a daily chart of the E-mini S&P 500 (ES), a trader may observe a consistent pattern of higher highs and higher lows—a hallmark of a well-established uptrend. This pattern signifies bullish momentum, where market participants are consistently willing to buy at increasingly higher prices, driving the market upward.

To confirm the presence of this uptrend, one key observation involves the price action relative to a rising moving average, such as the 20-period Exponential Moving Average (EMA). A reliable indicator of trend strength, the EMA provides a dynamic support level in bullish conditions. As the price climbs, it often retraces momentarily to touch or approach the rising EMA before bouncing upwards. This behavior reflects buyers stepping in at these levels, reinforcing the uptrend and providing potential entry opportunities for trend-following traders.

This phenomenon is not confined to the daily chart alone. On shorter timeframes, such as the 5-minute chart, the same principles apply. Traders may notice similar price behavior, with the EMA serving as a guidepost for identifying potential buying zones during intraday bullish movements. The consistent interaction between price and the EMA underscores its significance as both a trend indicator and a tool for pinpointing precise entry points during a rising market.

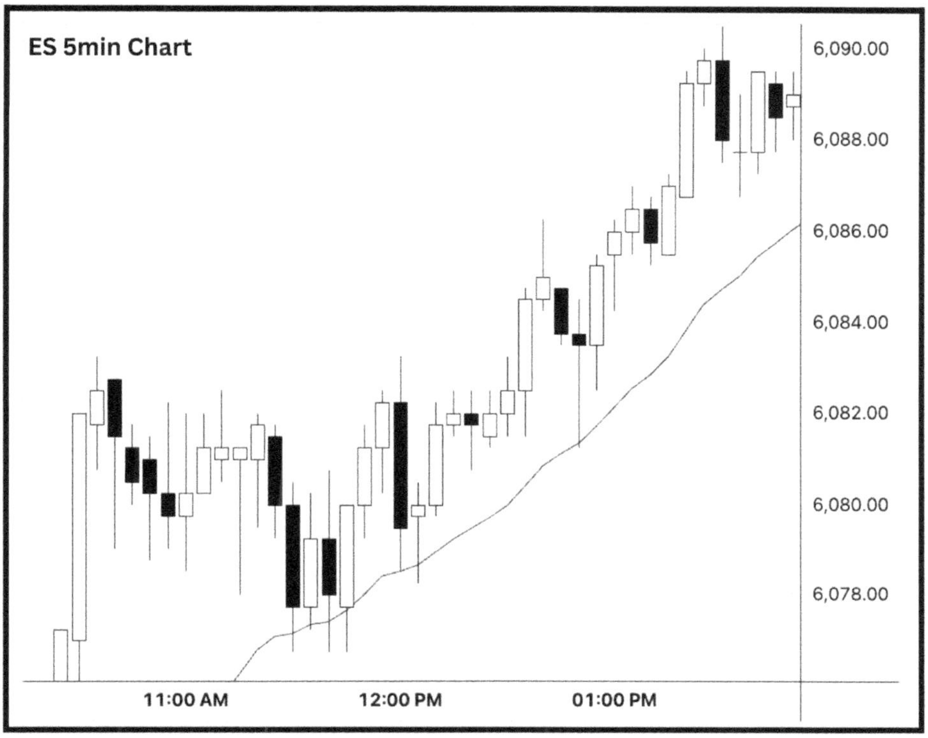

Tips for Identifying Trends

Use a higher timeframe (e.g., daily or 4-hour chart) to determine the primary trend. Observe the sequence of peaks and troughs to confirm the trend direction.

Trend Lines and Channels

Trend lines and channels provide a simple yet effective way to visualize and trade trends.

Drawing Trend Lines

Trend lines are straight lines connecting two or more significant price points, either **higher lows in an uptrend** or **lower highs in a downtrend**. For example, if the S&P futures form higher lows at 4000, 4100, and 4200, a trend line connecting these points indicates the trajectory of the trend.

Validation: The more times the price touches the trend line without breaking it, the stronger it is.

Breaks in Trend Lines: A break below an uptrend line or above a downtrend line signals a potential trend reversal or the end of the trend.

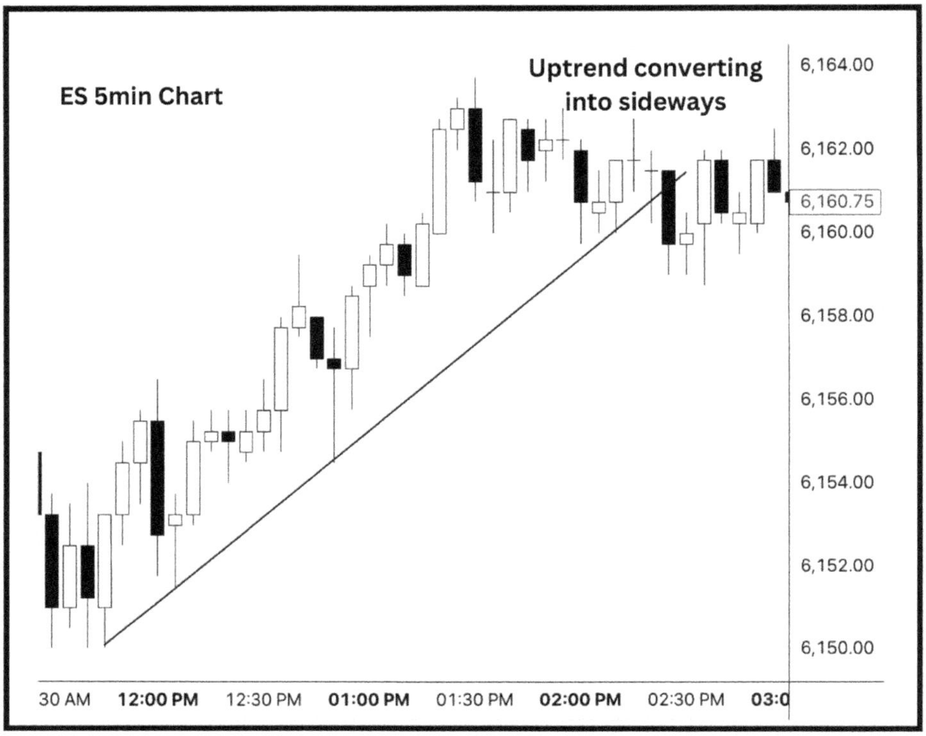

Using Channels

Channels enhance trend lines by adding a parallel boundary on the opposite side of the price movement. These boundaries help traders identify potential areas of support (bottom of the channel) and resistance (top of the channel).

Example of channel in 5 5-minute chart of ES:

In an ascending channel, S&P 500 futures might bounce between the two lines representing the upward channel (see the chart image above). Traders can buy near the lower boundary and sell near the upper boundary as long as the channel remains intact.

Example of a daily chart with a channel line of SPY:

Here is another example of channel lines on a higher time frame of the SPY daily chart for the year 2024. We can see the uptrend using these channel lines, as the price action occasionally tests the bottom channel line and the top channel line. (See the chart image that follows this paragraph.)

How to Trade Using Channel Lines on Higher Timeframes:

Traders can utilize higher timeframes to draw channel lines, helping to identify potential swing trade opportunities near the bottom or top of the channel where reversals may occur. It is essential to set appropriate stop-loss levels and utilize the channel boundaries to determine profit-taking zones effectively.

Use of Moving Averages in Identifying Trends

Moving averages are versatile tools for smoothing price data and identifying trends.

Types of Moving Averages

Simple Moving Average (SMA): A straightforward average of closing prices over a specific period

Exponential Moving Average (EMA): Places more weight on recent prices, making it more responsive to price changes.

Applications

Trend Confirmation: If the ES futures price is consistently above the 200-day SMA, the market is in a long-term uptrend.

Dynamic Support and Resistance: In an uptrend, the price often pulls back to the 50-day EMA before resuming its upward move.

Types of Trends

Trends vary in strength and duration, and understanding their types helps you align your strategy.

Primary Trends: Long-term trends lasting months to years. For example, the S&P 500 futures rallied from 2200 to 4500 during a multi-year bull market.

Secondary Trends: Medium-term trends that last weeks to months, often acting as corrections within primary trends.

Short-Term Trends: Intraday or daily movements driven by short-term catalysts like economic data or news events.

Adapting Strategies to Trend Types

For primary trends, use higher timeframes and larger stop-loss levels. For secondary trends, look for pullbacks within the broader trend for entry points. For short-term trends, focus on lower timeframes (e.g., 15-minute chart or 5-minute chart) and quick profit-taking.

Trend Reversals

Trend reversals occur when the market shifts direction, breaking the established pattern of higher highs or lower lows.

Example Chart of ES on a daily timeframe:

Signals of a Reversal

1. **Break of Trend Lines**: If S&P futures are in an uptrend and break below a long-held trend line, it could signal a reversal.

2. **Divergence**: For instance, if the S&P futures make higher highs but RSI makes lower highs, it indicates weakening momentum.

3. **Reversal Patterns**:

Double Top: Price fails to break above a previous high, forming two peaks at the same level.

Head and Shoulders: A high followed by a higher high and then a lower high signals a reversal in an uptrend

The V-Shaped Reversal - A Rare occurrence, but it does happen on certain days.

A "V-shaped reversal" is a sharp, rapid change in market direction where the price plummets and quickly rebounds with equal intensity, forming a "V" shape on a price chart. This pattern typically represents an extreme in market sentiment, with a dramatic sell-off followed by a swift recovery. Understanding the dynamics behind this reversal can help traders capitalize on these rare but powerful moves.

Anatomy of a V-Shaped Reversal

A V-shaped reversal starts with an aggressive downward move. Often, this sharp decline is driven by panic selling, negative news, or an overreaction to fundamental changes. As the price falls rapidly, traders and investors who hold long positions exit en masse, causing the market to fall further. Selling is often exacerbated by the triggering of stop-loss orders and margin calls, intensifying the decline.

At some point, the selling pressure subsides. Buyers recognize the oversold conditions or view the lower price as an opportunity. This buying interest causes a sharp reversal. The key characteristic of a V-shaped reversal is that the recovery is just as fast as the decline, leaving little time for hesitation. Short-sellers cover their positions, adding to the upward momentum, and the market quickly erases the losses incurred during the downturn.

Why V-Shaped Reversals Occur

1. **Overreaction to News**: Market participants sometimes overreact to news or data, causing a sharp decline. Once the panic subsides, the market often retraces, realizing the initial reaction was exaggerated.
2. **Liquidity Events**: During a sell-off, liquidity can dry up as buyers step aside, allowing the price to drop rapidly. When value buyers or institutional investors step in, the market quickly rebounds due to the pent-up buying demand.

3. **Short Squeezes**: When too many traders are short during a downtrend, a reversal can force them to cover their positions, driving prices up rapidly in a feedback loop of buying pressure.

How to Trade a V-Shaped Reversal

Identifying a V-shaped reversal is challenging, as it often happens unexpectedly and without clear signals. However, specific tools can help traders recognize potential reversals early. Watching for exhaustion in the downtrend, such as reduced volume on the downside or bullish divergence in momentum indicators (e.g., RSI), can provide early clues. Additionally, recognizing key support levels where buying pressure might increase can also help anticipate a turnaround.

Once the V-shaped reversal begins, there is little time to react. Traders need to be quick to enter long positions or cover short trades to take advantage of the rapid price recovery. Given the speed of this pattern, automated trading strategies or limit orders placed at key levels can be beneficial.

Risks of V-Shaped Reversals

One of the risks in trading V-shaped reversals is mistaking them for temporary pullbacks within a larger downtrend. A false reversal could lead to premature entries, resulting in losses. Therefore, confirming the reversal with other indicators, such as a break of key resistance levels or confirmation in volume, is crucial for avoiding false signals.

Conclusion

The V-shaped reversal is a sharp, powerful pattern that can offer significant trading opportunities. While it is challenging to predict, recognizing its formation and understanding the underlying reasons can enable traders to capitalize on the fast-moving price action. Since these reversals happen quickly, timing is key, and traders must be prepared to act decisively once the reversal begins.

Trading Ranges

When the market moves sideways, it creates a trading range, marked by clear support and resistance levels. Refer to the chart below, which shows the price fluctuating between 5987 and 5952 for most of the day. This is a 5-minute chart, showing each candle representing a 5-minute timeframe.

Strategies for Trading Ranges

Buy at Support: Look for bullish candlesticks or increased volume near the lower boundary. Enter a long trade near the bottom of the range after a confirmation of bull bar, and taking profit at the top of the range is a good strategy.

Sell at Resistance: Watch for bearish signals at the upper boundary. In the above example, selling near the top of the range after confirming the bearish candle and taking profit at the top of the range is a good strategy.

Practical Example on drawing a Trend line from a higher timeframe to a lower timeframe to take a trade:

Starting with a monthly time frame, let's draw a trend line connecting the lower low from the earliest month visible on the chart to the lower low in recent months. See the chart below, which shows a solid line indicating a support trend line. Please refer to the monthly timeframe chart on the next page.

Now let's change our chart setting to a weekly time frame and see if we can draw more support trend lines or resistance lines. Refer to the chart below, which includes another support trend line drawn to connect two of the most recent lower touch points. A and B, also notice the breakout to the downside marked with a circle. This circle is where traders should take their swing trade for a possible short position at Emini. Please refer to the weekly chart on the next page.

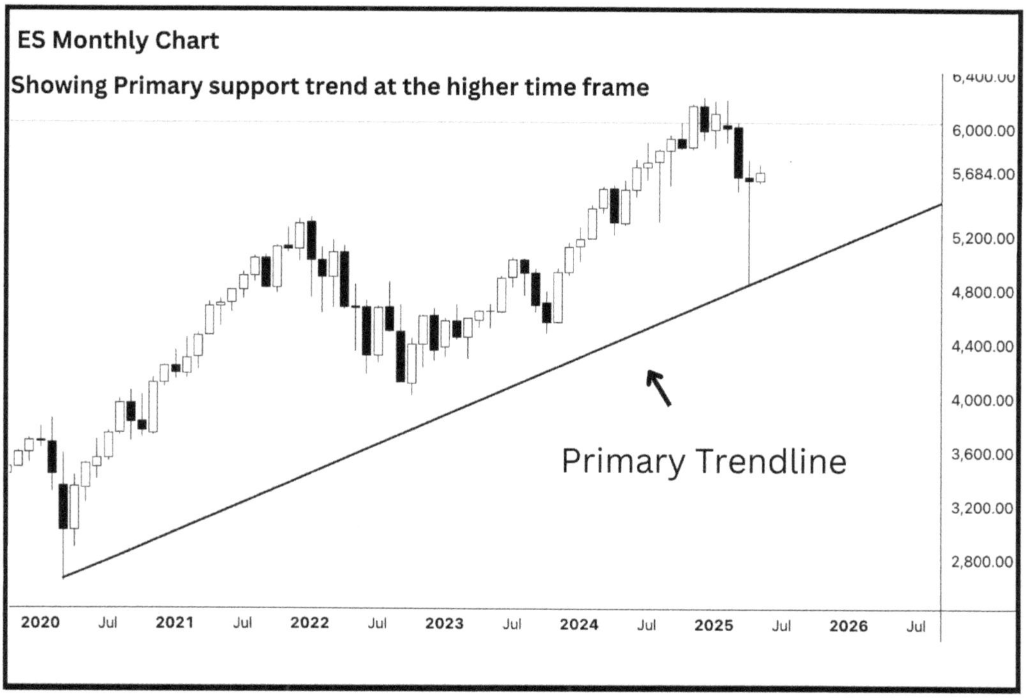

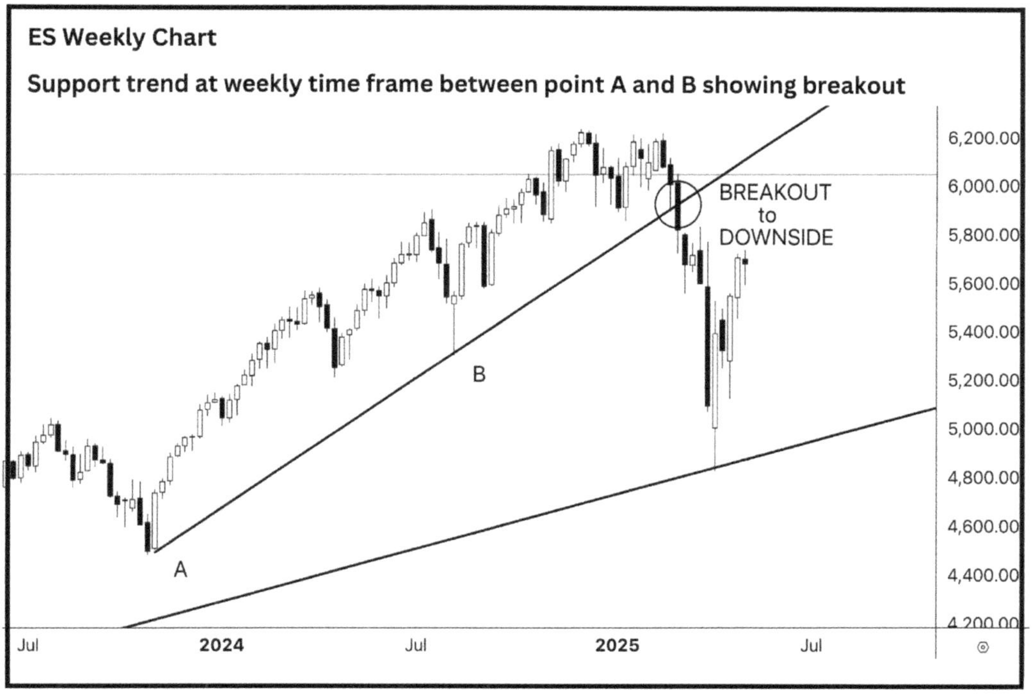

Now, repeat the process of drawing trend lines to further lower timeframes to a desired level, such as Daily, 4-hour, 1-hour, 15-minute, or 5-minute. Ultimately, whatever time zone you are in when taking a trade, let's say you are a day trader willing to spend 2 hours watching a trade, then you should reach the 5-minute level of trend breakout to take a trade. Suppose you are a larger account balance trader willing to hold an ES contract overnight and are looking for a swing trade setup. In that case, you should look for a 4-hour timeframe and look for a breakout within that time frame to take a trade and hold the contract for 4 hours or more, sometimes holding a contract for a few days to reach a desired take-profit level. In this swing trades there is a lot of overnight stress involved looking at the chart in the middle of the night and keep checking, however if you have proper stoploss in place, then you can keep moving your stoploss over the time to lock in some of the profits if the price action moves unexpectedly against your position.

Final thoughts on identifying the trends:

1. Use higher timeframes, such as Weekly, Daily, and 4-hour chart timeframes, to identify primary trends and confirm them with moving averages.
2. Employ trend lines and channels to visualize direction and entry points on the breakout from the trend in the opposite direction. For example, if the primary trend is bullish and the trend breaks downwards from the trend line, you take a short position.
3. Monitor for reversal signals to exit trades or prepare for a change in strategy.
4. Trade ranges using support and resistance levels.
5. Incorporate Fibonacci retracements to fine-tune entries and exits during pullbacks.

Achieving success in trend trading demands patience, discipline, and the agility to adapt to evolving market dynamics. By mastering the art of drawing trend lines and employing advanced techniques, you will be better prepared to navigate the complexities of the S&P futures market and seize opportunities to capitalize on prevailing trends.

CHAPTER NINE
Momentum Indicators

Momentum indicators are essential tools for traders in S&P futures, offering insights into the strength and direction of price movements. They help identify potential trend reversals, overbought or oversold conditions, and points of entry and exit. Among the most popular momentum indicators are the Relative Strength Index (RSI), the Moving Average Convergence Divergence (MACD), and the Stochastic Oscillator. In this chapter, we'll explore each indicator in detail, discussing how they work, their practical applications, and examples of how to integrate them into your trading strategy.

1. Relative Strength Index (RSI)

The Relative Strength Index (RSI) is a momentum oscillator that measures the speed and change of price movements over a specified period. Developed by J. Welles Wilder, RSI ranges from 0 to 100 and is typically used to identify overbought or oversold conditions.

Overbought: RSI above 70 suggests that the market may be overbought, indicating a potential reversal or pullback.

Oversold: RSI below 30 indicates the market may be oversold, signaling a potential bounce or trend reversal.

RSI Formula

The RSI is calculated using the following formula:

$$RSI = 100 - \frac{100}{1 + RS}$$

RS = Average gain over the selected period / Average loss over the chosen period

Practical Example

Let's say you're analyzing the E-mini S&P 500 futures (ES) on a daily chart. Over the last 14 days:

The market gained an average of 10 points on up days.

The market lost an average of 5 points on down days.

The relative strength (RS) is:

$$RS = \frac{10}{5} = 2$$

The RSI is then:

$$RSI = 100 - \frac{100}{1 + 2} = 66.67$$

With an RSI near 70, the market is approaching overbought territory.

Using RSI to find Overbought and Oversold Conditions(Refer to 30 min chart above):

If the RSI crosses above 70, consider it a warning that the market might reverse or consolidate. Refer to the image above: RSI crosses above 70, followed by a turn in price action to bearish.

If it falls below 30, it may signal an opportunity to buy as the market is oversold. See the image above: RSI crosses below 30, followed by a price action turn that signals a bullish reversal.

Divergences:

RSI divergence occurs when price makes a higher high, but RSI makes a lower high (bearish divergence) or when price makes a lower low, but RSI makes a higher low (bullish divergence). These are powerful reversal signals.

Example:

Suppose ES futures rally from 4000 to 4200, but RSI forms a bearish divergence by making a lower high. This divergence signals weakening momentum, and a potential pullback to 4100 might follow.

Trend Confirmation:

In an uptrend, RSI often stays above 40-50.

In a downtrend, RSI frequently remains below 50-60.

2. Moving Average Convergence Divergence (MACD)

What Is MACD?

The Moving Average Convergence Divergence (MACD) is a trend-following momentum indicator that reveals the relationship between two moving averages of a security's price.

- The MACD Line is the difference between a fast (short-term) exponential moving average (EMA) and a slow (long-term) EMA.
- The Signal Line is a 9-period EMA of the MACD Line.

The MACD oscillates around the zero line, which acts as a baseline:

- Above zero: Bullish momentum.
- Below zero: Bearish momentum.

Using MACD in S&P Futures Trading

Crossovers:

A bullish crossover occurs when the MACD Line crosses above the Signal Line, indicating upward momentum.

A bearish crossover happens when the MACD Line crosses below the Signal Line, signaling downward momentum.

Note: A MACD crossover on shorter timeframes can be helpful in identifying an earlier entry into your trade. Do not use a 1-minute chart, as you will get too many crossovers, which will make your trading day filled with many false alerts. Start with a higher timeframe MACD crossover, such as 15 minutes or 30 minutes, and make your trading decisions at a 5-minute timeframe. See below the chart image, which shows a 30-minute timeframe and a bullish MACD crossover.

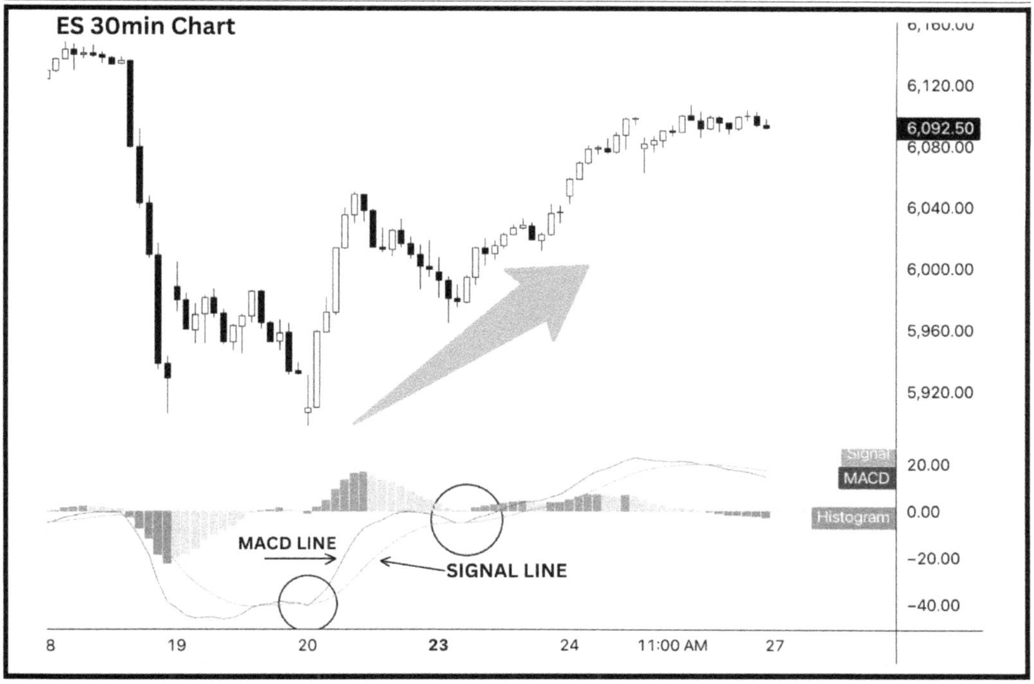

Zero Line Crosses:

- A cross above zero indicates bullish sentiment.
- A cross below zero signals bearish momentum.

Divergences:

- Bullish divergence: Price makes lower lows while MACD makes higher lows.
- Bearish divergence: Price makes higher highs while MACD makes lower highs.

Example:

If ES futures rise from 4200 to 4300 but MACD forms a bearish divergence, it could signal weakening momentum and an impending pullback.

3. Stochastic Oscillator

What Is the Stochastic Oscillator?

The Stochastic Oscillator compares a security's closing price to its price range over a specific period. It measures momentum and identifies overbought or oversold conditions.

The %K Line represents the current closing price relative to the range.
The %D Line is a 3-period moving average of %K.

Stochastic values range from **0 to 100**:

- Above 80: Overbought.
- Below 20: Oversold.

Applications in S&P Futures Trading

- Overbought and Oversold Conditions:
- Over 80: Be cautious of long positions; the market may reverse.
- Below 20: Consider buying opportunities; the market may bounce.

Crossovers:

A bullish crossover occurs when the %K Line crosses above the %D Line in oversold territory.

A bearish crossover happens when the %K Line crosses below the %D Line in overbought territory.

Divergences:

Bullish divergence: The price makes lower lows, but the stochastic oscillator makes higher lows.

Bearish divergence: Price makes higher highs, but stochastic makes lower highs.

Example:

On a 1-hour ES chart, the stochastic oscillator falls below 20 as the price touches a demand zone at 4100. A bullish crossover between %K and %D signals a potential reversal toward 4150.

Using the Indicators Together

Each of these indicators provides unique insights, but their real power emerges when used together:

Combine RSI with MACD:

Use RSI to identify overbought/oversold conditions and MACD to confirm trend momentum.

Example: If RSI falls below 30 (oversold) and MACD shows a bullish crossover, this alignment strengthens the buy signal.

Pair Stochastic with MACD:

Use stochastic to identify short-term extremes and MACD for longer-term trend direction.

Example: If stochastic signals are overbought (above 80) but MACD remains bullish, it may indicate a temporary pullback within an uptrend.

Triple Confirmation:

When RSI, MACD, and Stochastic align, confidence in trade decisions increases.

Example: On a 4-hour ES chart, RSI is oversold (below 30), MACD crosses bullish, and stochastic shows a bullish crossover. This confluence suggests a high-probability buying opportunity. Repeat the process in 2 hours and 1 hour, then dial it down to a smaller timeframe. Start with a higher time frame and then slowly change to a lower timeframe to dial in on your exact desired entry point.

Conclusion

Momentum indicators like RSI, MACD, and the Stochastic Oscillator are invaluable tools for trading S&P futures. They help traders navigate the complexities of price action, providing clarity on trend strength, reversals, and entry/exit points. By mastering these indicators and integrating them into a disciplined trading plan, you can enhance your decision-making and improve your overall trading performance. Always remember: no indicator is foolproof. Utilize these tools in conjunction with effective risk management to maximize their effectiveness.

CHAPTER TEN
Volatility Indicators

Day trading in S&P 500 futures isn't just about knowing the fundamental factors that drive the market; it's also about understanding and applying technical tools that help you make decisions quickly and confidently. As a day trader, you operate on short time frames, watching markets move by the minute, sometimes even by the second. Under these conditions, having the proper set of indicators can help you find trading opportunities, gauge how volatile the market might become, and spot when trends are about to turn.

In this chapter, we'll take a closer look at three key indicators that many experienced traders rely on: Bollinger Bands, the Average True Range (ATR), and the Volatility Index (VIX). You'll learn what each one measures, how to read their signals, and how to blend them into your daily trading routine. We'll also explore real-life examples to show how these indicators come into play when the market's in motion, whether it's calmly drifting along or suddenly roaring with unexpected energy.

Introduction to Volatility and Indicator Use in S&P Futures

Before we delve into these specific indicators, it's essential to understand why they are important. The S&P 500 futures are among the most actively traded contracts worldwide, reflecting a diverse range of investor opinions. Prices can fluctuate unexpectedly in response to economic reports, political news, Federal Reserve statements, or shifts in market sentiment. For a day trader, these swings can mean quick profits if you stay ahead of them, or painful losses if you don't see them coming.

Because you're trading over short periods, you need reliable ways to measure if the market is calm or jittery, if momentum is building or fading, and if a trend is likely to continue or reverse. Indicators like Bollinger Bands, ATR, and the VIX don't guarantee success, but they can act like a compass and a map, guiding you through uncertain market terrain and helping you make more informed choices.

1. Bollinger Bands: A Visual Guide to Market Volatility

What Are Bollinger Bands?

Bollinger Bands, created by John Bollinger, are a popular tool for picturing volatility right on your price chart. They consist of three lines: a middle line (usually a 20-period moving average) and two outer lines that sit a certain number of standard deviations above and below that average. When volatility increases, the bands stretch wider; when things calm down, they squeeze closer together. By looking at these bands, you get a visual sense of when the market might be overextended, either overbought at the top band or oversold at the bottom band.

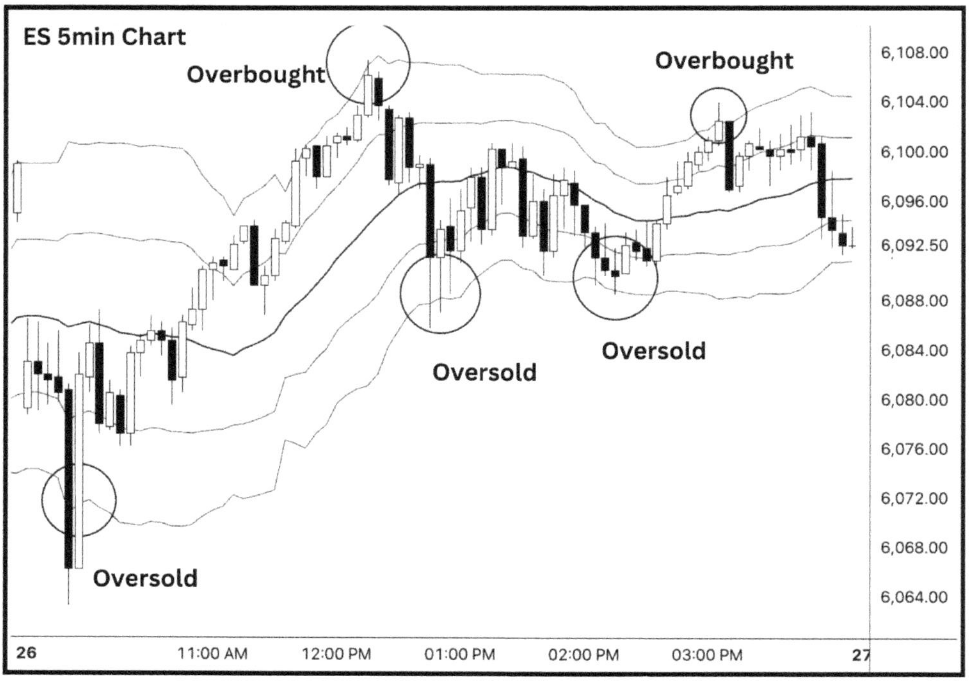

How to Use Bollinger Bands in Day Trading: Spotting Overbought/Oversold Conditions

If prices approach the upper band, the market may be getting overheated. If they approach the lower band, it may be getting oversold. For a day trader, these moments can offer clues on when to consider taking profits or placing countertrend trades, provided you have other signs that the move is running out of steam.

Riding Trends in Strong Markets:

In a powerful uptrend, prices can "hug" the upper band for a while, and in a strong downtrend, they can cling to the lower band. So, a touch of the upper band doesn't always mean "sell"—it might mean the trend still has energy left.

The Band Squeeze—A Sign of Potential Breakouts:

When the Bollinger Bands tighten up, it often signals that a bigger move could be on the horizon. While you won't know the direction in advance, the squeeze tells you to be alert and ready for a breakout trade.

Reversal Patterns Near the Bands:

If the market forms a double bottom near the lower band or a double top near the upper band, it can hint at a change in direction. Combine these patterns with other signals for stronger confirmation.

Practical Strategies with Bollinger Bands

Band Bounce: In a range-bound market, you might buy near the lower band and sell near the upper band.

Band Breakout: In trending or breakout conditions, you might initiate a trade when price pushes through the upper or lower band with convincing momentum.

2. Average True Range (ATR): Measuring Volatility in Numbers

What Is ATR?

The Average True Range (ATR) is a metric that indicates the average amount of price movement over a specified period, typically 14 price bars. It's not directly shown on the price chart, like Bollinger Bands, but rather as a line on a separate panel. When ATR is high, it means the market is swinging more wildly. When the market is low, it's calmer and moves in smaller increments.

How to Use ATR in Day Trading

Just glance at the ATR to see if today's market is unusually lively or surprisingly quiet. If ATR is high, expect larger price moves and consider using wider stop-losses to avoid being knocked out by normal price fluctuations.

Identify Breakout Potential:

When ATR starts rising after being low, it can signal that a more dynamic phase is beginning. This often means the market might soon break out of its usual ranges.

Set Your Stops and Targets Intelligently:

Traders often use the ATR to help position stop-losses. For example, if ATR is 2 points, you might set your stop 2×ATR away from your entry. This ensures that your stops reflect the market's current volatility, rather than a random number.

Adjust Position Sizes:

If the market is exceptionally volatile (high ATR), you might trade fewer contracts to keep risk under control. If it's quiet (low ATR), you might tighten your stops and reduce your profit targets, since you can't expect big moves.

ATR in Practice

If the ATR has doubled compared to usual, it might mean today's market is more dangerous—or more full of opportunities. Either way, you adjust your strategy accordingly.

3. Volatility Index (VIX): Measuring Market Mood

What Is the VIX?

Often called the "fear gauge," the VIX tracks how volatile investors expect the market to be over the next 30 days, based on S&P 500 index options. When the VIX is high, it suggests investors are nervous, expecting larger swings. When it's low, it implies calm and complacency.

How to Use the VIX in Day Trading

Contrarian Clues:

If the VIX suddenly spikes, it can mean panic is in the air. Sometimes, buying when others are scared can be profitable—if you see signs of the market stabilizing.

Inverse Relationship with S&P 500

Generally, when the VIX goes up, the S&P 500 goes down, and vice versa. Watching how the VIX moves alongside S&P futures can help confirm your market bias or warn you when something's not right.

Anticipating Volatility and Big Moves:

If the VIX suddenly jumps for no apparent reason, it could mean the market is bracing for something. Keep an eye out for a possible breakout or reversal in S&P futures.

Spotting Divergences:

If the S&P futures are climbing but the VIX is also creeping higher, it may mean the rally doesn't convince traders and they are quietly bracing for a downturn.

VIX Strategies

Look for extremes. A very high VIX might mean it's time to look for a bounce in S&P futures once the dust settles. A very low VIX could mean trouble ahead, as complacent markets can be caught off guard by sudden shocks.

Putting It All Together: A Holistic Approach

While each indicator has its merits, using them together often gives a richer picture:

Bollinger Bands + ATR:

A Bollinger Band squeeze combined with a rising ATR can alert you that a quiet market is about to wake up. This pairing helps you anticipate a big move and plan your trades accordingly.

VIX + ATR:

If both the VIX and ATR are climbing, the market is likely becoming increasingly volatile. Use smaller positions and wider stops to stay safe.

Bollinger Bands + VIX:

Tight Bollinger Bands and a low VIX could mean the market is "too quiet," setting the stage for a sudden spike in volatility. Watch for breaks out of the band, especially if the VIX starts ticking upward.

All Three Together:

When Bollinger Bands are tight, ATR is inching higher, and the VIX is moving up, you have a trifecta that screams, "Big move coming!" You won't know if it's going to blast up or crash down, but you'll learn to get your trading plan ready.

Practical Tips for Managing Risk

Always Use Stops:

Indicators help guide you, but they don't control the market. Use ATR-based stops to stay protected when prices jump around unpredictably.

Adapt to the Environment:

High VIX and ATR indicate more volatility and increased risk. Trade carefully and consider reducing your position size in wild markets.

Keep It Simple:

Don't get overwhelmed by indicators. Sometimes, a quick glance at price action and these tools is all you need to form a reasonable plan.

Practice First:

Test these indicators in a demo account or on historical data before risking real money. Understand how they behave in different conditions—quiet days, hectic news releases, earnings season—so you know what to expect.

Conclusion

Mastering Bollinger Bands, ATR, and the VIX won't guarantee success in S&P futures day trading, but these tools can give you a valuable edge. Bollinger Bands help you visualize volatility and potential turning points right on your price chart. ATR assigns a value to the market's typical volatility, informing your risk management strategy. The VIX offers a window into the market's emotional state, telling you when traders are calm or panicked.

No single indicator is perfect. By combining them—and using your judgment and experience—you can build a more complete understanding of what the market might do next. Over time, as you become comfortable with these tools, you'll rely on them like trusted partners, helping you spot better trades, manage risk more effectively, and adapt quickly to whatever surprises the S&P futures market has in store.

CHAPTER ELEVEN

Strategies

In this chapter, we will discuss various trading strategies frequently employed in S&P futures trading. These strategies are inspired by techniques used in advanced algorithm-based trading firms and manual day trading desks worldwide. Each example includes a scenario, trade execution details, four concise lines of strategy explanation, and guidance on handling unexpected outcomes. Our focus is on proven, profitable approaches that combine price action, order flow, technical indicators, and sophisticated concepts like volume profiles, volatility triggers, and algorithmic nuances. The strategies below encompass a wide range of methodologies—from classic breakouts and mean reversion to complex, algorithm-inspired techniques involving volume profiles, order flow analysis, and intermarket relationships. Each example gives you a structured framework for entries, stops, take profits, and insights on what to do if the market behaves differently than expected.

Breakout and Momentum Strategies

Strategy #1 Opening Range Breakout

During the first 2 hours after the market opens, a high and low are established, forming the opening range. In this scenario, the price action then consolidates just below the opening range high, suggesting a potential breakout if buying momentum returns. The trade execution plan is straightforward: place a buy stop order at the opening range high, ensuring entry only if the price breaks above that key level; set a protective stop loss just below the lower side of the initial range to manage risk if the breakout fails; and target a predefined extension of the range, such as an additional ten points above the entry, to capitalize on early-day volatility.

For example, between 9:30 AM and 11:30 AM ET, the price action ranges between 6081.00 and a high of 6090.00. After defining these boundaries, the price action often consolidates below the upper edge of that initial range; in this particular scenario, the price tests around 6090 and tests this high twice before breaking upwards.

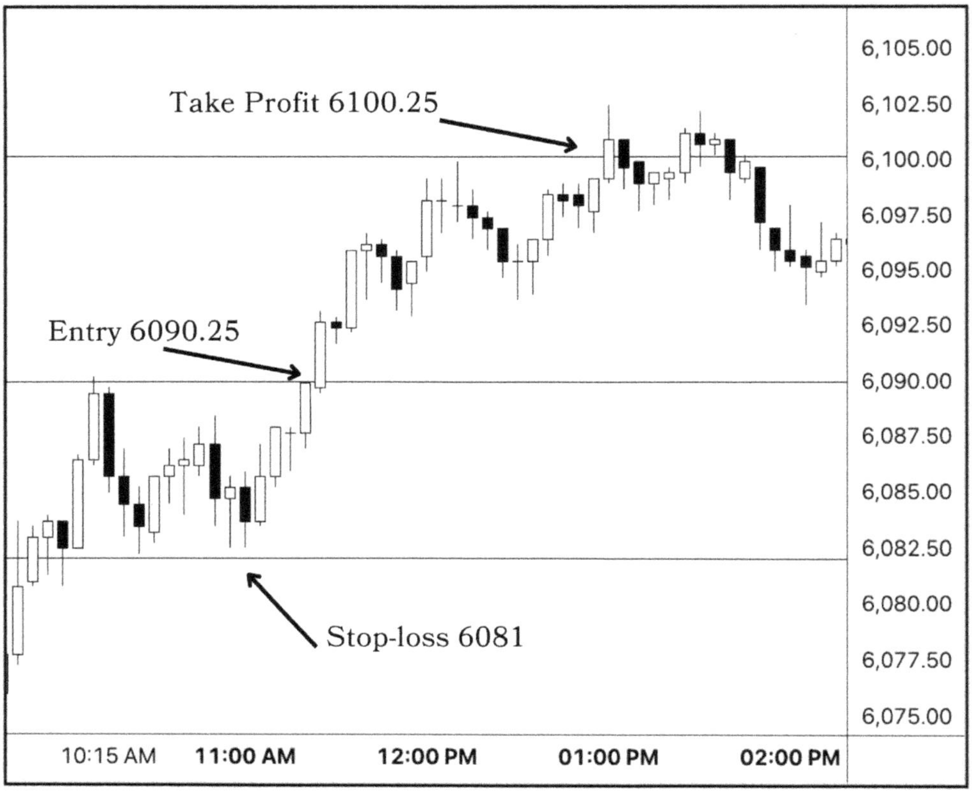

To capitalize on this pattern, you could implement a straightforward trade execution plan. First, place a buy stop order at one tick above the opening range high of 6090.00 (your entry at 6090.25), ensuring that you only enter the market if it breaks above the clearly defined upper boundary. Next, position your protective stop loss just below the lower of the initial range (your stop at 6081). Finally, aim for a predefined profit target that leverages the momentum of a successful breakout; if your strategy calls for a +10 point objective from the entry at 6090.25, you would place your take profit at 6100.25. In such a setup, if the market surges above the initial range high, you trigger a long position, manage risk with a tight stop, and define a clear reward level.

The underlying rationale for this approach hinges on four key points. First, it aims to capture the early-day volatility when institutional flows are at their heaviest, thereby increasing the likelihood of a directional thrust. Second, it aligns the entry with intraday bullish momentum by only buying above the established morning high. Third, placing a tight stop-loss provides a safety net in case the breakout attempt fails, thereby minimizing potential losses. Finally, targeting a reasonable profit extension of around ten points capitalizes on the common tendency for markets to continue in their breakout direction before settling into a more balanced state later in the trading day.

If the breakout fails immediately, you may experience a quick reversal as liquidity dries up. Unexpected selling pressure or a hidden sell iceberg can create a false start. In this scenario, honor your stop and reevaluate: if price returns inside the range, consider a mean reversion strategy rather than forcing another breakout attempt.

Strategy #2 Momentum Ignition Breakout (High-Frequency Tactic)

This Strategy seeks to capitalize on sudden market surges triggered by large orders or institutional flows that propel prices through key technical resistance levels. By entering the market as price approaches resistance amid increasing volume, the trader positions themselves to ride the wave of momentum if it ignites. A protective stop loss placed just a few points below the breakout level ensures controlled risk, while setting the take profit at approximately 1.5x or 2x the size of the preceding consolidation range allows the trader to maximize gains should the market continue to surge upward after breaking through resistance.

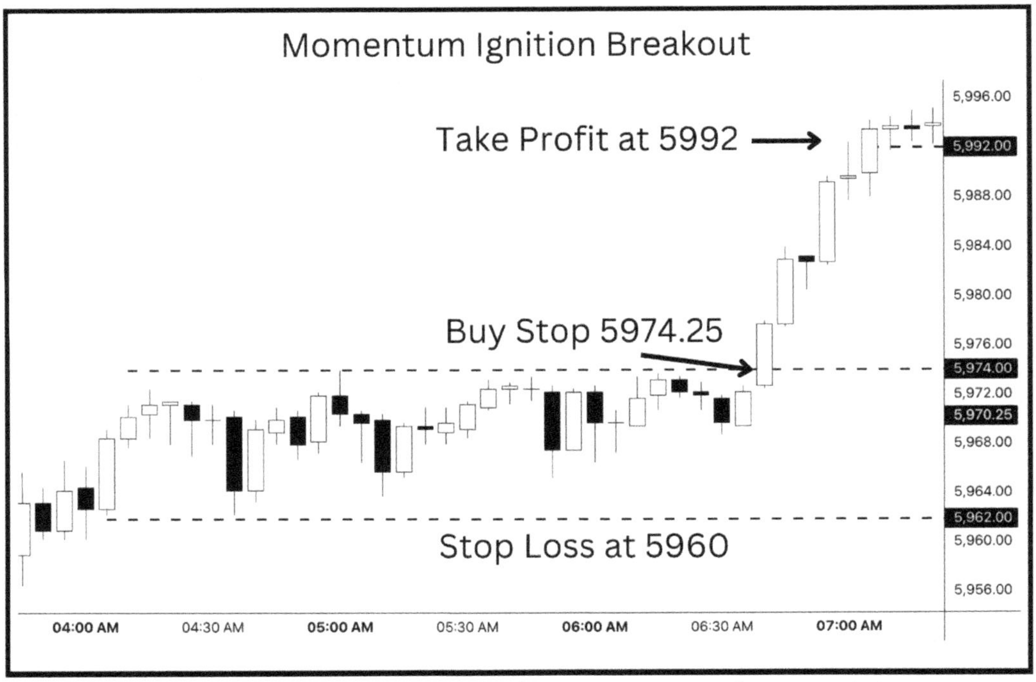

See the chart S&P E-mini futures (ES) settle into a tight consolidation range between 5962 and 5974. This narrow price band reflects a balance between buyers and sellers, with neither side able to exert decisive influence on the market. The quiet period, however, is suddenly disrupted when a noticeable spike in volume and order flow emerges at the upper boundary of the range. As the price approaches 5974, the tension builds, and a breakout above the consolidation area becomes a distinct possibility.

The trade execution plan for this scenario is straightforward yet disciplined. By placing a **buy stop order** at 5974.25, just one tick above the established consolidation high of 5974, you ensure that you enter the market only when there is a confirmed upward breach. Your risk management is equally clear-cut: position a protective stop loss at 5960, just below the lower boundary of the consolidation zone, to contain losses if the breakout fails. For the profit objective, consider a predefined extension based on the size of the initial range. With an 18-point range (5962 to 5974), aiming for a 1.5x extension yields a profit target of 5992. Alternatively, you can opt for a trailing stop, allowing the position to run and capture a larger-than-expected gain if buying momentum intensifies.

The logic behind this strategy revolves around harnessing microstructure signals and responding to the subtle cues provided by volume and order flow dynamics at a critical price level. Large players often trigger momentum by overwhelming liquidity at a key resistance point, initiating a chain reaction that forces short-sellers to cover their positions. This, in turn, amplifies the buying pressure. A stop loss below the consolidation zone guards against the sudden reversals that can result from spoofing or the unexpected appearance of large hidden orders. 1.5x profit-taking aligns with the short holding periods common in high-frequency trading approaches, capitalizing on the initial rush of breakout momentum. Meanwhile, as price propels higher, latecomers—often retail traders—may chase the move, further stoking the rally and increasing your odds of reaching the profit target.

What can go wrong with this strategy: A sudden shift in order flow (e.g., large hidden sellers) can slam the price back down instantly. Spoof orders might vanish, leaving you trapped at the top. If this occurs, exit immediately—no hesitation. Wait for genuine signs of committed buyers before attempting another long entry, ensuring that you only engage when conditions genuinely favor the continuation of upward momentum.

Strategy # 3 The EMA Pullback Strategy

In a strong uptrend, financial markets often experience brief retracements before continuing their upward movement. These pullbacks provide traders with valuable opportunities to enter the trend at advantageous levels. A highly effective approach involves using the 20-period Exponential Moving Average (EMA) as a dynamic support level. This method works particularly well in markets where trends are pronounced and directional. For example, after a sharp rally, the price may pull back slightly, approaching the rising 20-day exponential moving average (EMA). This retracement creates an ideal entry point for traders to position themselves for the continuation of the uptrend.

Trading setup under this strategy begins with a confirmed bullish bias, demonstrated by the ES's strong rally from 6014 to 6030, accompanied by high trading volume and consistent upward momentum. These elements reflect widespread buying interest and validate the trend's strength. As the price approaches the 20-EMA during the retracement phase, the EMA acts as a dynamic support level, guiding traders to a potential entry point. Around

6024.25, a bullish reversal candle, such as a hammer or an engulfing pattern, forms. This candlestick signal reinforces the notion that buyers are re-entering the market, poised to drive the price higher. Understanding this market structure is crucial, as it aligns the trade with the prevailing trend and increases the probability of success.

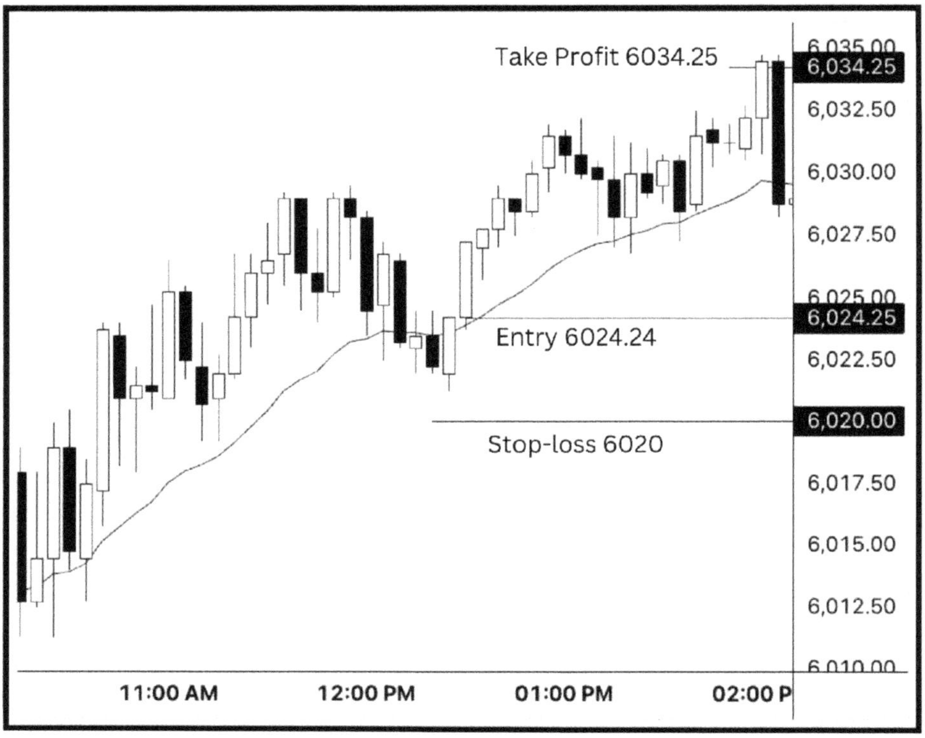

The execution of this strategy hinges on precise timing and effective risk management. The entry point is triggered when the price touches the 20-EMA and a bullish reversal candle confirms the continuation of the uptrend. At this moment, traders open a long position, entering the market at 6024.25. To protect against downside risk, a stop-loss order is placed a few points below the recent swing low of 6021, typically at 6020. This ensures that potential losses are contained in the event of an unexpected market reversal. For the take-profit target, the initial focus is on the prior high at 6030, aligning with the price's previous peak. If momentum continues to build, the profit target can be extended to 6034.25, capturing additional gains while still respecting the overall trend. If waiting for further gain, the trader should be vigilant for any unexpected reversal and can take profit immediately if there is any sign of price action falling below the rising EMA.

This disciplined strategy, rooted in the EMA pullback, provides a structured framework for trading in a strong uptrend, making it an invaluable tool for both novice and experienced traders.

What can go wrong with this strategy: Price may slice through the EMA if sentiment abruptly changes (e.g., unexpected news). If the candle confirming the bounce never appears or turns bearish, abort the trade. If stopped out, take a break and wait for stronger confirmation of trend resumption or switch to a breakout strategy if volatility emerges.

Strategy #4 Understanding Fibonacci Retracements in Trending Markets

In trending markets, Fibonacci retracement levels serve as a vital tool for identifying natural pullback zones where prices are likely to resume their primary trend. These levels, derived from mathematical ratios, help traders pinpoint areas of interest during a retracement. For instance, after a strong upward move, the price often retraces to one of the key Fibonacci levels, such as 38.2%, 50%, or 61.8%, before continuing its upward trajectory. This provides traders with a structured framework for identifying optimal entry points. Imagine the S&P E-mini futures (ES) making a strong bullish rally from 5909.5 to 5965.25. As the price retraces to the 38.2% Fibonacci level near 5944, it presents a high-probability opportunity to rejoin the trend.

Scenario: The bullish rally from 5909.5 to 5965.25 during the morning session reflects strong momentum, indicating a healthy uptrend. Traders apply the Fibonacci retracement tool to this price movement, identifying the 38.2% retracement level at 5944 using the formula: $5909.5 + (5965.25 - 5909.5) \times 0.382 = 5944$. Following the initial upward surge, the price begins to pull back, touching the 5944 level, where signs of buying interest emerge. This is often observed through a bullish reaction, such as a hammer candlestick or a volume spike. Such signals confirm that the Fibonacci level is acting as a support zone, offering an ideal entry point for traders to align themselves with the ongoing trend.

Executing the Trade: The trade execution process begins with entering a long position at 5950 when the price shows a bullish reaction above the 38.2% retracement level of 5944. This confirmation is crucial, as it reduces the likelihood of premature entry. To manage risk, a stop-loss order is placed slightly below the Fibonacci level at 5942. This position accounts for potential price noise, ensuring the trade remains viable while minimizing the downside. The initial profit target is set at 5965, the prior swing high, aligning with the trend continuation. If momentum remains strong, traders can aim for an extended target of 5975, capturing additional gains while maintaining alignment with the bullish market structure.

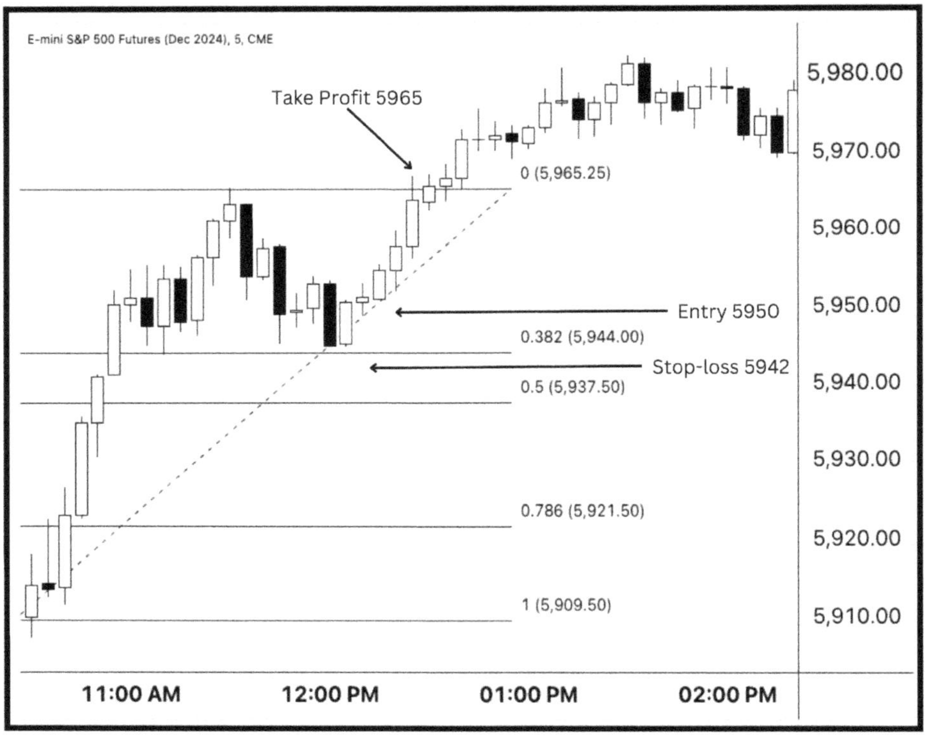

Strategy Components and Risk Management: This strategy hinges on three core elements: identifying Fibonacci levels, reacting to bullish signals, and managing risk effectively. Fibonacci retracement levels highlight natural zones where pullbacks are likely to end. Entering the trade only after observing a bullish reaction, such as a candlestick pattern or increased volume, improves the chances of success. Meanwhile, a well-placed stop loss below the Fibonacci level protects against deeper retracements or trend reversals. Profit targets focus on swing highs, ensuring the trade aligns with the prevailing trend. These elements collectively form a disciplined approach to trading pullbacks in trending markets, striking a balance between risk and reward.

What can go wrong with this strategy? Despite its effectiveness, the Fibonacci pullback strategy is not without risks. If the price grinds below the 38.2% level without forming a bullish signal, the setup may fail, resulting in a premature entry. Sudden market news or fundamental shifts can invalidate the retracement and negate the significance of Fibonacci levels. In such cases, traders must be prepared to reassess. If stopped out, the next step is to evaluate the strength of the trend and consider waiting for deeper retracement levels, such as the 50% or 61.8%, to re-enter the trade. This disciplined approach ensures that traders remain aligned with the market's structure while effectively managing risk and adapting to changing conditions.

Mean Reversion and Range Trading Strategies

Strategy #5: Understanding Bollinger Bands in Mean Reversion

Bollinger Bands are widely regarded as a robust volatility indicator that helps traders identify overbought and oversold market conditions. They consist of three components: the mid-band (a moving average) and two outer bands that adjust dynamically based on market volatility. When prices approach the upper Bollinger Band, it often signals overbought conditions, suggesting potential exhaustion of buying pressure. In this scenario, the S&P E-mini futures (ES) provide a textbook example. The price rallies steadily toward 5945.75, consistently testing the 2nd upper band without breaking higher. This persistent failure to breach the band indicates waning bullish momentum and sets the stage for a mean-reversion trade. As the price struggles at the upper band, a reversal toward the mid-band becomes increasingly probable, creating an ideal shorting opportunity.

Scenario: The market environment is characterized by a steady climb in the ES to 5945, where the price repeatedly touches the upper Bollinger Band. Notably, the Bollinger Bands remain relatively flat, reflecting a range-bound market rather than a strong directional trend. This lack of breakout momentum suggests that the upper band is acting as a resistance level. The repeated inability to surpass 5946 highlights overbought conditions and signals that the market may soon correct toward the mean. At 5944-5940, a bearish reversal candlestick or a bearish engulfing pattern confirms this resistance. This is a critical signal for traders, as it not only validates the overbought condition but also provides a clear entry point for a short trade targeting mean reversion.

Executing the Mean Reversion Trade: Enter a short position at 5943 immediately after a bearish reversal candle forms near the 1st upper Bollinger Band, signaling buying exhaustion and a likely retracement to the mid-band. Set a stop-loss just above 5947, slightly beyond the 2nd upper Bollinger Band, to account for volatility while limiting risk. Target the mid-band at 5936.75 for mean reversion, or adjust slightly below depending on conditions. For extended downside potential, use a trailing stop or take profit at the 1st lower Bollinger Band near 5930.5.

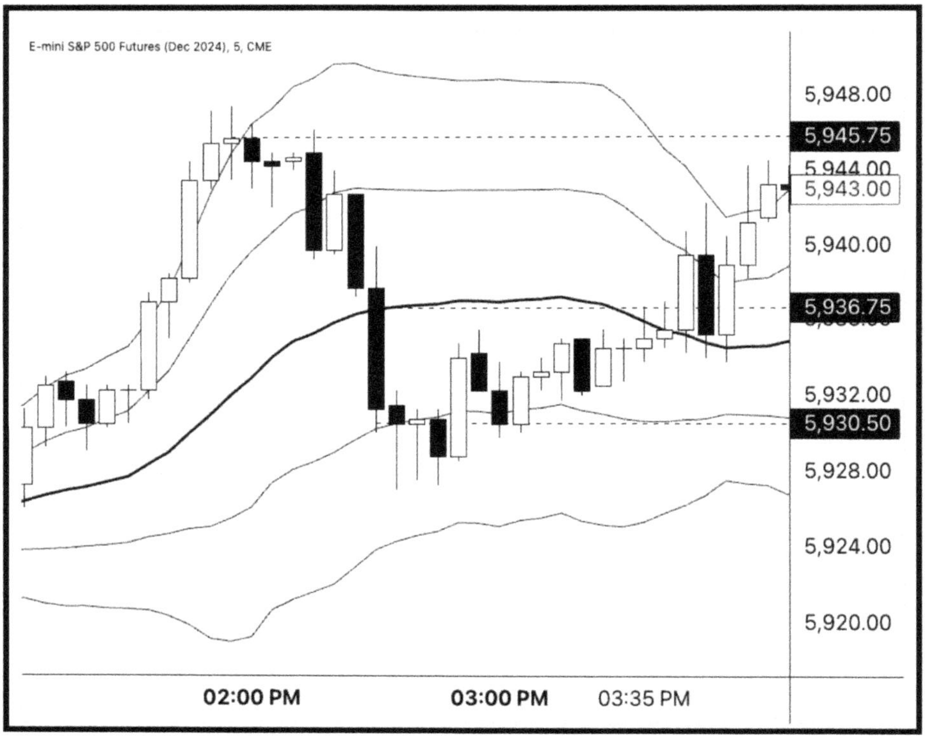

Strategy Insights: Why It Works: This Bollinger Band mean-reversion strategy relies on the principle that markets tend to oscillate between extremes of volatility before reverting to the mean. The upper Bollinger Band serves as an indicator of overbought conditions, making it a logical point to anticipate price exhaustion. By entering the short trade only after a bearish reversal candle forms, traders enhance their probability of success, as the candle confirms resistance and aligns with the expected reversion. The stop loss, placed just outside the upper band, provides a safety net while maintaining a favorable risk-reward ratio. Finally, targeting the mid-band for profit-taking aligns with the natural behavior of prices returning to the mean, which is a consistent feature of range-bound markets.

Managing Risks and Adapting to Challenges: Although the strategy is sound, certain risks should be considered. If the price breaches the upper Bollinger Band and closes above 5946, it could indicate a breakout rather than mean reversion, invalidating the setup. In such cases, the stop-loss placement minimizes potential losses. Additionally, traders should monitor for sudden fundamental shifts or news events, as these can disrupt the range-bound dynamics and lead to unexpected volatility. If the trade progresses as planned but shows strong momentum near the mid-band, trailing the stop can help lock in profits while allowing for further gains. This flexibility, combined with disciplined risk management, enables traders to execute the Bollinger Band mean-reversion strategy effectively while adapting to changing market conditions.

What Can Go Wrong: A sudden trend acceleration can push the price beyond the upper band, invalidating the mean reversion premise. If the price shoots above 5946 quickly, exit without argument. Reevaluate volatility conditions: if bands expand, consider joining the breakout rather than fighting it.

Strategy # 6 VWAP as a Mean Reversion Anchor

The **Volume Weighted Average Price (VWAP)** is a critical tool for traders, functioning as a dynamic benchmark of the average price at which a security has traded throughout the day. It acts like a gravitational center, around which price tends to oscillate in normal market conditions. However, extreme deviations from VWAP, such as those caused by a news-driven spike, can create compelling mean-reversion opportunities. Imagine a scenario where the S&P E-mini futures (ES) experience a sudden news spike, pushing prices 20 points above the VWAP level. This sharp overextension signals a potential pullback, as the cost is unlikely to sustain such a deviation for long without renewed buying pressure. The VWAP level becomes the natural target for the mean-reversion move, offering traders a structured strategy to capitalize on price normalization.

Scenario Background: Overextension Above VWAP Consider the ES surging to 4150 following an unexpected announcement, with the VWAP firmly anchored at 4130. This 20-point divergence reflects a significant overextension, as prices deviate far from the average traded level for the day. Despite the initial bullish momentum, the price begins to stall at 4150, with smaller candlestick bodies and decreasing volume signaling fading upward momentum. Such conditions suggest that the buying frenzy has cooled, increasing the likelihood of a reversal toward VWAP as the market normalizes. This setup presents a high-probability opportunity for mean-reversion traders to initiate a short position, targeting the VWAP as the anchor point for price correction.

Executing the Trade: A Step-by-Step Guide: The trade execution begins by observing for clear signs of stalling momentum above the VWAP deviation zone. For example, a bearish reversal candlestick, such as a shooting star or bearish engulfing pattern, forms near 4150, confirming resistance. At this point, traders initiate a short position, aligning their trade with the expectation of mean reversion. To manage risk, a stop-loss order is placed just above the recent spike high, at 4152. This placement ensures protection against unexpected upward continuation while minimizing risk. The profit target is set at the VWAP level of 4130, where price is likely to gravitate as the market reverts to its mean. By maintaining a disciplined approach, traders can balance risk and reward effectively while leveraging the VWAP's gravitational pull.

Why VWAP Reversion Works: The strategy hinges on the natural tendency of prices to revert to the VWAP after extreme deviations. VWAP represents the average traded price, a level of equilibrium that reflects fair value in the market. When prices deviate significantly from VWAP, the imbalance often attracts counter-trend activity, as traders seek to bring the price back in line with the average. The key to success lies in identifying fading momentum above the deviation zone. This indicates that the driving force behind the overextension, such as news or a surge in volume, has subsided. By combining a tight stop above the recent spike high with a clear target at the VWAP, traders can execute the strategy with a favorable risk-reward profile while staying aligned with market dynamics.

Managing Risks: While VWAP reversion is a reliable strategy, it is not without risks. If new information emerges, such as additional bullish news, sustained buying pressure may prevent the price from reverting to the VWAP. In such cases, the stop-loss order limits potential losses, allowing traders to quickly reassess their approach. Similarly, if the price shows no signs of fading momentum and continues to drift higher, it is crucial to cut the short trade early. Flexibility is key—traders must avoid becoming fixated on the mean-reversion idea and remain open to adapting their strategy. If the price refuses to bend toward VWAP, switching to a trend-following approach can help capitalize on the prevailing market conditions. By combining discipline with adaptability, traders can navigate the challenges of VWAP reversion and maintain an edge in dynamic markets.

What Can Go Wrong: While the VWAP reversion strategy is rooted in sound market dynamics, it can fail under specific conditions. One significant risk arises when new information or catalysts, such as unexpected news or economic data, reignite buying pressure, causing the price to drift further away from VWAP instead of reverting. In such cases, the overextension becomes a sustained trend, and traders holding onto the mean-reversion thesis risk compounding losses. Additionally, suppose the price shows no signs of fading momentum, such as consistent bullish candles, increasing volume, or repeated higher highs. In that case, this signals that the market is not ready to revert. To mitigate these risks, traders should closely monitor the price action. If momentum remains strong or the stop-loss is triggered, it's crucial to abandon the reversion idea and reassess the trend. A fallback option is to switch to a trend-following strategy, aligning with the market's newfound direction. This adaptability allows traders to pivot quickly, minimizing losses and potentially capturing gains in the prevailing trend. The key is to remain flexible and prioritize risk management over rigid adherence to a single strategy.

Strategy #7 Trading the Non-Farm Payroll (NFP) Spike: A Tactical Approach

The release of Non-Farm Payroll (NFP) data is one of the most anticipated events in financial markets, often triggering explosive price movements due to its implications for economic health and monetary policy. At precisely 8:30 AM, when the data is published, markets react almost instantly, reflecting traders' collective interpretation of the report. Imagine a scenario where the NFP data exceeds expectations, signaling robust job growth and triggering a bullish surprise in the S&P E-mini futures (ES). The price surges from 4100 to 4112 within seconds, propelled by a wave of buying. This initial reaction creates an opportunity for skilled traders to capitalize on the momentum by executing a well-timed entry during the first retracement.

Understanding the Market Reaction: In this example, the market's immediate bullish reaction to the NFP data reflects a clear directional bias. The price jumps to 4112, breaking through resistance levels, as traders rush to price in the implications of the surprise data. However, after the initial spike, markets often pause or pull back slightly as some participants take profits or reassess the move. This retracement phase is where the opportunity lies. At around 4108, the first retracement candle forms, signaling a temporary pause in the upward momentum. This pullback offers traders a chance to enter the market without chasing the initial spike, aligning their trade with the prevailing bullish trend while minimizing the risk of entering at an overextended price.

Executing the Trade - Timing and Risk Management: The trade is executed by entering a long position at 4108, during the first pullback after the bullish spike. This entry point capitalizes on reduced buying pressure while staying within the broader trend. To protect against downside risk, a stop-loss is placed at 4103, just below the retracement zone. This tight stop ensures that losses are contained in the event of an unexpected market reversal or if the initial reaction proves to be a false move. The profit target is set in the 4118–4120 zone (10 plus points from initial entry using buy stop), aligning with the expected continuation of the bullish momentum. This zone represents a natural extension of the initial spike, offering a favorable risk-reward ratio while capturing the bulk of the post-news price action.

Where to Place a Stop - A Wide Stop-Loss Approach: For traders preferring a broader stop-loss approach to accommodate the high volatility associated with NFP releases, placing the stop further below key support levels can help manage the inherent noise of post-news trading. Instead of using a tight stop at 4103, a wider stop could be set around 4098 or 4095, below the pre-news consolidation zone. This placement allows the trade more room to breathe, accounting for potential whipsaw movements and volatility spikes without prematurely exiting a position in a broader bullish trend. While this approach increases the risk per trade, it can enhance the probability of staying in the trade during minor fluctuations that often precede a continuation of the initial spike. To balance the increased risk, position sizing must be adjusted accordingly, ensuring that the dollar amount at risk remains within acceptable limits. This method is particularly suitable for traders who want to capture larger moves and are willing to withstand temporary drawdowns during volatile conditions.

Why This Strategy Works: The NFP spike strategy is rooted in the principle of capitalizing on directional surges following high-impact news. The initial spike reflects traders' consensus view of the data, providing a directional bias for trade. By waiting for a minor retracement before entering, traders reduce the risk of chasing the move at an unsustainable price. The tight stop-loss placement accounts for the possibility of whipsaw movements, which are common in volatile post-news environments. Meanwhile, targeting the 4118–4120 zone allows traders to benefit from the full extension of the initial momentum without overstaying their position. This disciplined approach ensures that the strategy is both proactive and well-hedged against unexpected reversals.

Managing Risks and Adapting to Challenges: Despite its robustness, the strategy is not without risks. One potential pitfall is that the initial reaction may fade quickly due to second thoughts from market participants. For example, traders may reassess the data, focusing on revisions or weaker underlying components, causing the price to retrace below the entry level. In such cases, it is crucial to exit immediately at the stop-loss to avoid larger losses. Another risk is the chaotic volatility that often accompanies NFP releases, which can lead to slippage and larger-than-expected losses. To adapt, traders must remain disciplined, cutting the trade promptly if the price fails to hold key support levels. Once volatility stabilizes, traders can reconsider re-entry opportunities based on the updated market structure, ensuring they remain aligned with the prevailing trend. Flexibility and quick decision-making are vital to navigating the unique challenges of trading the NFP spike.

What Can Go Wrong and Exit Strategy for a Wide Stop-Loss Approach: While a wider stop-loss provides flexibility to endure market noise, it comes with increased risk and requires careful management. One significant risk is that the initial bullish momentum from the NFP spike may fail to sustain, causing the price to retrace sharply and trigger the wider stop. If the price falls below key levels, such as 4098 or 4095, it may indicate that the market is reassessing the data and shifting sentiment, turning the trade idea invalid. Additionally, extended drawdowns during volatile conditions can create emotional pressure, making it harder to stick to the plan. To mitigate these risks, the exit strategy must be proactive. Suppose the price approaches the wider stop but shows no signs of bullish recovery, such as the absence of higher lows or increasing selling volume. In that case, it's crucial to exit manually to avoid unnecessary losses. Alternatively, suppose the price fails to regain momentum within a reasonable timeframe. In that case, traders should reassess the trade's validity and consider closing the position to prevent being stuck in a ranging or reversing market. This disciplined approach ensures that losses remain controlled, even when employing a wider stop-loss.

Strategy #8 Trading the FOMC Release: Fading the Knee-Jerk Reaction

The Federal Open Market Committee (FOMC) release is one of the most significant market-moving events, often creating rapid and exaggerated price movements as traders react to the latest policy announcements. At precisely 2:00 PM EST, the Fed's statement hits the wires, and markets respond instantly to interpret its tone—hawkish, dovish, or neutral. This knee-jerk reaction often results in overextended moves, which can later be retracted as sentiment stabilizes and traders fully digest the context of the statement. For example, imagine the S&P E-mini futures (ES) spike 15 points upward following the release, reaching 4150. Shortly after, the price stalls and forms a bearish reversal candle, signaling exhaustion in the initial upward momentum. This setup creates an opportunity to fade the reaction, targeting a partial retracement toward a more balanced price following the FOMC.

Scenario Background - Recognizing the Setup: The initial spike after the FOMC release is driven by algorithmic and knee-jerk human trading, often amplifying short-term sentiment before a broader market consensus emerges. In this case, the ES surges from 4135 to 4150 on a dovish-sounding statement, sparking immediate buying. However, as the initial euphoria fades, the price stalls near 4150, with the formation of a bearish reversal candle, such as a shooting star or bearish engulfing pattern. This stalling indicates that the initial reaction may have been overdone and is losing steam. Recognizing this pattern is crucial, as it signals a high-probability opportunity to short the market, anticipating a reversion to a more neutral level as traders recalibrate their expectations.

Executing the Trade - Entry, Stop Loss, and Take Profit: The trade is executed by entering a short position immediately after the reversal candle forms, ideally at 4148, near the top of the stalled move. A stop-loss is placed 5 points above the spike high, at 4155, to protect against a potential continuation of the bullish move. This tight stop ensures limited risk while providing enough room to account for minor volatility. The profit target is set at a mid-reversion level, halfway back to the pre-spike price. In this example, the target would be around 4142, offering a favorable risk-reward ratio. This approach allows traders to capitalize on the normalization of price action without overstaying their position in a highly volatile environment.

Why This Strategy Works: This strategy relies on the principle that markets often overreact to major news events like the FOMC release, only to retrace as the initial emotional response subsides partially. Fading the knee-jerk reaction takes advantage of this dynamic by waiting for clear signs of momentum exhaustion before entering. By using a nearby stop-loss, traders minimize potential losses if the spike continues, while the mid-reversion target aligns with typical post-news price behavior. The strategy is particularly effective in scenarios where the Fed's statement is ambiguous or lacks follow-through in sentiment, causing the initial move to appear overextended. This disciplined approach helps traders profit from market inefficiencies while maintaining strict risk management.

Managing Risks and Adapting to Challenges: While effective, this strategy is not without risks. If the Fed's tone is genuinely market-friendly or dovish, the initial spike may continue relentlessly, invalidating the fade trade. In such cases, the stop-loss prevents significant losses and allows traders to reassess the situation. Another risk is if no clear reversal candle forms after the spike, which may indicate that the market is consolidating rather than reversing. In this case, it's important to avoid forcing the trade and wait for a more reliable signal. If stopped out, traders should accept the loss and consider pivoting to a trend-following strategy if the bullish narrative proves durable. Flexibility and discipline are essential for navigating the fast-paced and unpredictable nature of FOMC-driven markets.

Strategy # 9 Order Flow and Microstructure Strategies: Trading Imbalances at Key Levels

Order flow trading, rooted in understanding the behavior of buyers and sellers, offers traders a unique edge by focusing on market microstructure. One effective strategy involves identifying order flow imbalances at critical price levels using tools like the Depth of Market (DOM). Imagine the S&P E-mini futures approaching a known resistance level at 4150. As the price nears this key level, the DOM reveals large offers beginning to pull back while smaller bids aggressively stack below, signaling a potential imbalance. This scenario suggests that sellers are retreating while buyers gain control, creating an opportunity for a momentum-driven trade as the price pushes through resistance.

Recognizing the Setup: A Play of Liquidity and Aggression

The DOM serves as a real-time window into the tug-of-war between buyers and sellers, and this strategy capitalizes on the subtle shifts in that battle. As the price approaches 4150, offers (representing sellers) begin to thin out, indicating a reduction in supply. Simultaneously, the bid side (representing buyers) shows signs of stacking aggressively, with smaller but persistent orders stepping in to absorb available liquidity. These micro-structural clues suggest that demand is overpowering supply, making a breakout through 4150 increasingly likely. Recognizing these dynamics in the DOM is crucial, as they reveal the market's true intent before the breakout materializes on the price chart.

Executing the Trade: Precision Timing with Defined Risk

The trade is executed by entering a long position as the ask stack thins and the price begins to push through the 4150 resistance level. Timing is critical—waiting too long risks missing the breakout, while entering prematurely may expose the trade to a failed attempt. A stop-loss is placed 4 points below the entry, at 4146, to protect against sudden reversals or fakeouts. The profit target is set for a quick scalp of 5–7 points, aiming to capture the immediate momentum as price lifts off from the breakout. This tight stop and short target align perfectly with the microstructure-driven nature of the strategy, allowing traders to capitalize on quick market moves while minimizing risk.

Why This Strategy Works: Exploiting Order Flow Shifts

The strength of this strategy lies in its alignment with the natural mechanics of liquidity and demand. By using the DOM to detect shifts in order flow, traders can position themselves to profit from moments when supply evaporates and demand overwhelms. The thinning of the ask stack, combined with aggressive bid stacking, is a telltale sign of algos and larger players stepping in to drive the market higher. These shifts are often brief, making a quick scalp the ideal approach. Additionally, this strategy improves odds by focusing on areas of liquidity, where algo-driven movements are more predictable, and where breakout moves often gain the most traction.

Managing Risks and Adapting to Challenges

Despite its advantages, this strategy carries risks that demand vigilance. One potential pitfall is spoofing activity—when large orders appear on the display order book (DOM) but are canceled before execution, creating a false sense of demand or supply. A sudden, unexpected sell order can also reverse the imbalance, invalidating the setup instantly. To mitigate these risks, traders must remain disciplined and exit swiftly if the price fails to lift off as anticipated. Clinging to a failing trade often leads to unnecessary losses. If stopped out, it's essential to reassess the order flow to determine whether the imbalance was genuine or manipulated. By staying nimble and adaptive, traders can navigate the challenges of order flow trading and position themselves for consistent success.

Strategy #10 Fading Iceberg Orders: A Tactical Approach to Hidden Liquidity

In the intricate world of trading, hidden liquidity, commonly known as "iceberg orders," can significantly impact market behavior. Iceberg orders, placed by large institutional players, conceal their full size, showing only a fraction of their actual volume on the order book. This allows them to absorb buying or selling pressure without tipping off retail traders. Imagine a scenario where the price of the S&P E-mini futures repeatedly tests the 4100 level, only to be absorbed each time by unseen resistance. These hidden iceberg orders prevent the price from breaking higher, creating a high-probability opportunity for a fade trade targeting the forced reversal caused by trapped buyers.

Recognizing the Iceberg Setup

The telltale sign of an iceberg order is persistent failure at a key level despite vigorous buying activity. In this case, the price attempts to breach 4100 multiple times, with aggressive bids pushing upward. However, each time the price approaches 4100, the momentum stalls as hidden sell orders absorb the buying pressure. This creates a visible struggle between buyers attempting to drive the price higher and institutional sellers quietly unloading their inventory—the inability to break through 4100 signals exhaustion among buyers, setting the stage for a short trade. The iceberg's presence not only caps the price but also creates a psychological barrier for market participants.

Executing the Fade: Entry, Stop, and Profit Targets

To capitalize on this setup, a short position is initiated at 4099 after observing another failed attempt to breach the 4100 level. This entry point positions the trader to take advantage of the subsequent downward pressure caused by trapped longs who are forced to exit their positions. A stop-loss is placed at 4104, just above the hidden resistance zone, to protect against unexpected breakouts or shifts in market dynamics. The profit target is set at 4090, aligning with the expectation of a pullback to lower support levels as the rejection intensifies. This tight risk-reward structure ensures that the trade remains profitable while effectively managing exposure.

Why the Iceberg Fade Strategy Works

The strength of this strategy lies in its ability to exploit hidden liquidity imbalances. Iceberg orders act as a stealth barrier, allowing large players to offload their positions without significantly impacting the price. As smaller buyers exhaust themselves against this invisible wall, the price is unable to gain traction, leading to a forced reversal.

By identifying the presence of these orders and fading the price under the iceberg, traders align their positions with the likely path of least resistance. The tight stop above the resistance zone further enhances the strategy by controlling risk, while the profit target focuses on capturing the move driven by trapped long positions unwinding.

Managing Risks and Adapting to Changes

Despite its effectiveness, this strategy is not without risks. If the iceberg orders are withdrawn or filled, the price may burst above 4100, triggering a breakout. In such cases, it is crucial to exit the trade immediately if strong follow-through occurs above the key level. Lingering in a losing position could lead to significant losses as buyers capitalize on the absence of resistance. After flattening the position, reevaluate the market structure. If the price is now free from iceberg pressure, a breakout strategy may become more appropriate. This flexibility allows traders to adapt to changing conditions, ensuring they remain aligned with the dominant market narrative.

Strategy #11: S&P-Nasdaq Correlation Break Strategy

Scenario Overview

In this strategy, we focus on leveraging the strong historical correlation between the S&P 500 and the Nasdaq indices. Imagine a situation where the S&P 500 drifts near a significant resistance level at 4160, showing limited momentum, while the Nasdaq surges decisively through its corresponding resistance level. This divergence presents a unique trading opportunity. The premise is simple: the S&P 500 is likely to play catch-up with the Nasdaq due to their correlated nature, offering a potential profit window for traders.

Trade Execution

Entry Point: Enter a long position on the S&P 500 when it breaches 4161. This level is slightly above the resistance, signaling the potential beginning of the anticipated catch-up rally.

Stop Loss: Place a stop-loss order at 4154. This level is just below a minor support zone, limiting downside risk in case the anticipated catch-up does not materialize.

Take Profit: Set your take-profit target at 4170. This target aims to capitalize on the S&P 500, aligning with the momentum seen in the Nasdaq.

Strategy Explanation

This approach relies on intermarket analysis and the inherent relationship between the S&P 500 and the Nasdaq. Here's a detailed breakdown of the logic behind the strategy:

Intermarket Analysis: A strong rally in the Nasdaq typically indicates broader market bullishness. This momentum often spills over into the S&P 500, making it reasonable to expect a follow-through in this index.

Leverage Lag: By buying the S&P 500 when it lags behind the Nasdaq, traders position themselves to benefit from the likely catch-up rally. This method leverages the predictable behavior of correlated markets.

Risk Management: Placing a stop-loss just below minor support (at 4154) helps limit potential losses if the correlation fails to hold or if external factors disrupt the market.

Profit Targeting: The take-profit level at 4170 is strategically placed to capture gains from the anticipated reassertion of correlation, without overstaying in the trade.

Potential Pitfalls

While this strategy is grounded in historical correlation, it is not without risks. Here are some potential challenges and how to address them:

Correlation Breakdown: If sector-specific news impacts Nasdaq stocks, the correlation may weaken or break down entirely. For instance, strong tech earnings might boost Nasdaq disproportionately, leaving the S&P 500 behind.

Stagnation Risk: If the S&P 500 fails to gain momentum after entry and remains stagnant near resistance, the trade's opportunity cost increases. In such cases, it's prudent to exit the trade early rather than waiting for the setup to fulfill its potential.

Divergent Signals: Forcing a trade based on correlation when signals diverge can lead to unnecessary losses. Instead, it's better to wait for clearer market clues or switch to a strategy that focuses solely on the S&P 500 without relying on external correlations.

Final Thoughts

The S&P-Nasdaq Correlation Break strategy is a powerful tool for traders who understand intermarket dynamics. However, discipline and adaptability are key. By adhering to the defined entry, exit, and risk management parameters, traders can effectively capitalize on correlation-driven opportunities while minimizing exposure to adverse outcomes. Always be prepared to adapt or abandon the setup if market conditions invalidate the underlying premise.

Strategy # 12: Bonds-Equities Inverse Relationship Strategy

Scenario Overview

This strategy capitalizes on the inverse relationship between bond yields and equity performance. Consider a scenario where the S&P 500 hovers near a significant support level around 4120, while bonds rally sharply, causing yields to drop. Historically, falling yields often boost equity valuations as lower borrowing costs and improved market sentiment support stock prices. This setup presents an opportunity to anticipate an equity bounce driven by the strength of the bond market.

Trade Execution

Entry Point: Enter a long position on the S&P 500 at 4121. This level lies just above the support, aligning the trade with the anticipated equity recovery.

Stop Loss: Place a stop-loss order at 4116, slightly below the support level. This minimizes downside risk if the correlation between bonds and equities is not realized.

Take Profit: Set the take-profit target at 4130 or higher, depending on the extent of the equity market's response to bond market optimism.

By structuring the trade with these parameters, the strategy strikes a balance between potential gains and controlled risk exposure.

Strategy Explanation

This strategy draws on the dynamics of inter-asset relationships. Here's the logic behind the setup:

Yield Impact: Falling bond yields often boost equity valuations, especially during intraday trading. This is because lower yields reduce the discount rate for future earnings, thereby enhancing the attractiveness of the stock.

Exploiting Sentiment Shifts: Buying the S&P 500 on bond strength leverages the positive sentiment shift across asset classes.

Risk Management: A nearby stop-loss at 4116 ensures minimal losses if the expected correlation does not play out.

Profit Targeting: The profit target assumes that equities will eventually reflect the bond market's optimism, capturing gains from the anticipated bounce.

Potential Pitfalls

While this strategy is rooted in well-documented market behavior, it is not foolproof. Here are the key risks and mitigation steps:

Ignoring Bond Cues: If equities fail to respond to falling yields—perhaps due to unrelated negative earnings data—the setup will not materialize as expected. Traders must remain vigilant for such divergences.

Breaking Support: If the S&P 500 convincingly breaks below 4116, it's critical to abort the trade immediately, as the breakdown invalidates the premise of the strategy.

Confirmation is Key: Before executing the trade, confirm that equities are beginning to respond to bond market movements. If there is no clear reaction, close the position early and reevaluate market drivers.

Final Thoughts

The Bonds-Equities Inverse Relationship strategy is a practical approach for traders who understand inter-asset correlations. However, success depends on disciplined execution and a readiness to adapt if market conditions change. By sticking to the defined parameters and remaining alert to potential pitfalls, traders can optimize their chances of achieving a profitable outcome.

Strategy #13 RSI Divergence at Support Strategy

Scenario Overview

This strategy leverages the predictive power of RSI (Relative Strength Index) divergence to anticipate potential market reversals. Picture a scenario where the price forms a lower low at 4030, while the RSI prints a higher low. This bullish divergence signals a potential shift in momentum, suggesting an upcoming reversal. When confirmed by price action, this setup offers an opportunity to enter a long position with a favorable risk-to-reward ratio.

Trade Execution

Entry Point: Enter a long position at 4033 upon confirmation of a bullish candle. This ensures alignment with the momentum shift indicated by the RSI divergence.

Stop Loss: Place a stop-loss order at 4028, just below the support level. This minimizes potential losses in the event of a reversal failure.

Take Profit: Set an initial take-profit target at 4040 to capture the immediate bounce. If momentum continues, consider extending the target to 4048.

Strategy Explanation

This strategy is built on the interplay of technical indicators and price action.

Momentum Shift: RSI divergence often signals a shift in momentum, hinting at a reversal even before price action confirms it. This makes it a leading indicator for potential entry points.

Support and Divergence: Entering at support combined with bullish RSI divergence increases the likelihood of a successful reversal, as the setup aligns multiple technical signals.

Risk Management: A tight stop-loss at 4028 ensures that risk is limited to a manageable level if the reversal does not materialize.

Profit Targeting: Initial and extended targets are designed to capture the short-term bounce as sellers exit, allowing traders to lock in gains efficiently.

False Signals: RSI divergence may occasionally fail to lead to a price reversal, especially during strong trending markets. Be cautious and ensure confirmation from price action.

Break of Support: If the price breaks decisively below 4028, it invalidates the setup. In such cases, exit promptly to avoid further losses.

Momentum Fades: If the bounce lacks follow-through, reevaluate the trade and consider taking profits early instead of holding for extended targets.

Final Thoughts

The RSI Divergence at Support strategy is a reliable tool for traders aiming to capitalize on momentum shifts at key levels. Success depends on disciplined execution, proper risk management, and adaptability to market conditions. By adhering to the defined parameters, traders can enhance their chances of profiting from reversal setups.

Strategy #14: MACD Momentum Cross with Volume Confirmation Strategy

Scenario Overview: This strategy focuses on identifying genuine momentum shifts by combining MACD (Moving Average Convergence Divergence) signals with volume confirmation. In this scenario, the MACD lines cross bullish at 4105, indicating a potential upward trend. Simultaneously, a spike in volume on green candles reinforces the signal, suggesting increased buying interest. This confluence creates an opportunity for a high-probability long trade.

Trade Execution

Entry Point: Enter a long position at 4106, right after a volume surge confirms the MACD bullish cross.

Stop Loss: Place a stop-loss order at 4100, slightly below a round number, to minimize risk from unexpected volatility.

Take Profit: Set an initial take-profit target at 4115. If momentum persists, extend the target to 4120 to capture additional gains.

This execution plan ensures disciplined entry and exit points while aligning with the underlying market momentum.

Strategy Explanation

The strategy integrates technical indicators and market psychology to maximize effectiveness.

Momentum Signal: The MACD bullish cross indicates a shift in momentum, while the accompanying volume spike confirms genuine buying interest.

Timing the Entry: Entering immediately after the cross leverages fresh buying activity, positioning the trade to benefit from early momentum.

Risk Management: A fixed stop-loss, set below a round number (e.g., 4100), protects against volatility while keeping losses manageable.

Profit Targeting: Incremental targets at 4115 and 4120 enable traders to lock in gains while allowing the trade to develop if momentum is sustained.

Potential Pitfalls

Despite its strengths, this strategy requires careful monitoring and flexibility. Here are potential challenges and solutions:

False Signals: MACD crosses, even with volume confirmation, can sometimes lead to false signals. To mitigate this, ensure additional context, such as broader market trends, supports the trade.

Momentum Failure: If the price fails to sustain momentum after entry, consider exiting early to preserve capital rather than holding for targets.

Volatility Spikes: Sudden volatility can trigger the stop-loss prematurely. Use a stop-loss placement that strikes a balance between protection and allowance for minor fluctuations.

Final Thoughts

The MACD Momentum Cross with Volume Confirmation strategy combines powerful technical indicators to identify and capitalize on short-term trends. Success hinges on disciplined execution, effective risk management, and the readiness to adapt in response to changing market conditions. By adhering to the defined parameters, traders can effectively exploit momentum-driven opportunities.

Strategy #15: Bull Flag Continuation Pattern Strategy

Scenario Overview: This strategy targets continuation patterns within strong trends, specifically the bull flag formation. Imagine a scenario where the price rallies from 4050 to 4065, forming a tight consolidation zone (4060-4063). This flag pattern suggests a brief pause in the uptrend, providing an opportunity to join the trend upon breakout.

Trade Execution

Entry Point: Enter a long position at 4064 once the price breaks out of the flag pattern, confirming renewed upward momentum.

Stop Loss: Place a stop-loss order at 4059, just below the lower boundary of the flag. This ensures minimal risk if the pattern fails.

Take Profit: Set the take-profit target at 4075, based on the measured move of the preceding rally. This captures the full potential of the continuation pattern.

Strategy Explanation

The bull flag continuation strategy is built on the principle of trend persistence.

Trend Pause, Not Reversal: Bull flags represent a pause in a strong trend, indicating potential continuation rather than reversal.

Breakout Alignment: Buying at the breakout aligns the trade with trend-following principles, maximizing the probability of success.

Risk Mitigation: A stop-loss just below the flag pattern's lower boundary prevents significant losses if the setup fails.

Profit Maximization: The measured move target captures the full expected continuation of the trend, ensuring optimal gains.

Potential Pitfalls

While this strategy leverages strong technical foundations, traders must remain vigilant for potential pitfalls:

Weak Breakouts: If the breakout candle lacks conviction or quickly reverses, the flag pattern is likely invalid. Exit promptly to avoid further losses.

Unexpected Selling: Macroeconomic shocks or unexpected selling pressure can disrupt the pattern. Monitor broader market conditions closely.

Retry Discipline: Avoid immediately reentering the trade if stopped out. Wait for a new pattern or a confirmed reversal signal before reengaging.

Final Thoughts

The Bull Flag Continuation Pattern strategy is a reliable method for trend-following traders. However, success requires disciplined execution, thorough pattern confirmation, and adaptability to market conditions. By adhering to the defined parameters and being vigilant for invalidation signals, traders can effectively leverage the power of continuation patterns to achieve consistent gains.

Strategy #16: Triangle Breakout Fade Strategy

Scenario Overview

This advanced strategy focuses on fading false breakouts from symmetrical triangles, exploiting the traps set for breakout chasers. Imagine a symmetrical triangle forming near 4125, where the price initially breaks out to 4127 but quickly reverses below 4125. This false breakout offers an opportunity to go short, anticipating a return to the triangle's midpoint.

Trade Execution

Entry Point: Enter a short position at 4124 after the false breakout is confirmed by a reversal below 4125.

Stop Loss: Place a stop-loss order at 4129, just above the false breakout high. This minimizes risk if the price retraces.

Take Profit: Set the take-profit target at 4115, near the triangle's midpoint, to capitalize on the mean reversion.

By structuring the trade in this manner, the strategy leverages market psychology while maintaining a tight risk-reward profile.

Strategy Explanation

This approach uses the dynamics of false breakouts and trapped traders to generate profits.

Trap Dynamics: False breakouts lure breakout chasers, creating a pool of trapped longs when the price reverses. This provides an opportunity to fade the move.

Short Entry Logic: Shorting after the reversal allows the trader to profit as trapped longs exit their positions, accelerating the downside move.

Risk Management: A stop-loss just above the failed breakout level ensures minimal risk if the trade does not play out as expected.

Profit Targeting: The midpoint of the triangle serves as a logical take-profit level, capturing the natural mean reversion within the pattern.

Potential Pitfalls

Despite its effectiveness, this strategy requires caution and adaptability. Here are potential challenges:

Secondary Fake-outs: If the price recovers immediately after the false breakout, the fake breakout could itself be a fake-out. Exit promptly if the price crosses 4129 again.

Messy Patterns: Inconsistent or unclear triangle formations can lead to multiple whipsaw losses. If the pattern is dirty, it's better to step aside and wait for clarity.

Emotional Trading: Avoid the temptation to reenter immediately after being stopped out. Switching to a neutral stance helps prevent unnecessary losses and maintains focus on clear setups.

Final Thoughts

The Triangle Breakout Fade strategy is a high-level technique for experienced traders. Success relies on understanding market psychology, disciplined execution, and strict risk management. By identifying and exploiting false breakouts, traders can turn failed moves into profitable opportunities while minimizing exposure to unnecessary risks.

Volume Profile and Market Profile Strategies

Strategy #17: Value Area Rotation Strategy (Volume Profile)
Scenario Overview

This strategy focuses on utilizing the value area concept from Volume Profile analysis to exploit predictable price rotations. Imagine a scenario where the price hovers within yesterday's value area, defined as 4100-4110. The price briefly breaks above the Value Area High (VAH) at 4110 but quickly returns inside the range. This re-entry presents a prime opportunity to short, anticipating a rotation back toward the Value Area Low (VAL).

Trade Execution

Entry Point: Enter a short position at 4109 as the price re-enters the value area after the failed breakout above VAH.

Stop Loss: Place a stop-loss order at 4114, just above the false breakout high, to manage risk if the breakout resumes.

Take Profit: Set the take-profit target at 4102, near the Value Area Low, to capture the full rotation within the value area.

By following these parameters, the strategy aligns with volume-driven market dynamics while maintaining tight risk controls.

Strategy Explanation

This strategy leverages the predictive power of Volume Profile's value area concept. Here's the rationale behind it:

Defining Fair Value: The value area represents price zones where the majority of volume was traded, indicating fair value. Re-entering the value area suggests a rejection of higher prices.

Fading Excursions: Shorting after re-entry fades the false breakout and profits from the likely rotation back to fair value.

Risk Management: A stop-loss above VAH limits potential losses if buying momentum resumes.

Targeting VAL: The take-profit target at VAL ensures traders capture the complete rotation, maximizing gains from the setup.

Potential Pitfalls

While this strategy is highly effective in balanced markets, traders must remain cautious of potential risks:

Strong Buyers Above VAH: If significant buying activity occurs above VAH, the price may not return to VAL. Exit promptly to avoid unnecessary losses.

Stalling at 4108: If the price struggles to move lower, consider taking a partial exit to lock in some profit while reducing exposure.

Bullish Volume Shifts: If volume dynamics turn bullish, adapt by closing the trade and waiting for a clearer signal. Avoid holding stubbornly in the face of changing conditions.

Final Thoughts

The Value Area Rotation strategy is a reliable technique for traders familiar with Volume Profile analysis. Its success depends on understanding value areas, disciplined execution, and quick adaptation to market changes. By adhering to these principles, traders can effectively capitalize on price rotations within established value zones.

Strategy #18: Market Profile 'P-Shaped' Day Fade Strategy

Scenario Overview

This strategy leverages Market Profile analysis to identify fading opportunities during P-shaped profile days. Imagine a scenario where an overnight short squeeze leads to the formation of a P-shaped profile, characterized by a long upward tail and price consolidating near the top of the distribution. The price hovers around 4160, close to the Value Area High (VAH), and begins to fail to push higher, presenting an ideal setup for a fade.

Market Profile is a charting tool that organizes price data into a distribution based on the amount of time the market spends at each price level. It provides insights into market structure, price acceptance, and rejection zones by using Time Price Opportunities (TPOs), which represent individual periods. The profile often takes the shape of a bell curve in balanced markets, helping traders identify key levels such as the Point of Control (POC), Value Area High (VAH), and Value Area Low (VAL). In contrast, **Volume Profile** focuses on the volume traded at each price level rather than time. It shows where the most trading activity occurred (high-volume nodes) and areas with little interest (low-volume nodes). The primary difference lies in their focus: Market Profile emphasizes time-based price acceptance, while Volume Profile highlights volume concentration. Both tools are valuable for analyzing market behavior, but they serve different purposes and offer complementary insights. For more details on how to set up "**Market Profile**", please refer to the chapter on "**Charting Tips**"

Trade Execution

Entry Point: Enter a short position at 4159 as the price fails to advance further in low-volume nodes near the top distribution.

Stop Loss: Place a stop-loss order at 4164, just above the thin volume zone, to manage risk if the price resumes the upward squeeze.

Take Profit: Set the take-profit target at 4150, near a prominent high-volume node, to capture the return to an area of fair value.

By adhering to these parameters, the strategy capitalizes on the imbalance fade while managing risk tightly.

Strategy Explanation

This advanced strategy uses Market Profile dynamics to identify profitable trades. Here's the breakdown:

Short-Covering Rallies: P-shaped profiles indicate short-covering rallies, often followed by consolidation as buying momentum fades.

Exploiting Imbalance: Shorting near low-volume nodes close to the top distribution capitalizes on the imbalance and the likelihood of price reverting to fair value.

Tight Risk Control: A stop-loss just above the thin volume zone protects against another upward squeeze.

Profit Targeting: Targeting a high-volume node ensures traders capture profits where the market is comfortable trading.

Potential Pitfalls

While this strategy is effective in balanced market conditions, traders should remain alert to potential risks:

Fresh Buying Momentum: A bullish catalyst or vigorous buying activity above 4164 can invalidate the fade. Exit promptly to minimize losses.

Building New Distribution: If the market begins to build acceptance at higher levels, it may indicate a shift in trend. Avoid fighting the move and adapt to the new structure.

Volume Shift: If volume dynamics change significantly, consider closing the trade early to avoid unnecessary losses.

Final Thoughts

The Market Profile 'P-Shaped' Day Fade strategy is an advanced technique for traders experienced in Market Profile analysis. Success depends on precise execution, disciplined risk management, and the ability to adapt to evolving market conditions. By following these principles, traders can effectively capitalize on fading opportunities within P-shaped profiles to achieve consistent profits.

Strategy #19: ATR-Based Trailing Stop Breakout Strategy

A higher ATR indicates that the market is more volatile, with larger price swings, while a lower ATR indicates smaller price movements. A rising ATR with bullish price action suggests a strong uptrend, making it an ideal time for buying, while a low ATR with weak price moves favors shorting opportunities. Imagine a scenario where ATR is rising along with the price moving up steadily from 4120 to 4130. The ATR suggests that daily volatility supports a 10-

point run, providing a framework to trail stops as the price climbs. Please refer to the chapter "**Charting Tips**" for how to add ATR to your chart.

Trade Execution

Entry Point: Enter a long position at 4132 on the close of the breakout candle to confirm the move.

Stop Loss: Use an ATR-based trailing stop starting at 4125 to manage risk as the price advances dynamically.

Take Profit: Do not set a fixed take-profit level. Instead, trail the stop dynamically as the price climbs, exiting when the stop is hit.

This execution approach ensures adaptability to market conditions while letting winners run.

Strategy Explanation

A higher ATR indicates higher volatility, characterized by larger price swings. A lower ATR indicates lower volatility, characterized by smaller price swings.

Trending Environment: When the ATR keeps increasing while price action is bullish, it indicates the market is trending higher and is suitable for going long. A lower ATR, along with lower price action, provides confirmation that market conditions are suitable for "shorting" the market.

False Breakouts: In cases of head-fake breakouts, losses are minimized by the ATR-based stop. Do not widen stops arbitrarily if volatility increases.

Re-Entry Discipline: If stopped out, re-enter only after fresh breakout confirmation to avoid chasing false signals.

Final Thoughts

The ATR-Based Trailing Stop Breakout strategy is a flexible and adaptive approach to trading breakout scenarios. By leveraging ATR for risk management and allowing trades to run in trending environments, traders can optimize their potential returns while maintaining disciplined execution. Stick to ATR rules for stop adjustments and be prepared to adapt to shifting market conditions for consistent success. Combine this strategy with **strategies #17 and #18, and make trading decisions in a comprehensive and logical manner for a** higher rate of success. *This strategy is suitable for experienced traders with prior trading experience, but it may not be ideal for beginners.*

Psychological Levels and Liquidity Pockets

Strategy #20: Trading Around Big Round Numbers

Scenario Overview

Big round numbers, such as 6000, often act as psychological levels where large institutional orders cluster, creating strong reaction zones. In this scenario, the price hovers near 6000, presenting an opportunity to trade around this key level based on market reactions.

Trade Execution

Entry Point: If the price bounces off 6000 and forms a bullish candle, go long at 6002 to ride the level's support.

Stop Loss: Place a stop-loss order at 5996, slightly below the psychological level, to limit potential losses if the level fails.

Take Profit: Set the initial take-profit target at 6010 to capture the typical rebound off significant round figure support.

Strategy Explanation

This strategy leverages the natural clustering of orders and market psychology around significant round numbers.

Institutional Flow: Round numbers, such as 6000, attract significant institutional activity, making them strong zones for price reactions.

Bullish Bounce: Entering after a bullish bounce at 6000 allows traders to align with the level's support, increasing the probability of success.

Tight Risk Control: A stop-loss is placed slightly below the psychological level, ensuring minimal loss if the level fails to hold.

Capturing Rebounds: The profit target at 6010 captures the typical rebound off such levels, maximizing gains while minimizing risk exposure.

Potential Pitfalls

While this strategy leverages predictable market behavior, traders must be cautious of potential risks:

Breaking the Level: If a large seller breaks 6000 with ease, the trade setup fails. Exit immediately by honoring the stop-loss to avoid larger losses.

No Averaging Down: Avoid adding to a losing position. Instead, switch tactics if the level completely fails.

Sustained Breakdown: If the price builds acceptance below 6000, consider flipping to a short position to align with the new trend.

Final Thoughts

Trading around psychological levels and liquidity pockets is a time-tested strategy for capturing predictable price reactions. By maintaining disciplined execution and adapting to market conditions, traders can effectively capitalize on opportunities around significant round numbers, such as 6000, while managing risk and staying aligned with market dynamics.

Using EMA crossovers

Strategy # 21: Trading 8 EMA Crossover with 21 EMA on a 5-Minute Chart

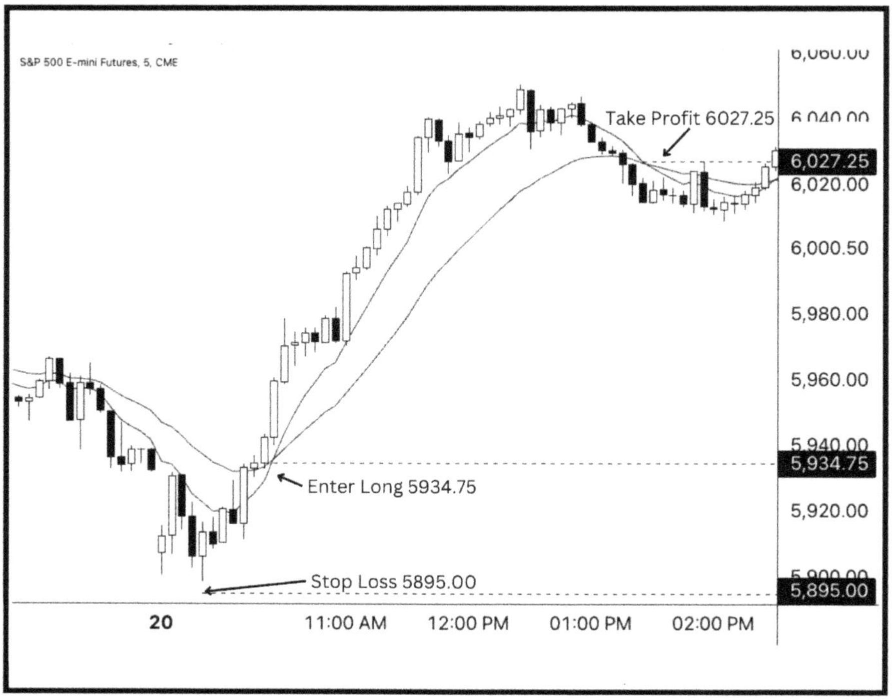

Scenario Overview

The 8 EMA (Exponential Moving Average) crossing above or below the 21 EMA on a 5-minute chart is a widely used strategy for intraday traders to identify potential short-term trends. This strategy leverages the crossover as a signal for potential momentum shifts and directional moves.

In this scenario, the 8 EMA crosses above the 21 EMA at 5934.75, signaling a bullish trend. Traders can enter a long position, setting appropriate risk and profit-taking levels.

Trade Execution

Entry Point: Enter a long position at the EMA crossover point of 5934.75, confirming the bullish momentum.

Stop Loss: Place a stop-loss order at 5895, slightly below the recent swing low, to limit potential downside risk.

Take Profit: Close the position when the 8 EMA crosses below the 21 EMA at 6027.25, signaling the end of the upward momentum.

Strategy Explanation

This strategy capitalizes on short-term trend changes signaled by EMA crossovers. The combination of the 8 EMA (fast-moving) and the 21 EMA (slower-moving) ensures that entries are based on a confirmed shift in market sentiment.

Risk Management:

The stop-loss is placed at 5895, below the recent price structure, ensuring minimal loss if the market reverses unexpectedly.

Profit Capture with Trend Confirmation:

Closing the trade at the next crossover (6027.25) ensures profits are locked in when momentum shifts. This dynamic exit aligns with the strategy's goal to ride trends while avoiding unnecessary risk.

Potential Pitfalls

While this strategy provides a clear framework for trading short-term trends, traders should be aware of potential challenges:

False Signals:

In choppy markets, EMA crossovers may produce false signals. Use additional confirmation, such as volume or price action, to validate entries.

Late Exits:

Waiting for the next crossover to exit may result in giving back some profits. To mitigate this, consider trailing stops or partial profit-taking at key resistance levels.

Volatility Risks:

Sudden spikes in volatility can cause quick whipsaws, triggering stop-loss orders. Do not trade this strategy on high-volatility days, such as FOMC announcements. Furthermore, if crossover occurs too frequently on the same day, avoid this strategy and wait for a better setup.

Final Thoughts

Trading EMA crossovers is a straightforward and effective method for capturing intraday trends. By combining disciplined entry and exit points with robust risk management, traders can consistently profit from market momentum. Staying vigilant of false signals and adapting to market dynamics will enhance the strategy's effectiveness.

Strategy #22: Trading After a Large Move

Scenario Overview

The market experienced a sudden 20-point surge in just 20 minutes. As the dust settles, the order book shows a telltale sign: a liquidity vacuum. This thin liquidity zone presents a ripe opportunity for countertrend traders to capitalize on the inevitable market rebalancing.

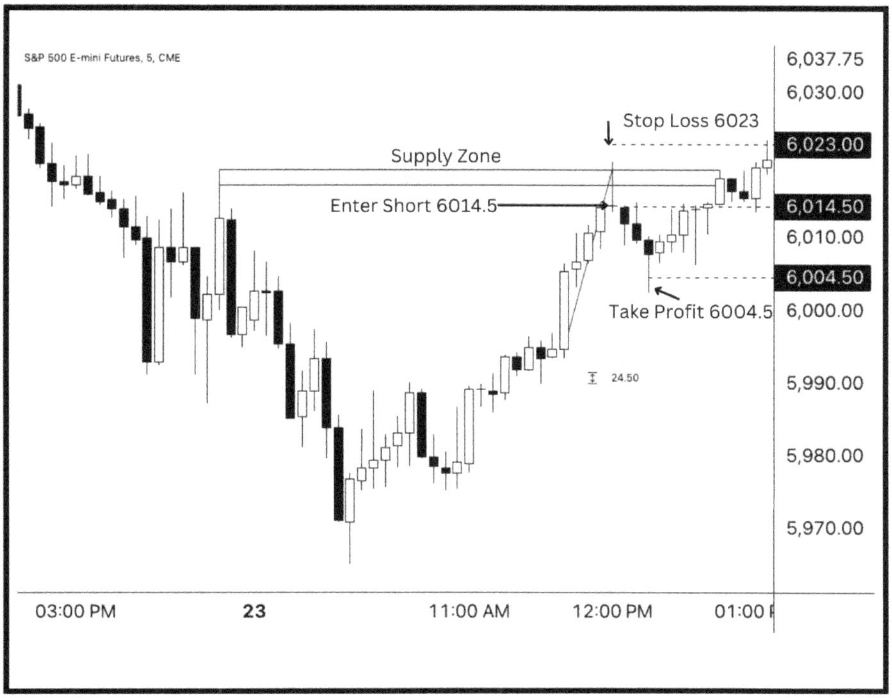

Trade Execution

Entry: Initiate a countertrend short position a few points below the recent spike high, once momentum stalls. Wait for a confirmation bear candle in the next 5 minutes for better entry.

Stop Loss: Place your stop loss 3 points above the spike high to cap potential losses.

Take Profit: Target a profit zone 5 to 10 points lower, where liquidity begins to re-enter the market.

Strategy Explanation

a. Rapid price movements often leave behind liquidity voids, creating an imbalance that the market tends to correct.

b. Shorting near the spike high exploits the likelihood that the price will normalize as regular trading activity resumes.

c. A tight stop just above the spike high limits risk if the surge regains momentum.

d. Profit-taking is timed to coincide with the market "filling in" the liquidity vacuum.

Risks and Mitigation

Momentum Exhaustion: If the momentum isn't exhausted and buyers continue to push the price higher, your stop loss will trigger quickly.

Lack of Liquidity: If liquidity fails to return and price drifts upward instead of reversing, cut your losses and exit the trade.

Do not move or delete your stop loss; take a loss if momentum reverses in the opposite direction.

Strategy # 23: Scaling In on a Pullback (Partial Position Management)

Scenario Overview

The market is in a strong uptrend, moving from 5995 to 6020. You anticipate a pullback near key levels of 6010 and 6005 before the trend resumes upward. This setup provides an opportunity to scale into an extended position and ride the next leg higher.

Trade Execution

Entry: Open a half-sized position at 6010 and scale in with the remaining half at 6005.

Stop Loss: Place a stop at 5990, just below the recent bull channel start.

Take Profit: Take half of your profit when the price retests 6020 and the remaining half at 6030 for a 10+ point gain.

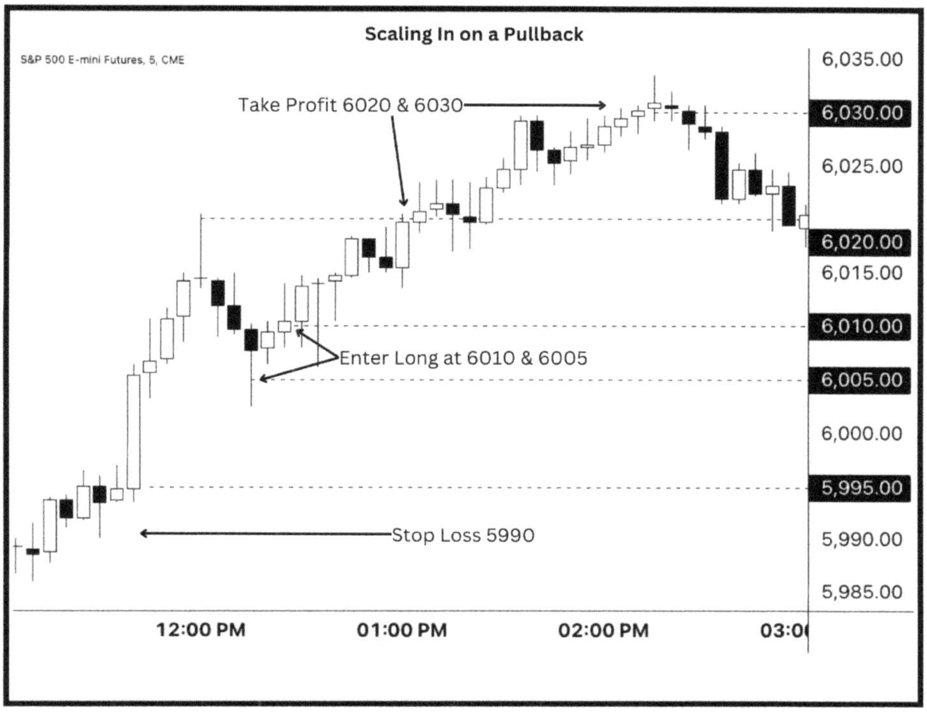

Strategy Explanation

Scaling into the trade near expected pullback levels improves your average cost and mitigates timing errors. Entering the first half early ensures you're not left behind if the pullback is shallow. A stop loss below the bull channel start limits downside risk and ensures discipline. Profit targets are set to recover the full swing high, allowing for participation in the broader trend.

Risks and Mitigation

Extended Pullback: If the price fails to bounce and continues to drop, your average position will hit the stop-loss. Accept the loss and refrain from adding to the trade.

Trend Reversal: If the trend breaks down, resist the temptation to scale further into the position. Instead, switch to a neutral stance or consider a reversal strategy once stopped.

This strategy is designed for advanced, experienced traders who excel at identifying recent highs and crafting precise entry and exit plans before committing to a trade. Once you've entered the trade, resist the urge to adjust your stop-loss position, as doing so could lead to larger losses than initially anticipated based on your calculated risk-reward ratio.

Strategy #24: Scaling Out for Emotional Comfort and Re-Entry Scenario Overview

You entered a long position at 5990, and the price has now climbed to 6010. While you anticipate further upside, there's a lingering concern about a potential reversal. This setup is ideal for a scaling-out strategy to balance risk, profit-taking, and emotional ease.

Trade Execution

Partial Exit: Sell half of your position at 6010 to lock in some profits.

Stop Loss: Adjust your stop loss to breakeven at 5990, eliminating downside risk.

Target: Hold the remaining half for a potential move to 6020.

Strategy Explanation

Scaling out secures partial profits, reducing psychological pressure, and allowing you to think more clearly. With risk minimized, you can comfortably hold onto the remaining position to capitalize on additional gains. Moving your stop loss to breakeven guarantees a no-loss scenario for the remaining position.

This flexible approach promotes better decision-making by reducing emotional baggage and regret.

Risks and Mitigation

Partial Profits: If the price reverses immediately after the partial exit and hits your breakeven stop, you'll only secure half of the potential profits.
Missed Opportunity: If the price continues higher, you'll earn more, but not as much as if you had held the entire position.

This strategy carries minimal downside but requires acceptance of its limitations. No approach is flawless—what you sacrifice in potential gains, you make up for in emotional stability and adaptability to evolving market conditions.

"When in doubt, don't let greed take the wheel—sell half, stand tall. A safety net now saves tears later when the market takes a tumble."

Strategy #25: Handling a Breakout Reversal: Honoring Your Stop Loss

Scenario Overview

You take a breakout long position at 4100, expecting upward momentum. However, the price reverses almost immediately, putting your trade in jeopardy. This is the moment to stay disciplined and stick to your stop-loss strategy.

Trade Execution

Stop Loss: Place your stop loss at 4094, just below the breakout level.
Action: Honor your stop promptly if it is triggered, without hesitation or adjustment.

Strategy Explanation

Accepting small losses is a natural and necessary part of consistent, successful trading. Promptly stopping execution prevents emotional escalation and safeguards your mental clarity. Discipline in honoring stops helps preserve capital for better, more favorable trade setups. This method builds long-term resilience and reinforces confidence in your trading system.

Risks and Mitigation

Temptation to Adjust: You might feel the urge to move your stop lower or hold the position "just in case" the price rebounds. Resist this impulse.

Revenge Trading: If the stop is hit at 4094, exit immediately and avoid impulsively jumping back into the market.

By adhering to your plan, you protect your capital and mental state. A disciplined approach allows you to reset, reassess, and prepare for the next rational opportunity without the baggage of emotional mistakes.

Chasing losses with revenge trades is like trying to extinguish a fire with gasoline. Step back, cool off, and trade with clarity, not emotion.

CHAPTER TWELVE

Gap Fill

Introduction to Gap Fill Trading

Gap fill trading revolves around the concept of "gaps"—significant price movements that occur between two consecutive trading sessions. These gaps create empty spaces on price charts, signaling potential trading opportunities for those who understand how to interpret and act upon them. A gap materializes when the opening price of a security is markedly higher or lower than its closing price from the previous session. For S&P futures, gaps are especially prevalent due to extended market closures such as weekends, holidays, or significant overnight news events. These interruptions allow substantial developments to occur, which can drastically influence market sentiment and, consequently, future price movements. Understanding the dynamics of gap fill trading involves delving into the various types of gaps, identifying their causes, and implementing a systematic approach to capitalize on the predictable behavior of price retracements.

Understanding the Concept of Gap Fill

The phenomenon of gap filling is central to this trading strategy. Gap filling occurs when the price retraces to the level where the gap originated, effectively "closing" the space on the chart. This retracement behavior is driven by the market's tendency to return to equilibrium after an overreaction caused by the initial gap. For traders, this presents a lucrative opportunity to anticipate and act upon these predictable movements, transforming gaps into strategic tools for profit.

The Significance of Gaps in S&P Futures Trading

S&P futures are particularly susceptible to gap formations due to the nature of their trading environment. The S&P 500 E-mini futures (ES), for instance, trade almost 24 hours a day during weekdays, allowing for continuous price discovery. These gaps are not random; they are typically the result of substantial news releases, economic data reports, or geopolitical events that influence investor behavior. For example, a significant economic announcement released after the market closes can lead to a substantial gap up or down when the market reopens. Understanding the underlying causes of these gaps is crucial for traders aiming to leverage them effectively.

Causes of Gaps in Financial Markets

Here are some primary factors that lead to gap formations:

1. **Earnings Reports:** Corporate earnings announcements can significantly impact stock prices. When a company's earnings exceed or fall short of market expectations, it can lead to substantial price movements, resulting in gaps. For instance, an unexpectedly strong earnings report might cause a stock to open significantly higher, creating a gap up.
2. **Geopolitical Developments:** Political events, such as elections, policy changes, or international conflicts, can introduce uncertainty or optimism in the market. For example, the announcement of a new trade agreement might lead to a gap up in S&P futures, reflecting increased investor confidence.
3. **Economic Releases:** Key economic indicators, such as GDP growth rates, unemployment figures, or inflation data, play a crucial role in shaping market sentiment. An unexpected surge in GDP growth might result in a gap up, signaling economic strength, while higher-than-anticipated inflation data could trigger a gap down.
4. **Unexpected News:** Sudden events, such as natural disasters, corporate scandals, or technological breakthroughs, can lead to immediate and significant price adjustments. These unexpected developments often cause gaps as the market rapidly assimilates new information. Despite their varied origins, a common thread ties these gaps together: their potential to create trading opportunities through the gap fill phenomenon.

The Tendency of Gaps to Fill

While gaps can initially appear as stark price deviations, market dynamics often drive prices back to equilibrium, resulting in the gap being filled. This retracement occurs as traders reassess the reasons behind the gap and adjust their positions accordingly. The tendency of gaps to fill is not guaranteed, but historical patterns suggest a notable propensity for this behavior, making it a valuable consideration for traders employing gap fill strategies. Gap filling is rooted in the market's natural inclination to correct overextensions caused by gaps. When a significant price movement occurs, it often represents an overreaction to news or events. As the market digests the information and reassesses valuations, prices tend to move back toward their previous levels, effectively closing the gap. This behavior transforms gaps from mere price anomalies into actionable trading opportunities.

The Gap Fill Trading Strategy

The gap fill trading strategy revolves around identifying gaps, assessing their likelihood of being filled, and executing trades that capitalize on the anticipated retracement. This strategy is built on the premise that markets, after reacting to new information or events, often revert to prior price levels as the initial overreaction is corrected. Implementing this strategy effectively requires a combination of technical analysis, market awareness, and disciplined execution.

Key Components of the Gap Fill Strategy

1. **Gap Identification:** The first step involves recognizing the presence of a gap. This is typically done by analyzing short-term price charts, such as 5-minute or 15-minute intervals, to spot significant price differences between consecutive trading sessions.
2. **Likelihood Assessment:** Not all gaps are equal in their probability of filling. Factors such as the size of the gap, the volume of trading, and the underlying cause of the gap influence the likelihood of it being filled. Smaller gaps in low-volatility environments are more prone to being filled quickly, while larger gaps driven by substantial news events may be less likely to retrace fully.
3. **Trade Execution:** Once a gap has been identified and its likelihood of being filled assessed, traders proceed to execute trades based on this

analysis. This involves entering positions that align with the anticipated retracement, setting target levels for the gap fill, and establishing stop-loss orders to manage potential risks.

4 **Risk Management:** Integral to any trading strategy, risk management ensures that potential losses are minimized. In gap fill trading, this involves setting appropriate stop-loss levels, managing position sizes, and avoiding overtrading based on unfounded assumptions.

The Necessity of a Systematic Approach

While the concept of gap fill trading is straightforward, its successful execution demands a systematic and disciplined approach. Traders must meticulously analyze each gap within its broader market context, considering factors such as prevailing trends, volume dynamics, and external catalysts. This methodical process enhances the probability of accurately predicting whether a gap will fill and executing trades that align with these predictions, thereby maximizing potential returns while mitigating risks.

Understanding Types of Gaps

Gaps are not monolithic; they manifest in various forms, each carrying distinct implications for traders. Recognizing the type of gap is pivotal in determining the appropriate trading strategy and anticipating the likelihood of a gap fill. The primary categories of gaps include common gaps, breakaway gaps, runaway gaps, and exhaustion gaps, each characterized by unique attributes and behavioral patterns.

Common Gaps

Characteristics: Common gaps are the most frequently occurring type of gaps in financial markets. They typically arise in sideways or low-volatility markets where there is a lack of significant news or events driving substantial price movements. These gaps are relatively small in size and often result from normal market fluctuations rather than major shifts in market sentiment.

Behavior: Due to their minor nature and the absence of strong underlying momentum, common gaps are likely to fill quickly. They do not signify the start or continuation of a trend but rather represent temporary imbalances in supply and demand that are corrected as the market stabilizes.

Example: Consider the S&P 500 E-mini futures (ES) closing at 4500 on a Monday. On Tuesday, due to minor after-hours news, the market opens at 4505, creating a 5-point gap up. Given the low follow-through buying volume and the lack of significant catalysts, a trader might interpret this as a common gap. The trader could decide to short at 4505, anticipating a retracement to the previous close at 4500, and place a stop-loss order at 4508 to manage potential risks if the gap fails to fill.

Strategic Implications: Common gaps offer straightforward trading opportunities. Since they are prone to quick fills, traders can employ short-term trading strategies to capitalize on these retracements. The simplicity of common gaps makes them an attractive entry point for novice traders looking to understand gap fill dynamics.

Breakaway Gaps

Characteristics: Breakaway gaps occur when the price decisively breaks through significant support or resistance levels, signaling the initiation of a new trend. These gaps are larger compared to common gaps and are often accompanied by high trading volume, indicating firm market conviction.

Behavior: Breakaway gaps are less likely to fill quickly because they signify a fundamental shift in market sentiment. The breakout from a key support or resistance level suggests that the market has overcome previous barriers, and the new trend is likely to continue in the direction of the gap.

Example: Imagine the S&P futures closing at 4450 on a Friday. Over the weekend, positive GDP data were released, indicating strong economic growth. On Monday, the market opens at 4465, creating a 15-point gap up. Given the significant nature of the GDP announcement and the substantial volume accompanying the gap, traders might interpret this as a breakaway gap. In this scenario, traders may choose to go long at 4465, anticipating further upward momentum, while placing a stop-loss order at 4458 to protect against any unexpected reversals.

Strategic Implications: Breakaway gaps are signals of robust market moves and are best approached with trend-following strategies. Traders should be cautious about assuming these gaps will fill, as they often represent the beginning of new, sustained trends. Instead, breakaway gaps can be used to align trades with the emerging trend, enhancing the probability of capturing significant market movements.

Runaway Gaps (Continuation Gaps)

Characteristics: Runaway gaps, also known as continuation gaps, occur within established trends and indicate ongoing momentum. These gaps are typically larger than common gaps and emerge as the trend accelerates, reflecting strong market participation and confidence in the prevailing direction.

Behavior: Runaway gaps act as stepping stones within a trend, reinforcing the existing market direction. They are less likely to fill immediately because they are driven by sustained buying or selling pressure. Instead, they signify the continuation of the trend, providing traders with opportunities to ride the momentum further.

Example: Suppose the S&P futures are in a strong uptrend, closing at 4520 on a Wednesday. The following day, driven by continued positive market sentiment, the market opens at 4530, resulting in a 10-point gap up. Given the context of an ongoing uptrend and the absence of significant resistance levels impeding the move, traders may interpret this as a runaway gap. In this case, traders might choose to trade in the direction of the trend, avoiding bets on an immediate gap fill and instead positioning themselves to benefit from the continued upward momentum.

Strategic Implications: Runaway gaps are indicative of robust trends and are best leveraged through trend-following strategies rather than gap-fill approaches. Traders should recognize that these gaps reinforce the existing trend, providing an opportunity to add to positions or enter new ones in the direction of the trend, thereby aligning with the market's momentum.

Exhaustion Gaps

Characteristics: Exhaustion gaps typically manifest near the end of strong trends and may signal that the prevailing trend is losing momentum. These gaps are often accompanied by declining trading volume, indicating waning market participation and potential exhaustion of the current trend.

Behavior: Exhaustion gaps suggest that the market is reaching a point of saturation, where the trend may be poised for a reversal. The lack of follow-through volume indicates that the initial enthusiasm driving the trend is fading, increasing the likelihood of a gap fill as the market reassesses its direction.

Example: Imagine the S&P futures rallying from 4400 to 4600 over two weeks, demonstrating a strong uptrend. On the final day of this rally, the market gaps up from 4600 to 4615 with declining volume, creating a 15-point exhaustion gap. Recognizing this as an exhaustion gap, a trader might interpret it as a signal that the uptrend is losing steam and that a reversal is imminent. Consequently, the trader might decide to short at 4610, targeting a gap fill to 4600, while placing a stop-loss order at 4620 to manage potential risks if the reversal does not materialize as expected.

Strategic Implications: Exhaustion gaps are prime candidates for gap fill trades, as they often precede trend reversals. Traders can utilize exhaustion gaps to anticipate the end of a trend and position themselves to benefit from the ensuing price retracement. This requires a keen understanding of market sentiment and the ability to distinguish exhaustion gaps from other types, ensuring that trades are based on accurate interpretations of market signals.

Identifying and Trading Gap Fills

Identifying and trading gap fills is a multifaceted process that extends beyond merely recognizing price gaps. It involves a systematic approach encompassing gap identification, assessment of the likelihood of a fill, precise timing for trade entries and exits, and robust risk management. This section explores the comprehensive methodology necessary to execute a successful gap-fill trading strategy.

Identifying Gaps

Chart Analysis and Monitoring: The initial step in gap fill trading is the identification of gaps. Traders typically employ short-term price charts, such as 5-minute or 15-minute intervals, to monitor price action at the market open. These charts provide granular visibility into price movements, enabling the detection of significant discrepancies between the previous session's closing price and the current session's opening price.

Criteria for Gap Detection: A gap is identified when there is a substantial price difference between the previous day's close and the current day's open. The definition of "substantial" can vary based on the trader's criteria, but it generally involves a price movement that is significant relative to recent volatility levels. For instance, a 3-point gap in S&P futures may be considered substantial in a low-volatility environment, while a 10-point gap might be the threshold in a high-volatility context.

Marking the Gap Fill Target: Once a gap is identified, the previous day's closing price is marked as the potential target for the gap fill. This level serves as the anticipated point where the price may retrace, effectively closing the gap. By setting this target, traders establish a clear objective for their trades, enhancing the precision of their trading strategy.

Assessing the Likelihood of a Gap Fill

Not all gaps possess an equal probability of being filled. Several factors influence the likelihood of a gap fill, and assessing these factors is crucial for determining the viability of a trade. The primary considerations include gap size, market context, and volume dynamics.

Gap Size: The size of the gap is a fundamental determinant of its likelihood to fill. Smaller gaps, such as a 3-point difference between a close at 4500 and an open at 4497, are more susceptible to quick fills, especially in low-volatility markets. Conversely, larger gaps resulting from significant news events or economic releases may be less likely to fill immediately, as they reflect substantial shifts in market sentiment.

Market Context: The broader market context plays a pivotal role in the likelihood of a gap fill. If the overall market trend is substantial and directional, gaps in the same direction as the trend are less likely to fill quickly. For example, in a robust uptrend, a gap up is more likely to persist, while a gap down might attract gap fill trades if it deviates from the prevailing trend.

Volume Dynamics: Volume analysis is integral to assessing the strength and sustainability of a gap. Gaps formed on high volume indicate firm market conviction and are less likely to fill quickly, as the price movement is supported by significant trading activity. In contrast, gaps formed on low volume with no follow-through momentum suggest weaker market support, increasing the probability of a fill.

External Catalysts: The underlying cause of the gap also influences its likelihood of being filled. Gaps driven by fundamental news or economic data releases may have different retracement behaviors compared to gaps arising from technical factors or minor news events. Understanding the catalyst behind the gap provides insights into its potential sustainability and the likelihood of a fill.

Trading the Gap Fill

Once a gap has been identified and its likelihood to fill assessed, the next step is to execute the trade. Trading the gap fill involves precise timing and confirmation to ensure that the trade aligns with the anticipated retracement.

Waiting for Confirmation: Entering a trade immediately after a gap forms can be precarious, as the initial price movement may not sustain. Instead, traders should wait for confirmation signals that validate the likelihood of a gap fill. This approach reduces the risk of premature entries based on speculative movements.

Reversal Signals: Confirmation of a gap fill often comes in the form of reversal signals, which are technical indicators that suggest the initial gap movement may be reversing. Common reversal signals include:

Bearish Engulfing Candles for Gap-Ups: A bearish engulfing pattern occurs when a larger bearish candle completely engulfs the previous bullish candle, indicating potential downward momentum.

Bullish Hammers for Gap-Downs: A bullish hammer is a candlestick pattern characterized by a small body and a long lower shadow, suggesting that buyers are stepping in to reverse the price movement.

Example: Consider the S&P futures closing at 5992 and opening at 5957, creating a 35-point gap down. If a bullish hammer candle forms at the bottom, it signals that buyers are entering the market to support the price, indicating a potential gap fill. The trader might then enter a long position at 5967 at the next candle after the bullish confirmation, set a target to fill the gap at 5992, and place a stop-loss order at 5948 below the bullish hammer candle to manage potential risks. In this example, the trader risks 19 points to gain 25, resulting in a risk-reward ratio of 1.31.

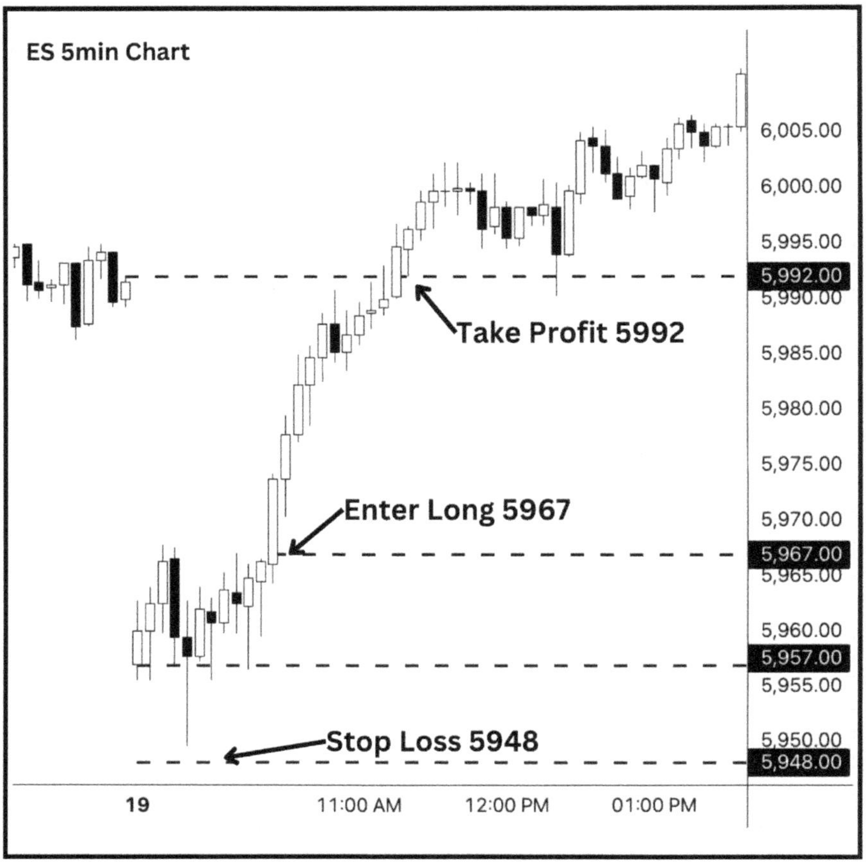

Setting Targets and Stop-Losses:

Target Level: The target is typically set at the previous session's close, as this is the level where the gap is expected to be filled.

Stop-Loss Order: A stop-loss order is placed to limit potential losses if the gap fails to fill and the price moves against the trader's position. The placement of the stop-loss should be strategic, often just beyond recent support or resistance levels to avoid being prematurely triggered by normal price fluctuations.

Managing Risk in Gap Fill Trading

Risk management is an indispensable component of gap fill trading, ensuring that traders can protect their capital and sustain their trading activities over the long term. Given the inherent uncertainties in the market, robust risk management practices are crucial for mitigating potential losses and maintaining a disciplined trading approach.

Key Risks in Gap Fill Trading

Non-Fill Risk: The primary risk is that the gap may not fill as anticipated, especially in cases of breakaway or runaway gaps that signal strong trends. When a gap fails to fill, the trader may incur losses if the price continues in the direction of the gap.

Mitigation: Implementing stop-loss orders is crucial to limit potential losses. By setting a stop-loss just beyond a key support or resistance level, traders can exit trades before significant adverse movements occur.

Example: In a scenario where the S&P futures gap down from 4530 to 4520, and the trader anticipates a gap fill, they place a short position at 4520 with a stop-loss at 4518. If the gap fails to fill and the price moves lower, the stop-loss ensures that losses are contained within predefined limits.

False Signals:

The market may initially appear to retrace the gap before reversing direction, leading to false signals that can result in premature or incorrect trades.

Mitigation: To reduce the likelihood of acting on false signals, traders should wait for clear confirmations, such as reliable candlestick reversal patterns or a break of key support/resistance levels. Utilizing multiple confirmation signals can enhance the reliability of trade entries.

Example: After a gap up, a trader observes a bearish engulfing candlestick pattern forming at the resistance level near the gap fill target. Before entering a short position, the trader ensures that the RSI is overbought, providing dual confirmation that the gap fill is likely, thereby reducing the risk of acting on a false signal.

Overtrading:

Entering too many trades, particularly on small or insignificant gaps, can erode profits and increase transaction costs, undermining the overall effectiveness of the strategy.

Mitigation: Establishing strict criteria for trade entries, such as a minimum gap size (e.g., 5 points), helps prevent overtrading. Additionally, setting protective stops just below the day's low for long trades or above the day's high for short trades ensures that losses remain manageable.

Example: A trader sets a rule to only trade gaps of 5 points or more in the S&P futures. By adhering to this criterion, the trader avoids overtrading on minor gaps that may not provide meaningful trading opportunities, thereby conserving capital and reducing transaction costs.

Advanced Risk Management Techniques

Beyond the basic strategies, traders can employ advanced techniques to further enhance risk management in gap-filling trading.

a. Position Sizing: Determining the appropriate size of each trade based on account size and risk tolerance is vital. By risking only a small percentage of the trading capital on each trade, traders can withstand a series of losses without significant detriment to their overall portfolio.

b. Diversification: Spreading trades across different market instruments or timeframes reduces exposure to any single position, thereby mitigating overall risk. By not relying solely on S&P futures, traders can spread their risk and protect their portfolio from sector-specific or instrument-specific downturns. **c.**

c. Hedging Strategies: Hedging involves taking offsetting positions to protect against potential losses. For instance, if a trader is long on a gap fill trade, they might hedge by taking a short position in a correlated asset to mitigate downside risk.

Example: A trader employs dynamic position sizing by calculating the Average True Range (ATR) to gauge market volatility. In periods of high volatility, the trader reduces position sizes to account for larger price swings, while increasing positions in low-volatility environments to optimize returns without disproportionate risk exposure.

Psychological Resilience and Discipline

Effective risk management transcends technical measures; it also involves managing the psychological aspects of trading. Emotional discipline, such as maintaining patience, avoiding impulsive decisions, and adhering to predefined trading plans, is crucial for successful gap fill trading. Traders must cultivate the ability to accept losses as part of the trading process and resist the temptation to deviate from their strategies based on short-term market fluctuations.

Maintaining Emotional Control: Traders must cultivate the ability to remain calm and composed, even in the face of losses or unexpected market movements. Emotional decision-making can lead to impulsive trades that deviate from the trading plan, increasing risk exposure.

Building Confidence Through Preparation: Confidence in trading decisions stems from thorough preparation and adherence to a well-defined strategy. By trusting their analysis and maintaining a disciplined approach, traders can reduce the influence of emotions on their trading performance.

Example: After experiencing a series of false signals, a trader reinforces their risk management practices by strictly adhering to their confirmation criteria and position sizing rules. This disciplined approach helps mitigate the emotional impact of losses and enhances the importance of strategic consistency.

Enhancing the Gap Fill Strategy with Indicators

Integrating technical indicators into the gap fill trading strategy can significantly enhance decision-making, providing additional layers of confirmation and increasing the likelihood of successful trades. This section explores various technical indicators that complement gap fill strategies, detailing their applications and benefits.

Volume Analysis

Importance of Volume in Gap Fill Trading: Volume is a critical indicator of market participation and conviction behind price movements. Analyzing volume alongside gap formation provides insights into the strength and sustainability of the gap, influencing the likelihood of a gap fill.

Application:

High Opening Volume without Follow-Through: When a gap forms with high initial volume but subsequent candles show declining volume, it suggests that the initial enthusiasm driving the gap may be waning, increasing the probability of a retracement to fill the gap.

Low Volume Gaps: Gaps formed on low volume typically indicate weak market conviction, making them more susceptible to being filled quickly as the lack of strong buying or selling pressure allows prices to retrace.

Example: Suppose the S&P futures gap up from 4520 to 4530 with substantial opening volume. However, in the following minutes, the volume declines significantly as buyers lose momentum. This scenario suggests that the gap up may not be sustainable, and a retracement to fill the gap is likely, presenting a potential trading opportunity.

Moving Averages

Role of Moving Averages: Moving averages smooth out price data to identify trends and provide dynamic support and resistance levels. They are essential tools for determining the direction and strength of trends, which are crucial considerations in gap fill trading.

Types of Moving Averages:

Exponential Moving Average (EMA): Places greater weight on recent price data, making it more responsive to new information.
Simple Moving Average (SMA): Calculates the average price over a specified period, providing a smoother and less volatile indicator.
Application:
Support and Resistance: Moving averages can act as support in uptrends and resistance in downtrends. A gap struggling near a moving average may indicate a potential reversal and a likelihood of a gap fill.
Trend Confirmation: The position of the price relative to moving averages can confirm the direction of the trend. For instance, prices above a moving average suggest an uptrend, while prices below indicate a downtrend.

Example: If the S&P futures gap up to 4525 and encounter resistance near the 20-period EMA at 4525, traders may interpret this as a sign that the gap may not sustain, increasing the likelihood of a gap fill to 4515. Conversely, if the price maintains its position above the moving average, it may indicate that the gap will persist.

Relative Strength Index (RSI)

Understanding RSI: The Relative Strength Index (RSI) is a momentum oscillator that measures the speed and change of price movements. It oscillates between 0 and 100, indicating overbought or oversold conditions.

Function of RSI in Gap Fill Trading:

Overbought Conditions (RSI > 70): Suggests that the asset may be overvalued and due for a correction, increasing the likelihood of a bearish gap fill.
Oversold Conditions (RSI < 30): Indicate that the asset may be undervalued and poised for a rebound, suggesting a potential bullish gap fill. **Application:**
Confirming Gap Fill Opportunities: An RSI reading above 70 during a gap up signals that the asset may be overextended, making a gap fill more probable.

Conversely, an RSI below 30 during a gap down suggests that the asset may be oversold, increasing the chances of a gap fill.
Example: In the case of a gap down from 4520 to 4510, if the RSI drops below 30, it indicates that the S&P futures may be oversold. This scenario could prompt traders to anticipate a bullish retracement, targeting a retracement to 4520.

Pivot Points and Candlestick Patterns

Pivot Points: Pivot points are technical indicators used to determine potential support and resistance levels. They are calculated based on the previous period's high, low, and close prices, providing traders with reference points for price retracements.

Candlestick Patterns: Candlestick patterns are visual representations of price movements and are used to identify potential reversals or continuations. Common reversal patterns include shooting stars, hammers, and dojis.

Application:

Support and Resistance Alignment: Pivot points can align with gap fill targets, providing additional confirmation for trade entries and exits.
Visual Reversal Cues: Candlestick patterns near pivot points or moving averages can offer strong signals for entering or exiting trades, enhancing the precision of gap fill strategies.
Example: If the S&P futures gap up and approach a pivot point that coincides with the previous close, and a shooting star candlestick pattern forms at this level, it can serve as a strong signal for a bearish gap fill, prompting traders to enter short positions with targets at the pivot level.

Integrating Multiple Indicators

Synergizing Multiple Indicators: Using a combination of indicators enhances the reliability of trading signals by providing multiple layers of confirmation. This approach reduces the likelihood of false signals and increases the probability of successful trades.

Example: A trader identifies a gap down from 4520 to 4510. They observe a bullish hammer candlestick pattern near the previous close at 4508, with the RSI below 30 indicating oversold conditions, and the price approaching a pivot point at 4520. The convergence of these indicators provides robust confirmation for a bullish gap fill, prompting the trader to enter a long position with a well-defined target and stop-loss.

Limitations and Considerations: While technical indicators enhance gap fill trading strategies, they are not foolproof and should be used in conjunction with other forms of analysis. Traders should be wary of relying solely on indicators without considering broader market context and fundamental factors that may influence price movements.

A Comprehensive Gap Fill Playbook

Implementing a successful gap-fill trading strategy requires a disciplined and structured approach. This comprehensive playbook outlines a step-by-step guide to executing gap fill trades effectively, ensuring that traders can systematically identify, assess, and capitalize on gap fill opportunities while managing risks appropriately.

Step-by-Step Playbook

Step 1: Pre-Market Preparation

- **Review Overnight News:** Assess any significant news or events that occurred outside of regular trading hours, as these can influence gap formations.
- **Analyze Economic Indicators:** Check for scheduled economic releases or data announcements that could impact market sentiment and lead to gap formation.
- **Set Alerts:** Use trading platforms to set alerts for significant price movements or gaps at the market open.

Step 2: Identifying the Gap

- **Monitor Short-Term Charts:** At market open, observe 5-minute or 15-minute charts to detect any significant price gaps.
- **Determine Gap Size:** Assess whether the gap meets the predefined criteria for significance (e.g., 5 points or more).
- **Classify the Gap:** Identify the type of gap (everyday, breakaway, runaway, exhaustion) based on its characteristics and market context.

Step 3: Assessing the Gap Fill Likelihood

- **Analyze Volume:** Evaluate the volume accompanying the gap. High volume suggests firm conviction, while low volume indicates potential retracement.
- **Evaluate Market Context:** Consider the prevailing market trends and how the gap aligns with them.
- **Check Technical Indicators:** Utilize moving averages, RSI, pivot points, and candlestick patterns to assess the probability of a gap fill.

Step 4: Waiting for Confirmation

- **Look for Reversal Signals:** Wait for candlestick patterns or other technical signals that indicate a potential retracement.
- **Confirm with Indicators:** Ensure that multiple indicators align with gap fill expectations to enhance trade reliability.

Step 5: Executing the Trade

- **Enter the Position:** Based on confirmed signals, enter a long or short position at the gap open price.
- **Set Target and Stop-Loss:** Define the target at the previous session's close and establish a stop-loss order to manage risk.

Step 6: Managing the Trade

- **Monitor Price Movements:** Keep a close watch on price action to ensure the trade is progressing as anticipated.
- **Adjust Stops as Needed:** If the trade moves in favor, consider moving the stop-loss to lock in profits or reduce exposure.
- **Take Profits:** Exit the trade upon reaching the target or if reversal indicators suggest a change in trend.

Step 7: Post-Trade Analysis

- **Review Trade Performance:** Analyze the outcome of the trade, assessing whether it met the expected criteria and results.
- **Document Insights:** Record key observations, including what worked well and areas needing improvement.
- **Refine Strategy: Utilize insights from the trade analysis to refine** and enhance the trading strategy for future trades.
- **Example Playbook Execution: Scenario:** The S&P futures close at 4520 on a Monday. Overnight news indicates a minor positive economic development, leading to a gap up to 4530 on Tuesday morning.

Action Steps:

1 . **Identify the Gap:** Detect a 10-point gap up to 4530 on the 5-minute chart.

2 . **Assess the Gap Fill Likelihood:** Volume is high at the open but declines in subsequent candles. The gap up aligns with a medium-term uptrend but lacks strong continuation signals. RSI approaches overbought territory at 72.

3 . **Wait for Confirmation:** Observe a bearish engulfing candlestick forming at 4530, indicating potential downward momentum.

4 **Execute the Trade:** Enter a short position at 4530. Set a target at 4520 (previous close) and place a stop-loss order at 4535 to manage risk.

5 **Manage the Trade:** Monitor the trade as the price begins to retrace toward 4520. If the price reaches 4520, take profits by closing the position. If the price moves to 4535, the stop-loss is triggered, limiting the loss.

6 **Post-Trade Analysis:** The trade successfully filled the gap, resulting in a 10-point profit. Document the effective use of confirmation signals and volume analysis in predicting the gap fill.

7 . **Ensuring Consistency and Discipline:** Adhering to this playbook requires unwavering discipline and consistency. By following a structured approach, traders can mitigate the influence of emotions, maintain focus on strategic objectives, and enhance the overall effectiveness of their gap fill trading strategy.

Risk Management in Gap Fill Trading

Risk management is the bedrock of successful trading, ensuring that traders can sustain their activities over the long term by protecting their capital from significant losses. In the context of gap fill trading, where price movements can be swift and unpredictable, robust risk management practices are paramount. This section examines the key aspects of risk management relevant to gap fill trading, providing strategies and techniques to effectively mitigate potential risks.

Understanding and Mitigating the Risk of Non-Fill

Nature of Non-Fill Risk: The primary risk in gap fill trading is that the gap may not fill as anticipated, especially in cases of breakaway or runaway gaps that signal strong trends. When a gap fails to fill, the trader may incur losses if the price continues in the direction of the gap.

Mitigation Strategies:

Stop-Loss Orders: Implementing stop-loss orders is crucial to limit potential losses. By setting a stop-loss just beyond a key support or resistance level, traders can exit trades before significant adverse movements occur.

Position Sizing: Carefully determining the size of each trade based on account size and risk tolerance ensures that a single loss does not disproportionately impact the trading capital.

Example: In a scenario where the S&P futures gap down from 4530 to 4520, and the trader anticipates a gap fill, they place a short position at 4520 with a stop-loss at 4518. If the gap fails to fill and the price moves lower, the stop-loss ensures that losses are contained within predefined limits.

Managing False Signals

Nature of False Signals: False signals occur when the market initially appears to retrace the gap but subsequently reverses direction, leading to premature or incorrect trade entries. These signals can result in losses if the trader acts on them without sufficient confirmation.

Mitigation Strategies:

Waiting for Clear Confirmations: Traders should refrain from entering trades based solely on the presence of a gap. Instead, they should wait for additional confirmation signals, such as candlestick reversal patterns or breaks of key support/resistance levels, before executing trades.

Using Multiple Indicators: Combining multiple technical indicators increases the reliability of trade signals. For instance, a bullish hammer candlestick pattern coupled with an oversold RSI reading provides stronger confirmation than either signal alone.

Example: After a gap up, a trader observes a bearish engulfing candlestick pattern forming at the resistance level near the gap fill target. Before entering a short position, the trader ensures that the RSI is overbought, providing dual confirmation that the gap fill is likely, thereby reducing the risk of acting on a false signal.

Preventing Overtrading

Nature of Overtrading: Overtrading involves entering too many trades, often based on minor or insignificant gaps, leading to increased transaction costs and potential losses. It can erode profits and undermine the effectiveness of the gap fill strategy.

Mitigation Strategies:

Establishing Trade Criteria: Setting strict criteria for trade entries, such as a minimum gap size of 5 points, helps prevent overtrading. This ensures that only significant gaps with higher probabilities of filling are considered for trading.

Adhering to Trading Plans: Developing and following a comprehensive trading plan helps maintain discipline and prevents impulsive trading decisions based on emotions or short-term market fluctuations.

Example: A trader sets a rule to only trade gaps of 5 points or more in the S&P futures. By adhering to this criterion, the trader avoids overtrading on minor gaps that may not provide meaningful trading opportunities, thereby conserving capital and reducing transaction costs.

Psychological Resilience and Discipline

Effective risk management transcends technical measures; it also involves managing the psychological aspects of trading. Emotional discipline, such as maintaining patience, avoiding impulsive decisions, and adhering to predefined trading plans, is crucial for successful gap fill trading. Traders must cultivate the ability to accept losses as part of the trading process and resist the temptation to deviate from their strategies based on short-term market fluctuations.

Maintaining Emotional Control: Traders must cultivate the ability to remain calm and composed, even in the face of losses or unexpected market movements. Emotional decision-making can lead to impulsive trades that deviate from the trading plan, increasing risk exposure.

Building Confidence Through Preparation: Confidence in trading decisions stems from thorough preparation and adherence to a well-defined strategy. By trusting their analysis and maintaining a disciplined approach, traders can reduce the influence of emotions on their trading performance.

Example: After experiencing a series of false signals, a trader reinforces their risk management practices by strictly adhering to their confirmation criteria and position sizing rules. This disciplined approach helps mitigate the emotional impact of losses and enhances the importance of strategic consistency.

Conclusion

Gap fill trading represents a sophisticated and strategic approach within the realm of S&P futures trading, leveraging the market's inherent tendencies to retrace significant price gaps. By understanding the various types of gaps, identifying and assessing their likelihood to fill, and executing trades with precision and discipline, traders can capitalize on these predictable market movements to achieve consistent profitability. The integration of technical indicators such as volume analysis, moving averages, RSI, pivot points, and candlestick patterns enhances the gap fill strategy, providing additional layers of confirmation and increasing the probability of successful trades. Moreover, robust risk management practices, including the use of stop-loss orders, position sizing, and the prevention of overtrading, are indispensable for protecting capital and ensuring long-term trading sustainability. A comprehensive gap fill playbook serves as a practical guide, outlining a systematic approach to identifying, assessing, and executing gap fill trades. This structured methodology enables traders to navigate the market's complexities with confidence and precision, adapting to varying market conditions and thereby enhancing their trading performance.

Key Takeaways:

1. **Discipline and Patience:** Essential for waiting for proper confirmations before entering trades, avoiding impulsive decisions based on preliminary observations.
2. **Thorough Understanding:** Grasping the different types of gaps and their implications is crucial for accurately assessing trade opportunities and risks.
3. **Risk Management:** Protecting capital through stop-loss orders, position sizing, and avoiding overtrading is fundamental to sustaining trading activities and minimizing potential losses.
4. **Technical Integration:** Enhancing gap fill strategies with volume analysis, moving averages, RSI, pivot points, and candlestick patterns provides a more robust framework for making informed trading decisions.
5. **Continuous Learning and Adaptation:** Regularly reviewing and refining the trading strategy based on performance analysis and market developments ensures that the strategy remains effective and aligned with evolving market dynamics. By mastering the nuances of gap fill trading, traders can gain a significant edge in the dynamic and competitive landscape of S&P futures trading. Whether navigating modest 5-point gaps in low-volatility environments or managing substantial 20-point gaps driven by significant news events, a structured and disciplined approach ensures sustained profitability and fosters a deeper understanding of market mechanics.

Final Thoughts: Gap fill trading is not a one-size-fits-all strategy; it requires customization and adaptation to individual trading styles, risk appetites, and market perspectives. Success in gap fill trading hinges on the ability to combine technical analysis with disciplined execution, continuously refining strategies based on empirical observations and performance metrics. As traders immerse themselves in the art of gap fill trading, they develop a more nuanced appreciation of market dynamics, ultimately contributing to their long-term success and resilience in the ever-evolving financial markets. *Note:* This comprehensive exploration of gap fill trading serves as an extensive guide for traders seeking to implement this strategy within the S&P futures market. By delving into detailed explanations, practical examples, and strategic methodologies, this guide equips traders with the knowledge and tools necessary to navigate the complexities of gap fill trading effectively.

CHAPTER THIRTEEN

Swing Trading

Swing trading in the S&P 500 futures market is an art that blends technical analysis, risk management, and market psychology to capture medium-term price moves. Unlike day trading, which focuses on intraday price action, swing trading looks to profit from trends that unfold over several days or weeks. In this chapter, we will delve into three critical components of a successful swing trading strategy: identifying swing trades, setting stop-loss and take-profit orders, and position sizing for swing trades. Each section will provide actionable insights and examples to help you become a more disciplined and profitable swing trader.

Understanding Swing Trading in Futures

Swing trading involves capturing price swings—the natural ebbs and flows of the market—to profit from both trending and range-bound markets. In the context of S&P 500 futures, traders seek opportunities to capitalize on price movements that emerge as the index responds to economic data, earnings reports, or shifts in monetary policy. The key to successful swing trading lies in identifying setups that offer a favorable risk-reward ratio while aligning with the prevailing market trend.

Swing trading differs significantly from other trading styles, such as scalping or long-term investing. Scalpers focus on quick profits by executing multiple trades in a single session, while investors hold positions for months or years. Swing traders sit between these extremes, aiming to capitalize on medium-term price moves. For example, a swing trader might have an S&P 500 futures contract for several days, benefiting from a trend triggered by Federal Reserve announcements or quarterly earnings reports. This balance of frequency and duration allows traders to participate in the market without being glued to their screens or committing to long-term risks.

Using Technical Analysis to Spot Opportunities

Technical analysis is the cornerstone of swing trading. Here are some key tools and techniques to identify swing trade setups in the S&P 500 futures:

Trendlines and Channels: Draw trendlines to identify the general direction of the market. Channels can highlight potential entry points when price approaches support or resistance within the channel.

Moving Averages: Use a combination of short-term (e.g., 20-period) and long-term (e.g., 50-period) moving averages to confirm the trend. For example, when the 20-period moving average crosses above the 50-period moving average, it may signal a bullish trend.

Fibonacci Retracements: Identify retracement levels (e.g., 38.2%, 50%, 61.8%) within a larger trend to pinpoint areas where price might reverse or consolidate.

Candlestick Patterns: Look for reversal patterns like hammers, shooting stars, or engulfing patterns near key support or resistance levels.

Oscillators and Momentum Indicators: Tools like the Relative Strength Index (RSI) or MACD can provide additional confirmation. For instance, an RSI reading below 30 indicates oversold conditions, which may signal a potential bullish reversal.

Fundamental Drivers for Swing Trades

In addition to technical analysis, understanding the fundamental factors driving the S&P 500 futures is crucial. Keep an eye on:

- **Economic Indicators**: Pay attention to employment data, inflation reports, and GDP growth. These can provide clues about market sentiment.
- **Federal Reserve Policy**: Changes in interest rates or quantitative easing can significantly impact the index's direction.
- **Earnings Reports**: Monitor the earnings season, as strong or weak corporate performance can shift the market's trajectory.

- **Global Events**: Geopolitical developments, such as trade agreements or conflicts, can introduce volatility, creating opportunities for swing traders.

Practical Example

Imagine the S&P 500 futures are trending upward, with price consistently bouncing off the 20-period moving average. A strong jobs report causes a minor retracement, and the price pulls back to the 50% Fibonacci level, forming a bullish engulfing candle. This setup signals a potential swing trade opportunity to enter long with a target near the recent high. By combining technical and fundamental analysis, traders can confidently identify trades that align with prevailing market conditions.

Setting Stop-Loss and Take-Profit Orders

The Importance of Risk Management: Properly setting stop-loss and take-profit orders is essential for preserving capital and ensuring consistent profitability. Without these protective measures, emotions like fear and greed can derail even the most well-planned trades. Swing trading inherently involves holding positions overnight or across multiple sessions, which exposes traders to additional risks, such as gaps caused by after-hours news or economic data. Having well-placed stop-loss and take-profit orders ensures you are protected against unexpected market movements while maintaining the discipline to lock in profits when your targets are met.

Setting a Stop-Loss: A stop-loss order is designed to limit losses by automatically closing your position when the price reaches a predetermined level. Here's how to determine the optimal stop-loss placement:

Technical Levels: Place the stop-loss just beyond a support or resistance level. For example, if you're long, set the stop-loss slightly below the nearest swing low.

ATR (Average True Range): Use the ATR to account for market volatility. Multiply the ATR by a factor (e.g., 1.5x) and set your stop-loss accordingly.

Fixed Dollar Amount: Determine how much you're willing to lose on the trade and calculate the stop-loss distance based on your position size.

Using a combination of these methods can provide a balanced approach. For example, placing a stop-loss below a significant swing low while factoring in the ATR ensures that your trade is protected from minor market noise but still allows for natural fluctuations.

Setting a Take-Profit Order: Take-profit orders lock in gains by closing the position when the price reaches your target. Here's how to put them:

Risk-Reward Ratio: Aim for a risk-reward ratio of at least 1:2. For example, if your stop-loss is 10 points, set your take-profit target 20 points away.

Technical Levels: Identify key resistance levels or Fibonacci extensions as potential profit-taking zones.

Scaling Out: Consider taking partial profits at intermediate targets to reduce risk while keeping some exposure to potential gains.

Take-profit orders should be placed thoughtfully. For instance, if the market approaches a critical resistance level near your profit target, it might be wise to take partial profits and let the remaining position run with a trailing stop to maximize gains.

Practical Example: Suppose you entered a long trade at 4100, with your stop-loss set at 4090 (10 points risk) and your take-profit at 4120 (20 points reward). This 1:2 risk-reward setup ensures that even if you lose half your trades, you'll remain profitable over time. By adjusting your take-profit strategy to include partial exits, you can further optimize your overall returns.

Position Sizing for Swing Trades: Position sizing determines how much of your account you allocate to each trade. It's a critical component of risk management, ensuring that a single loss doesn't wipe out a significant portion of your capital. Position sizing also affects your psychological comfort. Trading too large can lead to fear-driven decisions, while trading too small might result in missed opportunities. Striking the right balance ensures you remain disciplined and consistent.

Calculating Position Size: Decide what percentage of your account you're willing to risk on a single trade (e.g., 1%). Calculate the risk per contract by subtracting the entry price from the stop-loss level and multiplying by the contract size. For the S&P 500 futures, each point typically represents $50. Divide your account risk by the dollar risk per contract to determine how many contracts to trade. Position sizing calculators, available in many trading platforms, can simplify this process. Using these tools ensures that you adhere to your risk management plan without manually recalculating for every trade.

Adjusting for Volatility: In volatile markets, reduce your position size to account for larger stop-loss distances. Conversely, in quieter markets, you can afford slightly larger positions while staying within your risk tolerance.

Practical Example

Imagine you have a $50,000 account and are willing to risk 1% per trade ($500). If your stop-loss distance is 10 points, your risk per contract is $500 (10 points x $50/point). In this case, you'd trade just one contract to stay within your risk parameters. If the market becomes volatile and the ATR suggests a stop-loss distance of 20 points, you might reduce your position size to half a contract or consider sitting out the trade.

Scaling In and Out: Advanced traders often scale into or out of positions. For example, you might enter half your position size at the initial setup and add the rest as the trade moves in your favor. Similarly, you can scale out by taking partial profits at intermediate levels. Scaling techniques not only enhance flexibility but also reduce the psychological pressure of managing prominent positions. By scaling out, you lock in gains while allowing a portion of the trade to benefit from extended moves.

Conclusion

Swing trading the S&P 500 futures requires a blend of technical expertise, disciplined risk management, and adaptability. By mastering the art of identifying high-probability setups, setting precise stop-loss and take-profit orders, and sizing your positions appropriately, you can navigate the futures market with confidence. Remember, success in swing trading isn't about winning every trade—it's about managing your risk and consistently executing a well-defined strategy. With these principles in mind, you'll be well on your way to becoming a profitable swing trader in the dynamic world of S&P 500 futures.

Swing trade example:

On certain days, the market opens, briefly tests the low of the day in the first 60 minutes, and then continues to rise steadily throughout the day until close. The following characteristics can be recognized these days:

Price action remains consistently above the 20 EMA line, indicating strong upward momentum with minimal price corrections. Moreover, there are no substantial pullbacks to challenge this trend, and the market continues trading well above the VWAP. Even though the Point of Control (POC) appears on the chart, it exerts minimal downward pressure, allowing the upward trajectory to persist. When minor pullback candles do form, they tend to be short-lived—often limited to one or two bars—before bullish price action resumes, reversing the temporary sell-off and maintaining the overall bullish bias.

Look at the chart above, ideally we take a trade and go long as soon as we see a bullish hammer followed by a bullish candle, as the price action elevates above the 20 EMA line, we stay long until the price reaches significant upward levels and starts to touch the EMA line again and goes sideways.

In this example, the risk-reward ratio is calculated by subtracting the entry price from the target price (6160.25 – 6144.25) and then dividing that result by the difference between the entry price and the stop-loss price (6144.75 – 6137.25). The outcome is 2.13, which means that for every $1 of risk, the potential reward is approximately $2.13. This calculation is fundamental in determining whether a trade's prospective profit justifies the inherent risk.

By way of illustration, if a trader realizes $2.13 in profit on one trade and loses $1 on another, the net gain remains $1.13. Traders—especially those new to swing trading—need to incorporate regular risk-reward assessments into their routine until it becomes second nature. As a general rule, avoid trades that present a risk-reward ratio lower than 2. Once your success rate becomes more consistent, you may consider adjusting this ratio slightly, but you should do so only after building a substantial foundation of experience. Above all, have a solid plan in place and adhere to it diligently.

When it comes to best practices in swing trading futures, it is crucial to establish a clear and consistent trading plan. This plan should outline criteria for both entries and exits, as well as define precise risk parameters through the use of stop-loss orders. Additionally, conducting thorough technical and fundamental analyses can help you anticipate shifts in market sentiment and identify optimal swing-trade opportunities. It's also wise to maintain discipline by avoiding impulse trades and chasing rapidly moving prices—both of which can undermine your long-term profitability. Keeping track of key economic releases and staying informed about relevant market news can further enhance your readiness for sudden price volatility. By balancing a well-researched strategy, disciplined execution, and prudent risk management, you can improve your chances of success in swing trading futures over the long haul.

CHAPTER FOURTEEN

Risk Management

"Trading without a stop-loss is like driving without brakes—sooner or later, the road will remind you why they're essential."

Risk management is the cornerstone of successful trading in S&P futures, or in any other financial instrument. While many new traders focus on identifying profitable entries and exits, veteran traders understand that longevity in the market is not achieved through predictions alone but through effectively managing downside exposure. The S&P futures market—a highly liquid, leveraged, and widely followed derivative—provides numerous opportunities for gain, but also carries inherent risks that need careful navigation. With leverage, small market moves can translate into disproportionately large gains or losses, making strict controls over risk not only prudent but essential.

The fundamental logic behind risk management is to preserve capital over the long term. Without a robust risk management framework, even the most accurate trading strategy can fail, as one significant adverse move can wipe out weeks, months, or even years of accumulated profit. In the context of S&P futures, where overnight gaps, geopolitical events, unexpected Federal Reserve decisions, and extreme volatility can all send prices swinging, the necessity of having a well-defined approach to controlling losses cannot be overstated. In this chapter, we will explore some of the core components of a solid risk management plan. We will begin by examining the importance of risk management itself, delve into position sizing methodologies, and then look closely at how to employ stop-loss and take-profit orders effectively. Understanding and applying these concepts will help traders maintain consistent performance and mitigate the harmful effects of adverse price movements.

The Importance of Risk Management

The allure of trading S&P futures often revolves around the potential for significant returns. These contracts are highly leveraged; a slight fluctuation in the underlying index can yield substantial profit for the savvy trader. However, leverage is a double-edged sword. Just as it magnifies gains, it can also magnify losses. Without a rigorous framework for mitigating downside risk, traders may find themselves exposing too much capital to market swings, jeopardizing their entire trading account.

Effective risk management begins with a mental shift. Rather than viewing every trade as an opportunity for profit, seasoned traders see it as a potential risk to be managed. They understand that the market is dynamic and unpredictable, and that even the best analysis may yield trades that go wrong. By embracing the possibility of loss and planning for it, traders insulate themselves from the catastrophic impact of unexpected market events. Every trade should have a predetermined exit strategy—both in terms of profit and loss—long before the trader clicks the "buy" or "sell" button.

The importance of risk management in S&P futures is not just theoretical. Historical market shocks—such as the 2008 financial crisis, the COVID-19 pandemic sell-off in March 2020, or sudden flash crashes—serve as powerful reminders that markets can turn violent rapidly. Traders who diligently manage their risk may suffer manageable drawdowns during these turbulent periods but live to trade another day. Those who neglect risk controls often find themselves at the mercy of a few bad trades that erase all prior gains. Ensuring that each position is in line with one's overall risk tolerance, capital, and objectives is a prerequisite for building a sustainable trading career. In short, successful risk management practices allow traders to remain disciplined, consistent, and robust enough to handle whatever challenges the S&P futures market may throw at them.

Position Sizing

Position sizing is one of the most critical yet frequently overlooked aspects of trading S&P futures. Determining how many contracts to trade is not merely a function of capital available—it is a strategic decision that directly impacts a trader's ability to withstand volatile market conditions. Proper position sizing ensures that even if a trade moves against you, the potential loss is only a small, manageable percentage of your total account. This careful calibration prevents excessive drawdowns and maintains a trader's psychological equilibrium.

The general rule of thumb is never to risk more than a small percentage of your total trading capital on any single trade. While the exact number varies depending on risk tolerance and strategy design, many professional traders adhere to risking no more than 1% or 2% of their account equity per trade. For example, if you have a $100,000 trading account and want to limit risk to 1% per trade, the maximum loss you can accept on a single S&P futures position would be $1,000. Given that each S&P E-mini contract has a set dollar value per tick, you can back-calculate how many contracts to trade and where to place your stop-loss.

Position sizing is not static; it may evolve as the account grows, as volatility changes, or as your confidence in a particular strategy increases. During periods of heightened volatility, when the S&P futures contract might be experiencing large intraday swings, wise traders reduce their position size. By doing so, they ensure that a wider stop-loss, which may be necessary to avoid getting whipsawed by volatile price action, does not expose their capital to unacceptable risk. Similarly, suppose a trader's confidence in a certain setup or market condition is high. In that case, they might choose to take a slight risk while still staying within their overall risk parameters.

In practice, position sizing entails continuous evaluation. It requires keeping a close eye on account equity, volatility measures, and the current financial environment. By adhering to disciplined position sizing principles, traders are less likely to panic during drawdowns and can maintain a consistent risk profile across varying market conditions. This not only supports longevity in the market but also helps build confidence, knowing that no single trade can be ruinous.

Stop-Loss Orders

Stop-loss orders are the trader's primary defensive tools. A stop-loss order is a pre-determined price level at which a position will be automatically closed if the market moves against it. In S&P futures trading, setting a proper stop-loss is essential because these contracts often move quickly, and a trader might not have time to close a losing position manually if the market turns sharply. By placing a stop-loss order, you effectively program your exit plan into the system, ensuring that your losses remain within your predefined tolerance levels.

Determining where to place a stop-loss is part science and part art. From a technical perspective, traders often identify critical support and resistance levels or significant technical markers, such as recent swing highs or lows, moving averages, or Fibonacci retracement levels. Placing the stop just beyond these levels can make sense—if the market invalidates your trade thesis by pushing past your "line in the sand," the best decision is to exit rather than to hope the market will turn back in your favor. From a risk management perspective, the distance between your entry price and stop-loss price determines the monetary risk on the trade. This risk, combined with your chosen position size, ensures your loss remains within your acceptable parameters.

However, stop-loss placement is not a one-size-fits-all approach. Market volatility, current liquidity conditions, and individual trader risk tolerance all influence the best stop location. During periods of elevated volatility, tighter stops might lead to premature exits, while stops placed too far away might risk more capital than intended. As conditions evolve, traders may need to adjust their approach, experimenting with different methodologies until they find a sweet spot that aligns with their overall trading style and objectives.

Another key consideration is that once a stop-loss is set, it should not be moved further away to accommodate a losing trade. This is a common mistake that often leads to escalating losses. Instead, if the market is nearing your stop, it may be beneficial to re-evaluate your strategy. If the original trade thesis no longer holds, allow the stop to be triggered. Consistency in executing your stop-loss rules is critical in risk management. Over time, adhering to your predefined stop levels will reinforce discipline and reduce the emotional strain associated with active trading, thus providing a stable foundation for long-term success in the S&P futures market.

Take-Profit Orders

While stop-loss orders focus on minimizing downside risk, take-profit orders aim to secure profits at predefined levels. A take-profit order instructs your broker's system to automatically close a winning position once a certain price is reached. By employing take-profit orders, traders ensure they convert unrealized gains into realized profits before the market reverses. In the S&P futures arena, where intraday and overnight reversals are not uncommon, locking in profits at predetermined levels can prevent the disappointment of turning a winning trade into a break-even or losing one.

Setting take-profit levels involves striking a balance between ambition and prudence. On one hand, traders might be tempted to hold out for a larger gain, believing the market could run further in their favor. On the other hand, excessive greed can lead to holding positions for too long, thereby giving back profits as prices fluctuate. Seasoned traders often look to the same technical markers that guide their stop-loss decisions—support and resistance levels, key pivot points, or indicators like average true range—to identify logical profit targets. By using a systematic approach, traders remove emotion from the equation, focusing on the probabilities and patterns that historically have yielded favorable outcomes.

When determining take-profit placements, it helps to consider the overall risk-reward ratio of the trade. A sound guideline is that the potential profit should be equal to, if not greater than, the potential loss. For example, if your stop-loss is set to risk $1,000 on a trade, aiming for at least a $1,000 profit target ensures that you do not need a high win rate to remain profitable over time. Many successful traders strive for trades where the reward is at least two to three times the risk. This ratio can improve the overall profitability of a trading system, even if not all trades hit their full target.

In dynamic markets like the S&P futures, partial profit-taking strategies can also be beneficial. A trader might take off half the position at the first profit target, then move the stop-loss to breakeven for the remaining contracts. This approach secures a guaranteed profit while still leaving open the possibility of capturing larger gains if the trend persists. It also reduces the psychological pressure of "all-or-nothing" decision-making. Such flexible strategies underscore the importance of adopting a transparent, rules-based approach to taking profits, which, when combined with well-placed stop-loss orders and proper position sizing, creates a resilient framework for long-term capital growth.

Integrating Risk Management into a Trading Plan

Merely knowing the individual components—such as position sizing, stop-loss placement, and take-profit targets—is not enough. Effective risk management comes from seamlessly integrating these elements into a cohesive trading plan. This plan should clearly define your objectives, market conditions for trading, risk tolerance, and criteria for both entry and exit. When these rules are written down and followed consistently, they help eliminate emotional decision-making. Instead of reacting to every market fluctuation, you become a strategist, executing a well-thought-out blueprint.

A comprehensive trading plan includes guidelines on how to adapt to changing market conditions. For instance, if the VIX (Volatility Index) is signaling turbulent times, the plan might dictate reducing your average position size and widening your stops. Conversely, in calmer markets, you might increase your contract size slightly, assuming the reduced volatility decreases the likelihood of abrupt price swings. Similarly, the plan might dictate that if your equity drops by a certain percentage from a recent high watermark, you take a step back and re-evaluate your methods, temporarily suspending trading to prevent further damage.

The key to successful integration lies in discipline and review. Periodic performance analysis can highlight weaknesses in your approach, such as stops consistently placed too close, profit targets set unrealistically far away, or position sizes that are too large given your tolerance for drawdowns. By reviewing your trades, journaling the reasons behind each decision, and calculating metrics like maximum drawdown or average risk-reward ratio, you can fine-tune your risk management parameters over time. Continuous improvement is the hallmark of longevity in trading. The S&P futures market evolves, and so should your risk management plan.

Emotional Discipline and Risk Management

No matter how well-structured the risk management strategy may be, its effectiveness ultimately depends on the trader's ability to follow it. This is where emotional discipline comes into play. Fear, greed, and impatience are powerful emotions that can compel traders to deviate from their plans. For instance, a trader might move a stop-loss further away in the hope of avoiding a loss, or cancel a take-profit order prematurely out of impatience. Both actions undermine the logic and consistency behind risk management, often leading to suboptimal results.

To maintain emotional discipline, traders must cultivate a mindset that views losses as an inevitable part of the trading process, rather than a failure. When rules are established beforehand and consistently adhered to, the impact of emotions on decision-making diminishes. Using risk management tools effectively is not simply about mechanical execution; it's also about accepting the outcomes, both profits and losses, as a natural result of following a well-defined plan.

Practical steps to strengthen emotional discipline include practicing meditation, reducing screen time during volatile trades, and reviewing historical trading performance to reinforce the understanding that no individual trade determines long-term success. Similarly, understanding that stop-loss orders protect your capital and that take-profit orders safeguard your gains can help traders see these orders as safety nets rather than restrictions. Over time, disciplined adherence to these principles fosters confidence and a measured approach, making it easier to implement risk management strategies even under stressful market conditions.

Adjusting Risk Management in Different Market Environments

Market conditions in S&P futures are far from static. Periods of high volatility, influenced by major economic reports or geopolitical tensions, can give way to quieter times marked by narrow trading ranges. Each environment demands a slightly different approach to risk management. In highly volatile conditions, traders may opt for smaller position sizes to accommodate wider stops without increasing their absolute risk. They may also consider employing tighter initial stops if they anticipate sharp, short-lived moves or reducing the duration of their trades to avoid overnight uncertainties.

On the other hand, during low-volatility environments, traders might find that the traditional wide stops and small positions are leaving too many unrealized gains on the table. In these times, it might be appropriate to slowly increase position size or tighten profit targets to capture smaller, more frequent gains. The key is adaptation. Just as the economy cycles through periods of growth and contraction, markets fluctuate between periods of exuberance and caution. Risk management strategies should be flexible enough to adjust, ensuring they remain aligned with the prevailing conditions without compromising the underlying principles of capital preservation.

It's also vital to remember that market environments can shift suddenly. A planned Federal Reserve announcement or a surprise geopolitical event can turn a quiet day into a storm of price action. Traders who have a contingency plan ready, such as scaling out of positions before major announcements or temporarily suspending trading until the storm passes, will be better prepared to handle these transitions smoothly. By continuously refining and adjusting your risk management protocols in response to evolving market conditions, you ensure that your trading approach remains robust and capable of weathering any market scenario.

The 3% Rule

Never risk more than 3% of your account on any single trade, even if you are in a profitable position. Risk management is essential in trading because it ensures that no single loss will wipe out a substantial portion of your capital. Without proper risk management, even a series of winning trades can be undone by a single significant loss. The 3% rule is a widely accepted guideline in trading, which states that a trader should never risk more than 3% of their account balance on any one trade. For instance, if a trader has a $20,000 account, they should avoid risking more than $600 on a single position. This rule provides a balance between preserving capital and allowing enough risk to generate returns.

Example of Risk Management

Let's consider the example, the trader is engaged in multiple positions throughout the day, using stops to manage risk. Assume the trader starts with a

$20,000 account. If the trader takes a position and is in profit by $1000 but still has a stop that is $800 away from the current price, the risk on the trade is effectively $800. This exceeds the 3% rule (since 3% of $20,000 is $600), so the trader must adjust their risk accordingly.

This could be done in a few ways:

1. **Reduce Position Size**: One of the most effective methods to reduce risk is to decrease the size of the position. For example, if the initial trade was made with a larger number of contracts or shares, the trader could scale down the position to bring the risk within acceptable limits.
2. **Move Stop Loss Closer**: Alternatively, the trader could move the stop closer to the current price action, reducing the potential loss on the trade. However, this may increase the risk of being stopped out prematurely, which must be considered.
3. **Exit the Trade**: If neither of the above options is possible or desirable, the trader could exit the trade. Exiting locks in profit and reduces exposure to further risk.

Protecting Profits

Once in a profitable trade, protecting those profits is as important as limiting losses. As the chart illustrates, a trader can adjust their stop loss as the trade progresses. For example, once the market makes a higher high or lower low, the stop can be moved to a more favorable position, locking in some profit while still allowing for potential further gains. This method is often referred to as a "trailing stop."

Conclusion

Risk management in S&P futures trading is not a one-time exercise; it is the foundational principle that shapes every aspect of a trader's decision-making process. Far more than a mere safeguard, it represents the critical difference between short-lived success and enduring profitability. Properly calibrated position sizing, consistent use of stop-loss orders, well-thought-out take-profit targets, and the discipline to follow these rules—even when emotions run high—form the backbone of a resilient trading strategy.

At the heart of this discipline lies a set of guiding principles. One is adhering to rules, such as the 3% rule, which helps ensure that no single trade carries the potential to significantly undermine an account. Another is the judicious use of stop-loss orders, placed not arbitrarily, but near logical technical or fundamental levels that minimize unnecessary market noise. Adjusting position sizes in response to volatility and systematically evaluating risk-reward ratios further enhances a trader's ability to navigate changing market conditions. In addition, strict adherence to protective measures applies not only to losing trades but also to winning ones, because protecting profits remains as crucial as guarding against losses. Even a string of successful trades can be undone by a single uncontrolled risk event.

Successful trading, therefore, is not measured by the occasional home run or a series of winning trades alone. Instead, it is defined by a sustainable approach: one that nurtures capital growth over time, ensures survival through all manner of market turmoil, and builds confidence rooted in preparedness and discipline, regardless of whether a given trade yields a profit or a loss, the consistent focus on limiting downside risk ensures that traders stay in the game. In this way, effective risk management serves as the cornerstone of successful S&P futures trading, forging the path to longevity, resilience, and ultimately, long-term profitability.

No matter how solid your trading strategy or how promising the market setup, ensuring consistent success in S&P futures ultimately hinges on disciplined risk management. By adhering to guidelines like the 3% rule, you preserve capital and prevent a single adverse move from decimating your account. Stop-loss orders function as essential safety nets, automatically closing trades before losses escalate beyond acceptable thresholds. Equally vital are take-profit orders, which safeguard gains in a market known for rapid reversals. Proper position sizing adds another layer of protection, ensuring that no single trade carries disproportionately high risk relative to your portfolio. Emotional discipline—bolstered by a written plan, regular self-evaluation, and an unwavering commitment to your rules—allows you to trade methodically rather than impulsively. Furthermore, adapting to shifting market conditions by adjusting stops, profit targets, and position sizes keeps your approach dynamic yet consistently risk-aware. In the end, effective risk management is the bedrock of resilient trading, enabling you to navigate S&P futures with confidence and longevity.

CHAPTER FIFTEEN

Overtrading

Introduction to Overtrading

In the high-stakes environment of financial trading, the pursuit of profit can sometimes lead traders down a perilous path known as overtrading. Overtrading occurs when a trader engages in excessive buying and selling of securities, often driven by emotions rather than a well-thought-out strategy. This behavior can undermine profitability, erode trading capital, and lead to significant financial losses. Understanding the causes, recognizing the signs, and implementing strategies to prevent overtrading are essential for maintaining a disciplined and successful trading career.

Defining Overtrading

Overtrading is characterized by making an excessive number of trades, often without adequate analysis or justification. This can manifest in various ways, such as:

High Frequency of Trades: Executing more trades than the strategy warrants.

Chasing Losses: Attempting to recover losses by increasing trade frequency or size.

Lack of Strategy Adherence: Deviating from a predefined trading plan in response to market movements.

Emotional Decision-Making: Allowing emotions like fear and greed to dictate trading actions rather than rational analysis.

Overtrading can occur in any market—stocks, forex, commodities, or futures—and is not confined to any particular trading style or timeframe.

Causes of Overtrading

Several factors contribute to overtrading, often intertwining to exacerbate the behavior:

Emotional Influence: Emotions such as fear, greed, and excitement can drive impulsive trading decisions, leading to excessive trading activity.

Lack of a Trading Plan: Without a clear, structured trading plan, traders may make ad hoc decisions, increasing the likelihood of overtrading.

Revenge Trading: After experiencing a loss, some traders may attempt to quickly recover by increasing their trading frequency or taking larger positions.

Market Volatility: High market volatility can tempt traders to capitalize on every price movement, leading to an unsustainable number of trades.

Overconfidence: Success in initial trades can lead to overconfidence, prompting traders to take on more trades than advisable.

Technology and Access: The ease of executing trades through online platforms can make it tempting to trade more frequently than necessary.

The Dangers of Overtrading

Overtrading poses significant risks to traders, impacting both their financial standing and psychological well-being:

Financial Losses: Excessive trading increases transaction costs, including commissions and spreads, which can erode profits and amplify losses.

Capital Erosion: Continuously engaging in trades without adequate risk management can deplete trading capital, limiting future trading opportunities.

Psychological Stress: The pressure of managing numerous trades can lead to heightened stress, anxiety, and burnout, affecting decision-making and overall mental health.

Poor Performance: Overtrading often results in lower win rates and diminished returns, as traders may enter unfavorable trades without proper analysis.

Reputation Damage: For professional traders, consistent overtrading can harm their reputation, making it difficult to attract investment or secure trading opportunities.

Identifying Overtrading

Recognizing the signs of overtrading is crucial for taking corrective action. Common indicators include:

Excessive Number of Trades: Trading significantly more frequently than the strategy dictates.

Deviating from the Trading Plan: Ignoring predefined rules and guidelines in response to short-term market movements.
Increased Transaction Costs: Noticeable rise in commissions and fees due to the high volume of trades.
Chasing Losses: Attempting to recover losses by making more trades, often leading to further losses.
Reduced Focus on Analysis: Entering trades without thorough analysis or justification.
Emotional Trading Decisions: Allowing emotions to influence trade entries and exits instead of relying on rational analysis.

Preventing Overtrading

Implementing strategies to prevent overtrading is essential for maintaining discipline and ensuring long-term trading success:
Develop a Comprehensive Trading Plan: Outline clear rules for trade entries, exits, position sizing, and risk management. Adhering to this plan reduces impulsive trading decisions.
Set Trading Limits: Define daily, weekly, or monthly limits on the number of trades and the amount of capital allocated to each trade.
Use Stop-Loss Orders: Implement stop-loss orders to limit potential losses on each trade, preventing the need to chase losses through additional trades.
Maintain a Trading Journal: Document each trade, including the rationale behind it, outcomes, and lessons learned. This practice fosters self-awareness and accountability.
Practice Emotional Regulation: Develop techniques to manage emotions, such as meditation, exercise, or taking breaks from trading during high-stress periods.
Automate Trading Strategies: Utilize automated trading systems or algorithms that execute trades based on predefined criteria, reducing the influence of emotions.
Regular Performance Review: Periodically assess trading performance to identify patterns of overtrading and make necessary adjustments to strategies and behaviors.
Educate Yourself: Continuously seek knowledge about trading psychology and risk management to reinforce disciplined trading habits.

Risk Management in Overtrading

Effective risk management is integral to preventing and mitigating the impacts of overtrading:

Position Sizing: Determine appropriate position sizes based on account size and risk tolerance. Avoid risking too much on any single trade.

Diversification: Spread trades across different assets or markets to reduce exposure to any single position.

Risk-Reward Ratio: Ensure that each trade has a favorable risk-reward ratio, balancing potential losses against potential gains.

Leverage Control: Use leverage cautiously, as excessive leverage can amplify losses and contribute to overtrading tendencies.

Please review and adjust: Regularly review risk management practices and adjust them as necessary to align with changing market conditions and personal risk tolerance.

Psychological Aspects of Overtrading

Understanding the psychological drivers behind overtrading is essential for addressing the behavior:

Fear and Greed: Fear of missing out (FOMO) and greed for higher profits can drive traders to enter excessive trades.

Cognitive Biases: Biases such as confirmation bias, recency bias, and overconfidence can distort judgment and lead to overtrading.

Stress and Fatigue: Prolonged stress and fatigue can impair decision-making, increasing the likelihood of impulsive trading actions.

Addictive Behaviors: Trading can become addictive, leading to compulsive trading behaviors that are difficult to control.

Strategies for Building Psychological Resilience

Building psychological resilience helps traders maintain discipline and avoid overtrading:

Mindfulness and Meditation: Practices that enhance self-awareness and emotional regulation.

Physical Activity: Regular exercise helps reduce stress and improve mental clarity.

A healthy lifestyle, characterized by a balanced diet, adequate sleep, and hydration, supports overall well-being.

Setting Realistic Goals: Establish achievable trading goals to maintain motivation without succumbing to excessive trading pressures.

Seeking Support: Engaging with trading communities, mentors, or mental health professionals can provide guidance and support.

Implementing a Personal Overtrading Prevention Plan

Creating a personalized plan to prevent overtrading involves several key steps:

Self-Assessment: Evaluate personal trading habits to identify tendencies towards overtrading.

Define Rules: Establish clear, actionable rules for trade frequency, position sizing, and risk management to ensure consistent and effective trading.

Monitor Adherence: Regularly review adherence to established trading rules and make adjustments as necessary.

Reward Discipline: Implement a reward system for adhering to trading rules and achieving trading milestones.

Continuous Improvement: Use feedback from trading performance reviews to refine strategies and prevent future overtrading.

Case Studies: Overtrading in Action

Analyzing real-world examples can provide valuable insights into the consequences of overtrading and effective prevention strategies.

Case Study 1: The Cost of Chasing Losses

Scenario: A trader experiences a series of losing trades and, driven by the desire to recover losses quickly, increases their trading frequency and size. This leads to a significant depletion of their trading capital due to heightened transaction costs and additional losses.

Outcome: The trader's account balance drops drastically, leading to heightened stress and further poor trading decisions.

Lesson Learned: Chasing losses through overtrading can result in substantial financial harm. Implementing strict risk management and adhering to a trading plan can prevent such scenarios.

Case Study 2: Emotional Trading Success

Scenario: A disciplined trader faces a period of market volatility. Instead of increasing trade frequency in response to rapid price movements, the trader sticks to their predefined strategy, maintaining position sizes and adhering to risk management rules.

Outcome: Despite market turbulence, the trader preserves their capital and achieves steady, consistent profits.

Lesson Learned: Maintaining discipline and following a structured trading plan can safeguard against the temptations of overtrading, ensuring long-term trading success.

Conclusion

Overtrading is a common pitfall in the trading world, driven by a combination of emotional impulses, lack of discipline, and inadequate risk management. It poses significant risks to both financial capital and psychological well-being, undermining the potential for consistent trading success. By understanding the causes, recognizing the signs, and implementing robust prevention strategies, traders can navigate away from the dangers of overtrading and cultivate a disciplined, strategic approach to trading.

Key Takeaways:

Recognize the Signs: Identifying the indicators of overtrading is the first step towards addressing the behavior.

Develop a Trading Plan: A comprehensive, well-defined trading plan serves as a roadmap, reducing the likelihood of impulsive trading decisions.

Implement Strict Risk Management: Proper risk management techniques, including position sizing and stop-loss orders, are essential for protecting capital and preventing overtrading.

Cultivate Emotional Discipline: Managing emotions and building psychological resilience are crucial for maintaining trading discipline and avoiding overtrading.

Continuous Monitoring and Adaptation: Regularly reviewing trading performance and adapting strategies ensures ongoing alignment with trading goals and risk tolerance.

By mastering the intricacies of overtrading and implementing effective prevention strategies, traders can enhance their trading performance, sustain their capital, and achieve long-term success in the competitive landscape of financial markets.

Final Thoughts: Overtrading is not merely an issue of executing too many trades; it is a manifestation of deeper psychological and strategic shortcomings. Addressing overtrading requires a holistic approach that encompasses emotional regulation, disciplined strategy execution, and robust risk management. As traders become more self-aware and implement structured trading practices, they can overcome the temptations of overtrading, fostering a sustainable and profitable trading career.

Overtrading in S&P futures often begins innocently enough—perhaps you score one solid profit, get a rush of adrenaline, and suddenly you're chasing every price blip like a cat fixated on a laser pointer. Fear, greed, and a dash of overconfidence can drive traders into a manic loop of entries and exits, all while racking up transaction costs and whittling away hard-earned gains. Before you know it, your trading account's on life support and your stress levels are through the roof. The antidote? Discipline is rooted in a straightforward plan that spells out risk parameters, daily trade limits, and stop-loss orders. Think of it like a GPS for your trades, minus the annoying "recalculating" voice when you deviate from the route. And hey, keeping a journal isn't just for angsty teens: it helps spot reckless patterns before they spiral, while mindfulness practices can keep your head cool enough to avoid emotional "revenge trades."

Most importantly, remember that S&P futures trading is a marathon, not a breakneck sprint to glory. High-quality setups, backed by ongoing self-education and measured execution, are your friends here. By pairing systematic risk management with emotional discipline, you'll protect your capital, dodge the overtrading trap, and stand a fighting chance of enjoying a calmer, more profitable ride in the turbulent world of S&P futures.

CHAPTER SIXTEEN

Money Management Strategies

Introduction to Fixed Fractional Position Sizing

In the world of financial trading, managing the amount invested in each trade is crucial for achieving long-term success. One effective method for doing this is Fixed Fractional Position Sizing. This strategy involves allocating a fixed percentage of your trading capital to each trade, helping you control risk and maintain discipline. This chapter explores Fixed Fractional Position Sizing, focusing on two key approaches: Percentage-Based Position Sizing and the Kelly Criterion. We'll break down these concepts in simple terms to make them easy to understand and apply.

Understanding Fixed Fractional Position Sizing

Fixed Fractional Position Sizing is a method where you decide to risk a certain percentage of your trading account on every trade. For example, if you choose to risk 2% of your account on each trade and your account balance is $10,000, you would risk $200 on that trade. This approach ensures that no single trade can significantly harm your overall capital, helping you stay in the game longer and manage losses effectively.

Importance of Fixed Fractional Position Sizing

Using Fixed Fractional Position Sizing helps you manage risk consistently. By risking only a small portion of your capital on each trade, you protect your account from significant losses. This method promotes disciplined trading, preventing emotional decisions that can lead to overtrading or excessive risk-taking.

Percentage-Based Position Sizing

Percentage-Based Position Sizing is the simplest form of Fixed Fractional Position Sizing. It involves deciding on a fixed percentage of your trading capital to risk on each trade. This percentage remains the same regardless of whether your account balance increases or decreases.

How It Works

1. **Choose Your Risk Percentage:** Decide what percentage of your account you're comfortable risking on each trade. Common choices range from 1% to 3%.
2. **Calculate Your Risk Amount:** Multiply your account balance by the chosen percentage to determine how much you will risk on a single trade.
3. **Adjust as Needed:** As your account balance changes, recalculate the amount you risk to maintain the same percentage.

Example

Imagine you have a $50,000 trading account and decide to risk 2% of your account value per trade. This means you will risk $1,000 on each trade. If your account grows to $60,000, 2% of that is $1,200, so you will risk $1,200 on your next trade. Conversely, if your account drops to $40,000, you will risk $800 on a trade.

Benefits of Percentage-Based Position Sizing

- **Simplicity:** Easy to understand and implement, making it suitable for traders of all experience levels.
- **Consistency:** Maintains a steady level of risk across all trades, helping to protect your account from significant losses.
- **Scalability:** Automatically adjusts as your account balance changes, allowing your risk to grow or shrink with your capital.

The Kelly Criterion

The Kelly Criterion is a more advanced position sizing method that aims to maximize the growth of your trading capital over time. Unlike Percentage-Based Position Sizing, which uses a fixed percentage, the Kelly Criterion calculates the optimal amount of risk based on your trading performance.

How It Works

1. **Assess Your Success Rate: Calculat**e the percentage of your trades that are profitable.
2. **Evaluate Your Wins and Losses:** Calculate the average amount you win on successful trades compared to the average amount you lose on unsuccessful ones.
3. **Calculate Your Optimal Risk:** Use these statistics to find the ideal percentage of your capital to risk on each trade.

Example

Suppose you win 60% of your trades, and your average win is twice as significant as your average loss. The Kelly Criterion might suggest that you should risk around 10% of your trading capital on each trade. However, many traders choose to use only a portion of the Kelly suggestion (like half-Kelly) to reduce risk and volatility.

Benefits of the Kelly Criterion

- **Maximizes Growth:** Aims to increase your capital as efficiently as possible by optimizing your risk.
- **Data-Driven:** Uses your trading performance statistics to determine the best risk level.
- **Adaptable:** Adjusts your risk based on how well your trading strategy is performing.

Limitations of the Kelly Criterion

- **Requires Accurate Data:** Needs precise information about your win rate and the ratio of wins to losses, which can be hard to estimate accurately.
- **Higher Risk:** Can suggest larger position sizes, which may lead to bigger losses if your estimates are off.
- **Complexity:** More complicated to calculate compared to Percentage-Based Position Sizing, making it less accessible for beginners.

Comparing Percentage-Based Position Sizing and the Kelly Criterion

Both Percentage-Based Position Sizing and the Kelly Criterion aim to manage risk effectively, but they do so in different ways:

- **Simplicity vs. Sophistication:** Percentage-Based Position Sizing is straightforward to use, while the Kelly Criterion is more complex and requires detailed performance data.
- **Risk Management:** Percentage-Based Position Sizing offers a consistent and conservative approach to risk, whereas the Kelly Criterion seeks to maximize growth, which can involve higher risk.
- **Adaptability:** Both methods adjust with your account size, but the Kelly Criterion also adapts based on your trading performance.

Risk Management in Fixed Fractional Position Sizing

Effective risk management is essential when using Fixed Fractional Position Sizing. Here are some key practices:

1. **Diversification:** Spread your trades across different assets or markets to reduce exposure to any single position.
2. **Use Stop-Loss Orders:** Set predefined exit points to limit potential losses on each trade.
3. **Regular Review:** Periodically assess your position sizing strategy to ensure it aligns with your current account balance and market conditions.
4. **Avoid Overleverage:** Ensure that you're not risking too much of your capital on any single trade, preventing excessive losses.

Psychological Aspects of Position Sizing

Managing how much you risk on each trade also has significant psychological benefits:

- **Confidence:** Consistent position sizing builds confidence, as you're less likely to suffer significant losses that can shake your trust in your trading strategy.
- **Emotional Stability:** By controlling risk, you reduce the emotional highs and lows associated with trading, helping you maintain a balanced mindset.
- **Focus:** A clear position sizing strategy allows you to concentrate on market analysis and strategy execution rather than worrying about potential losses.

Implementing Fixed Fractional Position Sizing

To effectively implement Fixed Fractional Position Sizing, follow these steps:

1. **Assess Your Risk Tolerance:** Determine how much risk you're comfortable taking on each trade based on your financial situation and trading goals.
2. **Choose Your Position Sizing Method:** Decide whether Percentage-Based Position Sizing or the Kelly Criterion best suits your trading style and risk tolerance.
3. **Calculate Your Position Size:** Use your chosen method to determine how much to invest in each trade.
4. **Integrate with Your Trading Plan:** Ensure that your position sizing strategy aligns with your overall trading strategy and goals.
5. **Monitor and Adjust:** Regularly review your position sizing approach and make adjustments as your account balance and trading performance evolve.

Case Studies: Fixed Fractional Position Sizing in Action

Understanding how Fixed Fractional Position Sizing works in real scenarios can provide valuable insights.

Case Study 1: Consistent Risk Management with Percentage-Based Position Sizing

Scenario: A trader starts with a $100,000 account and decides to risk 2% ($2,000) on each trade. Over a series of 50 trades, the trader maintains this risk level, adjusting the position size as the account balance changes.

Outcome: Regardless of whether the account balance increases or decreases, each trade risks only 2%, allowing the trader to manage losses effectively and take advantage of winning trades without overexposing their capital.

Lesson Learned: Percentage-Based Position Sizing offers a straightforward yet effective approach for maintaining consistent risk levels and promoting disciplined trading behavior.

Case Study 2: Maximizing Growth with the Kelly Criterion

Scenario: A trader with a $50,000 account uses the Kelly Criterion to determine their position size based on a historical win rate of 60% and an average win that is twice the size of the average loss.

Outcome: The Kelly Criterion recommends allocating approximately 10% of the trading capital to each trade. The trader experiences significant account growth during winning streaks but also faces larger drawdowns during losing periods.

Lesson Learned: While the Kelly Criterion can enhance growth potential, it requires careful management and a thorough understanding of its inherent risks. Many traders opt to use a fraction of the Kelly suggestion to balance growth and risk.

Conclusion

Fixed Fractional Position Sizing is a fundamental strategy for effective trade management, offering traders a disciplined and systematic approach to risk. By allocating a fixed percentage of capital to each trade, traders can maintain consistent risk levels, protect their accounts from significant losses, and foster long-term trading success. Whether you choose the simplicity of Percentage-Based Position Sizing or the growth-oriented Kelly Criterion, understanding and implementing Fixed Fractional Position Sizing is essential for optimizing your trading performance and managing risk effectively.

Key Takeaways:

1 **Consistency in Risk Management:** Fixed Fractional Position Sizing ensures that each trade carries a consistent level of risk, promoting disciplined trading practices.

2 **Adaptability:** Position sizes adjust automatically with account growth or decline, maintaining proportional risk exposure.

3 **Strategic Flexibility:** Percentage-Based Position Sizing offers simplicity, while the Kelly Criterion provides a more growth-oriented approach for those willing to manage higher risks.

4 **. Risk Mitigation: Effective position sizing is crucial for preventing significant drawdowns and main**taining trading capital over the long term.

5 **Psychological Benefits:** Structured position sizing reduces emotional strain, fostering a balanced and focused trading mindset.

By mastering Fixed Fractional Position Sizing, traders can enhance their risk management strategies, achieve consistent profitability, and navigate the complexities of the financial markets with confidence and precision.

Final Thoughts: Position sizing is not just about numbers; it's a crucial aspect of your overall trading strategy that directly impacts both risk and reward. Fixed Fractional Position Sizing, with its blend of simplicity and effectiveness, offers a reliable method for managing trades systematically. Whether you opt for the straightforwardness of Percentage-Based Position Sizing or the calculated balance of the Kelly Criterion, integrating Fixed Fractional Position Sizing into your trading plan is essential for building a resilient and profitable trading career.

CHAPTER SEVENTEEN

The Psychology of Trading

Trading, by its very nature, is an emotional endeavor. Every decision to buy, sell, or hold is influenced by complex internal factors—fears, hopes, habits, and biases—that shape how traders perceive the market and respond to price fluctuations. While many aspiring traders dedicate themselves to finding that perfect strategy or technical system, seasoned professionals know that robust techniques are only part of the equation. Just as critical is the trader's mindset: the ability to remain focused, calm, and disciplined under conditions of uncertainty. In this chapter, we will explore the significance of trading psychology and examine how emotions, biases, and psychological tendencies influence trading outcomes. We will discuss the common emotional pitfalls, from overconfidence to fear and greed, and present practical steps to develop emotional control and a well-grounded trading psychology. We will also look at common mistakes traders make—particularly in their early days—and identify ways to avoid or correct them before they become ingrained habits.

Overconfidence: The Illusion of Control

Overconfidence is one of the most pervasive psychological pitfalls in trading. It often manifests after a series of winning trades, when a trader begins to believe they have a special insight or near-infallible system. This can lead to increasing position sizes, neglecting risk management, and ignoring market warning signs. The illusion of control that overconfidence imparts is dangerous because it blinds the trader to potential threats. Markets are dynamic, influenced by countless variables that no single participant can fully anticipate.

Overconfidence can transform a once prudent trader into a risk-taker who discards the very methods that initially brought success.

The antidote to overconfidence lies in humility and self-awareness. Seasoned traders understand that no matter how skilled or experienced they are, losses are inevitable. Embracing the unpredictability of markets and maintaining a level of skepticism about one's prowess can help keep risk management and disciplined execution at the forefront. In practice, this might mean sticking to predefined trade sizes, reviewing losing trades to understand what went wrong, and never assuming that a few profitable trades guarantee future performance. Over time, recognizing overconfidence as a form of bias can save traders from catastrophic drawdowns.

Fear and Greed: The Core Emotional Drivers

Two of the most basic yet powerful emotions that influence trading decisions are fear and greed. These are often cited as the forces driving market cycles and impacting individual psychology at a granular level.

Fear: Fear manifests in various forms—fear of losing money, fear of missing out on a profitable opportunity, or fear of being wrong. Fear can cause traders to hold onto losing positions for too long, hoping they will turn around, because admitting a loss is painful. It can also lead traders to exit winning trades prematurely, anxious that profits might vanish if they stay in too long.

Greed: Greed, on the other hand, pushes traders to chase after excessive returns. It tempts them to ignore their rules, overleverage their positions, and risk too much for too little reward. Greed may also lead to "revenge trading" after a loss, where the trader tries to recover quickly by doubling down without proper analysis.

Balancing fear and greed is about learning emotional equilibrium. Recognize when fear prevents logical action and when greed encourages reckless behavior. Setting clear, mechanical rules for when to enter and exit trades can mitigate the influence of these emotions. For instance, predefining stop-loss orders ensures that fear will not keep you clinging to a losing position indefinitely, while setting realistic profit targets and sticking to them curbs greed-driven decisions.

Emotional Control: Taming the Inner Beast

Successful trading demands emotional resilience. Markets are inherently volatile, and prices can fluctuate significantly for reasons that often defy expectations. Traders who tie their emotional well-being to each tick in the market usually find themselves on an emotional rollercoaster that impairs their judgment. Emotional control means acknowledging feelings like stress, frustration, excitement, or anxiety without letting them dictate trading actions.

A common mistake is to let a series of losses trigger emotional responses that lead to worse decisions. For example, after taking several losses, a trader might "revenge trade," risking more than usual in an attempt to recover losses quickly. This classic scenario often leads to even bigger drawdowns. Another emotional misstep is shifting strategies mid-trade out of impatience or fear, such as beginning a trade as a scalp and then converting it into a swing trade out of desperation, hoping the market eventually turns around.

To maintain emotional control, traders must practice self-awareness and patience. Techniques include taking breaks after significant losses to regain composure, keeping a trading journal to reflect on decision-making processes, and having a predefined trading plan that reduces the influence of impulsive choices. Over time, these habits build emotional resilience, making it easier to stay level-headed during chaotic market sessions.

The Role of Emotions in Trading

Emotions are not inherently evil. They can provide valuable information when properly understood and managed. Nervousness before a trade might signal that more analysis is needed, while a sense of unease during a position might indicate that the initial thesis no longer holds. The key is to interpret emotional signals objectively rather than react impulsively.

Furthermore, emotions inform traders about their psychological thresholds. For instance, if a trader consistently feels overwhelmed by uncertainty during Federal Reserve announcements (FOMC) or major news events, it might be wise to avoid trading during those times until they develop strategies or the emotional fortitude to handle such volatility.

Instead of seeing emotions as enemies, traders can view them as data points in their overall performance metrics. By recognizing patterns—such as feeling anxious every time they place a trade too close to the closing bell or feeling overconfident when using unfamiliar trading methods—they can tweak their approach, refine their trading plan, and adapt to their psychological makeup.

Developing a Trading Psychology: A Structured Approach

Developing a robust trading psychology is a gradual process that involves introspection, skill-building, and consistent effort. Just as you would not expect to become a proficient trader overnight, you cannot cultivate mental resilience instantly. The following steps can guide traders on the path to forging a strong psychological foundation:

a. **Self-Assessment: Start** by understanding your emotional landscape. Are you prone to anxiety, impatience, or overconfidence? Identifying these tendencies early on will help you create strategies to counteract them.

b. **Define Your Rules**: A trading plan is not just about entry and exit signals; it should also outline risk tolerance, profit targets, stop-loss levels, and criteria for when and when not to trade. Clear rules minimize the influence of emotions during volatile conditions.

c. **Risk Management:** Ensure proper position sizing and maintain a correct risk/reward ratio. Over-leveraging or taking on too much risk to achieve too little will only exacerbate emotional responses to market fluctuations.

d. **Routine and Discipline**: Consistency in your trading habits—from market preparation to journaling trades—builds the kind of discipline that helps control emotions. Over time, repetitive positive actions form mental frameworks that keep traders grounded, even when conditions are challenging.

e. **Continuous Improvement**: Regularly review trades, assess emotional triggers, and adjust strategies as needed. As you gain experience, patterns in your behavior will emerge, allowing you to address weaknesses and reinforce strengths.

Familiar Psychological Mistakes Traders Make

Many new traders repeat a familiar set of mistakes that stem from a lack of emotional control or a misunderstanding of market dynamics. Let's examine these pitfalls, understand the emotional drivers behind them, and consider how to overcome them.

1. **Holding on to Losses Too Long**: Refusal to accept a loss often comes from fear—fear of admitting failure or locking in a negative result. This can be avoided by having a well-defined stop-loss and committing to respecting it. Letting a slight loss grow into a significant one can severely damage both your account and your confidence.

2. **Taking Profits Too Early**: Fear of losing unrealized gains can cause traders to exit winning trades prematurely. Overcoming this involves trusting your strategy and allowing the market to reach predetermined profit targets. By doing so, you maintain a favorable risk / reward ratio over the long run.

3. **Incorrect Risk/Reward Ratio**: Risking too much to gain too little often stems from impatience or greed. Setting proper position sizes and predefining acceptable risk levels ensures that each trade fits into an overall profitable framework.

4. **Trading Unfamiliar Methods Without Practice**: Curiosity and greed might push traders to jump into options trading or complex strategies without proper research or backtesting. This lack of preparedness often leads to confusion, fear, and unnecessary losses. By practicing on a demo account and honing one method at a time, traders gain confidence and reduce costly mistakes.

5. **Overtrading**: Driven by excitement, impatience, or the urge to "do something," overtrading results in unnecessary exposure to market fluctuations and random outcomes. Having a structured trading plan—perhaps limiting the number of trades per day—can prevent the impulse to trade excessively.

6. **Trading Too Close to the Closing Bell**: The final moments of the trading day can be volatile and thinly traded. Impatience or a desire to "make something happen" before the session ends can lead to rushed decisions. Waiting for the next day's session when conditions are clearer and liquidity is higher often yields better results.

7. **Trading on Impulse** Without Proper Setups: Jumping into trades without a well-defined setup often comes from anxiety or FOMO (fear of missing out). Sticking to a trading plan and predefined criteria ensures that each trade has a logical rationale, reducing emotional guesswork.

8. Overreliance on Indicators: Excessive reliance on any single indicator or tool can lead to false confidence. Emotional attachment to an indicator's "signal" might prevent you from seeing contradictory market information. Using indicators as guides rather than absolute truths maintains a balanced perspective.

9. Following Social Media Hype: Listening to opinions from strangers on social media or livestream platforms can sway emotions. Greed and fear thrive on crowd psychology. Instead, focus on your research and strategy, trusting your process rather than others' claims.

10. Trading During Major News Events (e.g., FOMC): High-impact news increases volatility and uncertainty. Emotional reactions—fear of missing out on big moves or greed for quick gains—can lead to impulsive trades. Many disciplined traders stand aside until after the dust settles, then trade with clearer insights.

11. Changing Trade Objectives Mid-Trade: Starting a trade as a scalp and suddenly deciding to hold it overnight due to fear or greed disrupts the original plan. This inconsistency arises from emotional responses to price movement. Sticking to the initial objective or exiting if conditions no longer match the plan is crucial.

12. Not Respecting Stop-Losses or Moving Stops: Moving a stop-loss further away to avoid realizing a loss often leads to bigger losses, sometimes large enough to wipe out a significant portion of the trading account. This action stems from denial and fear. The solution is to trust your initial analysis and accept when a trade is not working out.

Building Psychological Resilience for the Long Term

Achieving a stable and healthy trading psychology requires time, patience, and practice. By consistently applying the principles outlined in this chapter—managing overconfidence, balancing fear and greed, developing emotional control, and recognizing the critical role emotions play in trading—you lay the groundwork for long-term success.

Like physical exercise, mental conditioning requires regular maintenance. Continually monitoring your emotional responses, refining your plan, and learning from mistakes ensures that your psychological framework evolves with your trading journey. Over time, these processes become second nature, allowing you to approach the markets with clarity, confidence, and resilience.

In this balanced state, the inevitable losses and setbacks become learning opportunities rather than demoralizing defeats, and profitable trades serve as confirmation that your disciplined approach is paying off.

Conclusion

The psychology of trading is the bedrock upon which technical skills and market knowledge rest. Emotions will always be present, but how you handle them determines your trajectory. By understanding emotional drivers like overconfidence, fear, and greed, developing robust emotional control, and methodically addressing common psychological mistakes, traders can cultivate a mindset that supports consistent, sustainable profitability. Beyond any specific strategy, indicator, or market condition, a well-honed trading psychology is a trader's most valuable asset.

CHAPTER EIGHTEEN

Developing a Trading Plan

Many aspiring traders rush headlong into the markets without first establishing a clear direction. They bounce between strategies, follow random tips from social media, and enter trades on a hunch rather than a plan. While such improvisation might occasionally produce a lucky win, it rarely leads to sustainable success. Just as a traveler would never embark on a journey without a destination or a map, a trader should not begin their market adventure without clearly defined goals and a systematic trading strategy.

In this chapter, we will focus on the foundational steps that set the stage for successful trading. We will begin by discussing how to define your personal trading goals—objectives that provide a sense of purpose and keep you focused on what truly matters. Next, we will explore how to create a trading strategy that aligns with these goals and works as a guiding framework for all your market decisions. Ultimately, we will stress the importance of adhering to your plan, recognizing that long-term success hinges not only on having a well-considered strategy but also on the discipline and consistency required to execute it.

Defining Your Goals

Goals are the compass that directs your trading journey. Without them, you risk drifting aimlessly through the markets, influenced by short-term emotions and unpredictable market noise. Clear goals remind you why you started trading in the first place—whether it's to generate steady income, build a long-term investment portfolio, or achieve financial independence. They also serve as benchmarks for progress, helping you measure how far you've come and whether you're on track.

When defining your goals, it's essential to be both specific and realistic. For example, stating "I want to make a lot of money" is too vague. Instead, consider a measurable, achievable objective, such as "I want to earn a consistent 5% return on my trading account every quarter." This target is clearer, and you can break it down into steps: identifying a strategy, determining risk per trade, and continuously reviewing your performance.

In addition to performance-based goals, consider goals related to skill development or risk management. For instance, a meaningful goal might be "to maintain a maximum drawdown of 10% or less," or "to learn and master one new technical analysis technique by the end of the month." These process-oriented goals focus on enhancing your competency and discipline rather than chasing a specific monetary outcome. Over time, improvements in skill, risk management, and market understanding naturally contribute to better results.

The final step in defining your goals is writing them down. A written record gives your objectives substance and serves as a reference point, helping you maintain direction when your emotions would otherwise push you off track. Keeping your goals visible—perhaps pinned above your monitor or listed in your trading journal—reinforces their importance and ensures they remain at the forefront of your mind.

Creating a Trading Strategy

A trading strategy is the roadmap that guides you from where you are now to the achievement of your defined goals. It outlines how and when you will enter trades, manage positions, and exit the market. A good strategy is tailored to your personality, risk tolerance, and schedule. Some traders thrive on short-term intraday opportunities, while others prefer longer-term trades that allow them to hold positions for weeks or months. There is no "one-size-fits-all" approach—only the right approach for you.

When building a trading strategy, start by considering the markets and instruments you want to trade. Will you focus on futures, stocks, forex, or options? Will you specialize in a specific sector or index, or cast a wider net?

Selecting the right markets often means choosing those you can analyze well and that fit your availability and comfort level. If you can only watch the markets for a few hours each evening, short-term scalping strategies might not be as suitable as swing or position trading methods.

Next, determine how you will identify setups. Your criteria might include chart patterns, trend-following indicators, support and resistance levels, fundamental news catalysts, or a combination of technical and fundamental analysis. The crucial point is that your entry and exit criteria are explicit and can be tested. Vague notions like "when I feel it's right" only invite emotional decision-making. Instead, strive for concrete signals, such as "buy if price breaks above yesterday's high and the 50-day moving average is upward-sloping," or "initiate a short position if the RSI (Relative Strength Index) is above 70 and price fails at a key resistance level."

Risk management principles are another vital component of your strategy. Decide in advance how much you're willing to risk per trade, what your ideal risk/reward ratio is, and how you'll protect yourself against significant losses (such as stop-loss orders or position sizing rules). Consider also how you'll take profits—whether you'll exit entirely at a certain price level, scale out incrementally, or trail your stop to lock in gains as the market moves in your favor. A robust trading strategy integrates these elements seamlessly, leaving as little room as possible for in-the-moment guesswork.

Before putting any money at risk, backtest your strategy using historical data and practice it in a simulated environment. This testing phase helps you understand the strategy's strengths, weaknesses, and potential win rates. Armed with this knowledge, you'll have a realistic expectation of your strategy's performance and be better prepared to handle its natural ebbs and flows without losing confidence.

Sticking to Your Plan

Even the most thorough, well-crafted trading strategy will fail if you don't stick to it. Consistency in execution is paramount. Over time, your approach should yield a consistent pattern of outcomes that aligns with your expectations, as determined by backtesting and practice. If you're constantly deviating from the plan—exiting trades too early out of fear, ignoring stop-losses in hopes of a reversal, or chasing a hot tip that doesn't fit your criteria—you'll never know if your strategy truly works.

The challenge is that sticking to your plan demands emotional discipline. Markets are unpredictable and can trigger strong reactions, such as fear and greed. When faced with a sudden price spike or a disappointing drawdown, it's tempting to abandon the rules and improvise. Yet, this kind of emotional trading sabotages the long-term reliability of your approach. If you stray from your plan whenever the market tests your nerves, your performance metrics become meaningless.

To reinforce discipline, create checks and balances. For example, commit to journaling every trade you make. Include why you entered, your planned exit points, and your rationale for any adjustments made during the trade. Reviewing this journal regularly helps you identify patterns of behavior, such as repeatedly cutting winners short or holding losers too long, that indicate you're not following the plan. Another tool is having a daily or weekly routine: review your charts, set alerts, and plan potential trades. Preparing while the market is closed and your emotions are calm makes it easier to follow through with your rules once the action begins.

A supportive environment can also help. You might join a community of like-minded traders who share a commitment to disciplined execution. Alternatively, consider hiring a mentor who can provide feedback and hold you accountable. Sometimes, knowing that you'll need to explain your decisions to someone else is a powerful motivator to remain faithful to your plan.

Integrating Goals, Strategy, and Discipline for Long-Term Success

Your trading goals, strategy, and adherence to your plan are interdependent. Goals provide the destination, your strategy is the roadmap, and discipline keeps you on the path. Over time, these three elements work together, guiding you toward steady improvement and consistent profitability.

As you gain experience, don't be afraid to reassess your goals or tweak your strategy. Markets evolve, and so do individual circumstances. Perhaps as you learn more, you discover that specific timeframes or instruments no longer suit your style. Adjusting your plan in a controlled, systematic way—rather than reacting impulsively—will ensure you continue to move toward your targets.

Above all, remember that trading is a journey, not a race. Defining realistic goals, creating a logical strategy, and practicing unwavering discipline is a recipe for long-term success. While you may face setbacks, the structure you've built provides stability and direction. Instead of being tossed by the winds of market volatility, you'll navigate with confidence, steadily progressing toward the kind of results that inspired you to start trading in the first place.

Conclusion

The difference between a floundering trader and one steadily moving toward success often comes down to clarity of purpose, methodical planning, and disciplined execution. By defining your goals, you establish a compelling reason to enter the markets—something more meaningful than random speculation. By creating a trading strategy tailored to your objectives, you build a framework for evaluating opportunities and managing risk. Finally, by committing to sticking to your plan, you ensure that your actions align with your vision, regardless of the emotional challenges that arise.

Together, these steps form the essential foundation for building a sustainable and rewarding trading career. Over time, as you refine your approach, measure your results, and become ever more disciplined, you will develop the confidence, consistency, and resilience needed to thrive in the world's financial markets.

CHAPTER NINETEEN

Continuous Learning and Adaptation

Financial markets are in constant flux, evolving as the global economic landscape shifts and new technologies emerge. Traders who fail to keep pace with these changes risk falling behind, locked into outdated assumptions or fixed strategies that no longer produce consistent returns. Trading success is about more than finding a single winning approach; it hinges on an ongoing process of learning, adapting, and refining your methods in response to a dynamic environment.

In this chapter, we will examine three key concepts that enable traders to remain effective in the long run. First, we'll discuss the importance of staying updated on market trends, highlighting how continuous learning and situational awareness give you a competitive edge. Next, we'll address the critical skill of learning from mistakes, showing how missteps, if processed correctly, become valuable stepping stones toward improvement. Finally, we'll examine why adapting to changing market conditions is not just advisable, but essential, and offer practical guidance on how to evolve your strategies and mindset as the market environment shifts beneath your feet.

Staying Updated on Market Trends

Markets are influenced by an array of factors—economic reports, geopolitical events, technological innovations, central bank policies, and investor sentiment, to name just a few. Staying updated on these trends is not a one-off exercise; it is a continuous, deliberate effort to remain informed and prepared.

1. Market Research and Analysis: Start by building a reliable source of information. Follow reputable financial news outlets, subscribe to research publications from respected analysts, and maintain a curated list of influential economists, strategists, and experienced traders. By regularly reviewing market commentary and economic calendars, you ensure that you are aware of upcoming events, like central bank announcements or company earnings, that could affect price movements.

2. Technical and Fundamental Indicators: While news feeds and economic data provide the backdrop, traders must also develop a consistent approach to analyzing market data. Whether you rely on technical indicators like moving averages or Fibonacci retracements, or on fundamental metrics like earnings growth or macroeconomic forecasts, updating your analytical toolkit ensures that you see both the forest and the trees. Periodically review which indicators have been most predictive or valuable for your strategy, discarding those that no longer add value.

3. Continuous Education: The learning never ends. New financial instruments, algorithmic trading technologies, and market structures continue to emerge. Taking courses, reading new books, joining trading communities, and participating in webinars help you stay abreast of these developments. In an information-driven field, knowledge is a competitive advantage, and ongoing education helps maintain that edge.

Staying updated on market trends means more than collecting information; it's about transforming that information into actionable insight. By incorporating the latest market intel and refining your interpretive frameworks, you ensure that your trading decisions remain timely, well-informed, and relevant.

Learning from Mistakes

No matter how experienced or skilled a trader may be, mistakes are inevitable. Poorly timed entries, overlooked news events, or misread technical patterns can lead to losses. Yet, what separates consistently profitable traders from those who continually struggle is not the absence of errors, but their response to them. Mistakes are a natural part of the trading journey. Learning from them is the true hallmark of professionalism and growth.

Analyzing Errors Objectively: When a trade goes wrong, the natural human reaction might be to blame the market, complain about volatility, or attribute losses to bad luck. However, progress comes from introspection and honest self-assessment. Did you deviate from your strategy? Did a passing news event too heavily influence you? Did emotions override your risk management rules? By identifying the root cause of the mistake, you lay the groundwork for a solution.

Maintaining a Trading Journal: A trading journal provides a structured way to review past trades and glean lessons from them. Record your entry and exit points, market conditions, your rationale for the trade, and, importantly, how you felt at the time. Over days, weeks, or months, patterns in your decision-making process will emerge. You may realize that you consistently take on excessive risk after a winning streak or become too cautious following a string of losses. Recognizing these tendencies is the first step toward corrective action.

Adopting a Growth Mindset: Instead of viewing mistakes as failures, treat them as opportunities for improvement. Each error provides a data point in your ongoing effort to refine your strategy and your mindset. Keep a calm, constructive outlook. Remind yourself that even the best traders experience losses and that resilience comes from learning how to bounce back stronger and wiser each time.

Over time, accumulating lessons from mistakes helps you build a personal guide to better trading. It sharpens your instincts, clarifies your rules, and encourages the kind of humility and diligence that are essential for navigating the uncertainties of financial markets.

Adapting to Changing Market Conditions

If there's one constant in trading, it is change. Market environments evolve as economic cycles turn, regulatory landscapes shift, and investor preferences move in and out of favor. A strategy that worked perfectly during a trending bull market may falter when volatility spikes and the market moves sideways. Traders who fail to adapt risk seeing their strategies become obsolete.

Recognizing Market Regimes: Not All Markets Are Created Equal. Strong trends and momentum characterize some periods, while others see mean-reverting price action with no clear direction. Still others may see heightened volatility due to geopolitical conflicts or crises. By recognizing these "market regimes"—and understanding which strategies work best in each—traders can dynamically adjust their approach. For example, you might favor trend-following techniques in strongly directional markets but switch to range-bound strategies when price action flattens out.

Adjusting Position Sizing and Risk Management: Changing conditions often necessitate adjustments in risk management strategies. In calm, low-volatility environments, you might trade slightly larger positions or set tighter stops. When volatility surges, reducing position sizes and widening stops could be more prudent, safeguarding your capital until conditions stabilize. Regularly revisiting your risk parameters ensures they remain appropriate for the current market climate.

Expanding Your Toolkit: Adapting may also mean learning new instruments or strategies. If you primarily trade equities, consider exploring futures, forex, or options when these markets present clearer opportunities. If you rely heavily on technical indicators, you might supplement them with fundamental analysis during earnings seasons or macroeconomic shifts. A flexible, open-minded approach to strategy selection keeps you agile and responsive.

Testing Changes Before Implementation: Before making dramatic shifts, test new strategies or adjustments on a demo account or with a reduced position size. Verify their effectiveness in current market conditions before committing significant capital. This cautious approach helps you avoid unnecessary losses and builds confidence as you integrate new methods into your trading arsenal.

Adaptation is not just about following the market—it's about anticipating potential changes and preparing for them. By staying attuned to shifts in volatility, liquidity, or economic conditions, you ensure that your trading methodology remains suited to the landscape you face today, rather than the one you traded last year.

Combining Updates, Learnings, and Adaptation for Continuous Improvement

These three elements—staying updated on market trends, learning from mistakes, and adapting to changing conditions—are deeply interconnected.

Each supports and informs the others, forming a cycle of continuous improvement:

- **Stay Informed**: By closely following market trends and conditions, you develop the situational awareness needed to spot emerging opportunities or warnings that a strategy may be losing its edge.
- **Learn from Mistakes**: When trades go wrong, your updated knowledge of current market dynamics can help you understand why. Armed with this insight, you can refine your approach, reinforcing good habits and discarding outdated assumptions.
- **Adapt Strategically**: As you learn from both your successes and failures, you naturally become more agile. Recognizing that markets don't stand still, you evolve your strategies, making incremental changes rather than lurching from one approach to another.

This continuous feedback loop fosters resilience, innovation, and self-improvement. Rather than feeling overwhelmed by market complexity, you see it as a resource—one that, if studied and understood, can lead to more informed decisions and greater consistency over time.

Conclusion

Longevity in trading is not simply a matter of finding a "perfect" system. Markets are too dynamic, and no single strategy remains infallible forever. Instead, enduring success stems from an ongoing commitment to learning, adjusting, and reinventing yourself as conditions demand. By consistently staying updated on market trends, you remain well-informed and ready to act when opportunities arise. By treating mistakes as learning moments, you turn setbacks into stepping stones toward greater skill and discipline. And by adapting your strategies to the ever-changing environment, you ensure your approach remains relevant, effective, and profitable over the long term.

Ultimately, trading mastery is not a static achievement—it's a journey that rewards curiosity, tenacity, and adaptability. By embracing the mindset described in this chapter, you set the stage for continuous growth, resilience in the face of uncertainty, and the capacity to thrive in any market climate.

CHAPTER TWENTY

Artificial Intelligence

Harnessing AI and ChatGPT for Trading S&P Futures

Introduction to AI in Futures Trading: In recent years, the financial markets have undergone a rapid evolution, driven by significant technological advancements and the widespread adoption of high-speed data analysis tools. No longer are traders reliant solely on gut instinct, economic calendars, and rudimentary technical indicators. Instead, the trading landscape—especially for highly liquid and closely followed assets like the S&P 500 futures—has become an arena where artificial intelligence (AI) and machine learning systems play a pivotal role.

The S&P futures market is a dynamic, constantly shifting environment influenced by broad economic trends, corporate earnings, government policies, and global risk sentiment. With so many moving parts, it's nearly impossible for a single human trader to parse every piece of relevant information and form a precise market forecast. This is where AI steps in. AI-driven systems can process vast amounts of market data, news reports, economic indicators, and even social media sentiment, helping traders discern patterns, anticipate volatility, and refine their timing of entries and exits.

Within the AI ecosystem, language models like ChatGPT offer a novel and complementary approach. At the same time, algorithmic trading engines use complex numeric inputs and outputs, and ChatGPT leverages natural language processing to understand and produce human-like text. This can help traders in various ways: summarizing economic releases, generating new trading ideas, brainstorming risk management approaches, or even coding snippets of Python for backtesting strategies. By combining the depth of AI-driven quantitative analysis with the adaptability of ChatGPT's natural language capabilities, traders can develop a more robust and informed framework for decision-making in the S&P futures market.

Understanding the S&P Futures Market: Before diving deeper into how AI and ChatGPT can help, it's crucial to understand what S&P futures are and why they're popular. S&P 500 futures are derivative contracts tied to the S&P 500 Index—an index that aggregates the performance of 500 leading U.S. companies. These futures trade nearly around the clock, providing ample liquidity and continuous market access for traders across the globe.

Traders are drawn to S&P futures because they offer efficient exposure to the broader U.S. equity market. They allow participants to hedge stock portfolios, speculate on directional moves, and implement sophisticated spread or options strategies. Moreover, their liquidity ensures relatively tight bid-ask spreads and allows for quick entry and exit of positions.

While the appeal is strong, the market's complexity can be daunting. Economic announcements, geopolitical tensions, corporate earnings, and Federal Reserve policy shifts can all send shockwaves through S&P futures prices. By utilizing AI-driven tools, traders can efficiently analyze these numerous influences. Meanwhile, ChatGPT can synthesize complex macroeconomic commentary, help interpret Federal Reserve statements, and even simplify lengthy reports into actionable insights.

The Role of AI in Market Analysis: AI's prowess lies in its ability to identify patterns and relationships within vast datasets that might be too subtle or complex for a human to discern. Traditional technical analysis often relies on a handful of indicators, such as moving averages, MACD, or RSI. AI, by contrast, can ingest countless data points—historical price action, options market data, volatility indices (like the VIX), and high-frequency order flow—then integrate them with fundamental factors such as GDP growth rates, inflation statistics, and global commodity prices.

Machine learning models can identify non-linear relationships and statistical correlations that aren't apparent in standard chart analysis. For example, an AI model might reveal that S&P futures frequently exhibit a specific response pattern to surprises in monthly employment data, or that a particular combination of technical indicators is associated with a heightened probability of a breakout. Armed with these insights, traders can develop more nuanced strategies.

However, while AI excels at pattern recognition and quantitative analytics, it isn't inherently adept at contextual interpretation of economic events or textual reports. This is where ChatGPT steps in. By using a language model trained on extensive textual data, traders can swiftly convert raw AI findings into actionable narratives, fusing quantitative precision with qualitative understanding.

Introducing ChatGPT into the Trader's Workflow: Integrating ChatGPT into a trader's daily routine can take several forms. In the early morning before the U.S. market opens, a trader might ask ChatGPT to summarize the key overnight developments: Asian and European session market moves, relevant macroeconomic news, and analyst commentary regarding the upcoming trading day. This allows traders to form a coherent mental picture of the landscape before placing their first trades.

As the day progresses, the trader may utilize ChatGPT to quickly digest economic data releases. For instance, when Non-Farm Payrolls (NFP) data is released, ChatGPT can instantly provide a summary of how the numbers compare to consensus expectations, what leading analysts are saying, and how the market might react. This is invaluable in futures trading since speed and clarity of information often determine how effectively a trader can position themselves ahead of major moves.

In addition, ChatGPT can serve as a research assistant, helping identify key technical levels, summarizing Federal Reserve speeches, or even generating trading plan outlines. Although ChatGPT may not be perfect—no AI tool is—it acts as a second pair of eyes and a sounding board that can refine a trader's thinking and confirm whether they've considered multiple angles before committing capital.

Utilizing AI for Strategy Development and Backtesting:

Beyond day-to-day market analysis, AI and ChatGPT can aid traders in developing and refining their strategies. Creating a robust trading strategy often involves iterative experimentation: proposing a hypothesis about how the market behaves, translating it into code or a set of rules, and then backtesting it against historical data to see if it yields consistent, profitable signals.

AI-driven quantitative models can help identify these hypotheses. For instance, a machine learning model might suggest that when the S&P futures price trades above its 50-day moving average and the VIX remains below a certain threshold, there's a statistically significant probability of upward price continuation over the subsequent two sessions. Armed with this statistical insight, the trader can then formalize a strategy and ask ChatGPT to help write initial code snippets in Python or to integrate the rule set into a backtesting framework.

Moreover, ChatGPT can assist in scenario analysis. Suppose the trader wants to understand how their strategy might perform under various market conditions, such as a sudden rate hike by the Federal Reserve or a geopolitical crisis. By framing these scenarios in natural language, ChatGPT can provide thoughtful guidance on what factors to consider, how other traders have reacted historically, and what risk management tactics might be prudent.

Risk Management and AI-Driven Insights: A cornerstone of successful futures trading is robust risk management. AI can contribute significantly here, as machine learning models can detect patterns of heightened volatility or identify early warning signals of trend reversals. These alerts can prompt traders to tighten stop losses, reduce position sizes, or close positions preemptively when risk conditions are unfavorable.

ChatGPT, for its part, can help distill complex risk management frameworks into easy-to-understand steps. A trader might ask ChatGPT to explain how to balance their portfolio across multiple asset classes or how to scale into a position gradually to mitigate initial volatility risks. It can also provide outlines for emergency procedures—what to do if a particular threshold is breached or if a strategy experiences consecutive losing trades beyond a certain tolerance.

Additionally, ChatGPT can streamline the documentation process. Keeping a journal is vital for any serious trader. ChatGPT can summarize the day's trades, highlight what went right, what went wrong, and store key lessons. Over time, these summaries form a valuable knowledge base that the trader can review periodically to identify longer-term performance trends and areas for improvement.

The Limitations and Challenges of Using ChatGPT and AI: It's important to acknowledge that while AI and ChatGPT can be powerful allies, they're not infallible. Language models like ChatGPT generate text based on patterns in data they've been trained on. They lack proper comprehension and the ability to verify the accuracy of real-time data. For example, ChatGPT might confidently describe a trading scenario that sounds plausible but lacks real-time price confirmation or timely fundamental inputs.

Moreover, markets evolve constantly. A strategy that was successful last year may not be effective this year. AI models trained on historical data risk overfitting—identifying patterns that no longer hold in a changed market environment. Traders must continuously monitor and update their models, ensuring they remain relevant in the face of new market regimes, shifting macroeconomic conditions, and regulatory changes.

Regulatory constraints also matter. Depending on where you trade and how you deploy AI, compliance requirements may dictate how you can use automated systems or rely on AI-generated recommendations. ChatGPT can guide you in understanding specific rules or summarizing complex regulatory texts, but ultimately, the trader must ensure legal and ethical compliance with all applicable guidelines.

Combining ChatGPT with Other Tools and Data Sources: Maximizing the effectiveness of AI and ChatGPT involves integrating these tools with other resources. Data feeds from reputable vendors provide real-time quotes, news analytics platforms scan thousands of headlines daily, and charting software offers a visual perspective on price action. By combining these diverse inputs, a trader can create a richer and more reliable decision-making environment.

For example, a trader might use ChatGPT to generate a list of potential bullish continuation signals based on the latest Federal Reserve remarks, then verify these signals against a technical analysis platform that calculates key support and resistance levels. Simultaneously, an AI-driven anomaly detection model could highlight periods of unusual order flow activity. The integration of multiple streams of information helps confirm or refute trading hypotheses more robustly than relying on any single source.

Many trading platforms now offer APIs, enabling programmatic access for custom algorithms and AI models. Traders comfortable with coding can ask ChatGPT to help refine their Python scripts, integrate new risk management rules, or connect to a broker's API to automate specific trading actions. The goal is not to let ChatGPT trade on your behalf but to let it simplify and streamline the tasks that inform your human-driven decisions.

Practical Examples and a Day in the Life of a Trader Using ChatGPT: Imagine starting your trading day at 6:00 AM Eastern Time. Over coffee, you ask ChatGPT to summarize the overnight sessions in Asia and Europe. It provides a concise rundown: the Nikkei closed lower on weaker-than-expected GDP data, European indices are mixed ahead of the ECB meeting, and several large-cap U.S. tech firms issued earnings guidance updates. Within minutes, you have a cohesive snapshot of global market sentiment.

Next, you open your AI-driven dashboard, which has detected an interesting statistical pattern: S&P futures have consistently rallied in the first hour after a particular economic report under conditions similar to those expected today. You ask ChatGPT to help write a brief Python script to backtest this pattern over the last two years, and it quickly provides a starting point. After refining the code, you run the backtest and confirm that the pattern has had positive expectancy over that period.

As the U.S. market approaches its opening bell, you turn your attention to a new Federal Reserve speech scheduled for midday. ChatGPT helps you craft a watchlist of key phrases to monitor in the Fed remarks, which your data feed will flag. If the Fed speaker hints at a change in monetary policy direction, you'll already know how such language historically correlated with short-term moves in S&P futures. Armed with this knowledge, you set alerts to adjust your positions accordingly.

The Future of AI-Enhanced Trading and Conclusion: Looking ahead, the integration of AI, natural language processing, and human discretion seems poised to shape the future of trading. As models like ChatGPT grow more capable, traders will rely on them to handle increasingly complex tasks: analyzing the subtle language used by central bankers, interpreting the nuances of corporate earnings transcripts, and generating multifaceted scenario analyses at a moment's notice. In turn, AI-driven quantitative models will become more adept at predicting market regimes and adapting strategies in real-time.

This synergy does not remove the human element. On the contrary, it empowers human traders to focus on creativity, risk management, big-picture thinking, and strategy refinement. By offloading the grunt work—data parsing, initial code drafting, quick summaries of market events—to AI tools, traders free up mental bandwidth for higher-order tasks, such as understanding the market's true narrative and adapting to the inevitable surprises that define trading in the real world.

In conclusion, utilizing AI and ChatGPT for trading S&P futures involves striking the right balance. Traders who embrace these tools can gain an edge by identifying patterns, accelerating their research, and responding more quickly to evolving market conditions. Yet no technology can replace the need for sound judgment, experience, and a careful approach to risk. With the right blend of human insight and AI-driven assistance, today's traders can navigate the complexities of the S&P futures market with greater confidence, clarity, and efficiency than ever before.

Quantum computing could revolutionize the trading world by delivering unprecedented speed, precision, and analytical power to both institutional and individual investors. Institutions may gain early advantages through real-time data analysis, hyper-accurate market predictions, lightning-fast arbitrage, enhanced portfolio optimization, and superior risk management, all powered by quantum technology. At the same time, retail traders could benefit from democratized access to advanced analytics, AI-driven insights, and quantum-enabled trading bots via fintech platforms. However, this technological leap also brings challenges—such as encryption vulnerabilities, ethical concerns, and the risk of market domination by early adopters. Ultimately, while quantum computing may initially widen the gap, it holds the promise of leveling the playing field over time.

CHAPTER TWENTY-ONE

A Conversation with Trader Joe

Setting the Scene

I'm sitting with Trader Joe, a seasoned pro in the S&P futures market, in a quiet corner of a busy trading floor. With decades of experience, Joe has a way of cutting through the noise and sharing insights that stick with you long after the conversation. This chapter brings together some of those memorable discussions, packed with advice that traders of all levels can use.

Q: "Joe, what's the single biggest mistake new traders make in the S&P futures market?"

Joe: "They trade without a plan. It's like walking into a battlefield with no strategy—you're bound to get ambushed. The S&P futures market is fast, volatile, and unforgiving. Without a clear entry, exit, and risk management plan, you're just gambling."

Follow-up: "But doesn't every trader think they have a plan?"

Joe: "Thinking you have a plan and having one are two different things. A plan isn't just 'buy low, sell high.' It's knowing your stop-loss before you enter, having a profit target, and understanding your edge in the market. If you can't articulate your edge, you're trading blind."

Q: "How do you handle losing streaks?"

Joe: "Losing streaks are inevitable. The key is not letting them define you. I reduce my position size, revisit my strategy, and take a step back if needed. Trading is a marathon, not a sprint. Most traders blow up because they double down on losses to 'get it back.' That's the gambler's mindset, not a professional trader's approach."

Follow-up: "Is it ever okay to chase losses?"
Joe: "Never. Chasing losses is like adding fuel to a fire. The market doesn't care about your need to recover. Focus on executing your plan, not on the money you've lost."

Q: "What's your take on indicators? Do you rely on them heavily?"
Joe: "Indicators are tools, not crutches. Many traders become obsessed with fancy indicators and forget that price action tells the real story. I keep it simple —moving averages, RSI, and volume. But even then, they're secondary. The structure of the market and understanding where buyers and sellers are positioned is far more important."

Follow-up: "So what's the best indicator in your opinion?"
Joe: "Your brain. Learn to read the market's rhythm. Indicators can help, but they'll never replace intuition and experience."

Q: "Let's talk about stop-losses. Are they really that important?"
Joe: "Are seatbelts important? A stop-loss isn't just a safety net; it's your lifeline in this business. Trading without a stop-loss is like saying, 'I'll jump out of the plane and figure out the parachute on the way down.'"

Follow-up: "But don't stop-losses sometimes trigger prematurely?"
Joe: "Sure, but that's not a reason to avoid them. It's a reason to refine your placement. Think of stop-losses like the cost of doing business. You'd rather pay for insurance than suffer a catastrophic loss."

Q: "What separates a consistently profitable trader from the rest?"
Joe: "Discipline. It's not about who has the best strategy or the fanciest tools. It's about who can stick to their rules, control their emotions, and stay consistent under pressure. Most traders lose because they sabotage themselves, not because the market beats them."

Follow-up: "What's the hardest rule for most traders to follow?"

Joe: "Cutting losses. People hate admitting they're wrong, but every trader is wrong at some point. The sooner you accept that, the faster you'll grow. The market doesn't reward ego; it rewards adaptability."

Q: "If you could give just one piece of advice to a new trader, what would it be?"

Joe: "Learn to love the process, not the outcome. Focus on making good trades, not on making money. If your process is solid, the profits will follow. If you chase money, you'll lose sight of the process—and that's when mistakes happen."

Follow-up: "What's a 'good trade' in your eyes?"

Joe: "A good trade is one where you followed your plan, regardless of the outcome. Wins and losses are part of the game. The only bad trades are the ones where you broke your rules."

Closing Thoughts

Trader Joe's insights reflect years of hard-earned experience. His emphasis on discipline, planning, and mindset serves as a powerful reminder that success in the S&P futures market isn't about luck or shortcuts—it's about consistency, adaptability, and a deep respect for the market. As Joe often says, "Trading is simple, but it's not easy. The difference lies in execution."

CHAPTER TWENTY-TWO
Conclusion

In the journey of trading S&P futures, the true wealth lies not in the profits amassed but in the wisdom gained along the way. Knowledge, as the foundation of trading, is a treasure that endures when markets shift and trends fade. It is through the acquisition of market insights, analytical prowess, and strategic understanding that a trader arms themselves for success. Yet, knowledge alone is insufficient without the patience to let it guide our actions. Patience, the steadfast ability to wait for the right opportunity amidst market turbulence, is a trader's greatest ally. It serves as a counterbalance to impulsive decisions that often lead to regret.

Discipline and self-control, like the steady hand of a seasoned sailor, steer the trader through the stormy seas of greed and fear. Contentment with calculated gains and the humility to accept losses create the foundation for sustainable success. Risk, the ever-present companion in trading, demands respect and careful management. A wise trader embraces the reality of risk, utilizing tools like stop-loss orders to safeguard against adversity while maintaining a steady course toward their goals.

Focus and clarity of purpose separate the successful trader from the distracted. The ability to adhere to a well-defined strategy, free from the noise of market chatter and emotional swings, is a hallmark of mastery. Impulsive actions, driven by fleeting emotions, are the enemies of consistent profitability. Reflection and deliberate decision-making transform uncertainty into opportunity.

Losses, though inevitable, are not defeats but lessons. The resilient trader views setbacks as stepping stones, learning from them with resolve and determination. Cautious action, rooted in a thorough evaluation of risks and rewards, ensures that each trade is a deliberate step forward. Financial management, the cornerstone of lasting wealth, requires discipline, diversification, and strategic foresight. Without these, even the most significant gains can slip away.

Ultimately, adaptability is the hallmark of the proficient trader. Like a crane poised for the right moment, the trader who remains flexible and attuned to market dynamics finds opportunities where others see chaos. It is this blend of knowledge, patience, discipline, resilience, and adaptability that defines success in trading. As you close this book, remember that trading is not merely a pursuit of profit but a path to personal growth and wisdom. Approach the markets with humility, curiosity, and a steadfast commitment to your principles, and you will find not only financial success but the enduring wealth of experience and insight.

If you found this book helpful and enjoyed reading it, I would be grateful if you could leave a review. Your honest feedback not only helps me, as the author, understand how the book has resonated with you, but it also assists other readers in deciding if this resource is right for them. Thank you very much for your time; I genuinely appreciate your support.

From the depths of my heart, thank you for embarking on this challenging journey of mastering the art of trading S&P futures. Your dedication and perseverance in pursuing this knowledge are truly commendable. As you move forward, I sincerely wish you not only good luck but also the confidence and discipline to achieve consistent success. Nothing would bring me greater joy than seeing each of you turn your efforts into daily triumphs. Remember, the markets reward those who never stop learning—keep striving, and your success will surely follow.

www.ingramcontent.com/pod-product-compliance
Ingram Content Group UK Ltd.
Pitfield, Milton Keynes, MK11 3LW, UK
UKHW060220061026
15625UKWH00007B/412

9 798999 471604